ROMAN SPRING

Mrs. Winthrop Chanler

ROMAN SPRING

MEMOIRS

by

MRS. WINTHROP CHANLER

Illustrated

BOSTON

LITTLE, BROWN, AND COMPANY

1934

Copyright, 1934,

By Margaret Chanler

———

Published September, 1934
Reprinted September, 1934

THE ATLANTIC MONTHLY PRESS BOOKS
ARE PUBLISHED BY
LITTLE, BROWN, AND COMPANY
IN ASSOCIATION WITH
THE ATLANTIC MONTHLY COMPANY

PRINTED IN THE UNITED STATES OF AMERICA

TO MY CHILDREN
WHO WANTED ME TO SET DOWN THESE MEMORIES
THIS BOOK IS FONDLY DEDICATED

CONTENTS

CONTENTS

ILLUSTRATIONS

ROMAN SPRING

I

ROMAN CHILDHOOD

My father, Luther Terry, left Connecticut in 1833 to study art in Rome. He was twenty years old. He was born and brought up on a farm near Hartford, at the old Terry homestead where the family had lived since earliest Colonial times. They claimed descent on the distaff side from the patriarchal Governor Bradford, who came to America in the *Mayflower*.

The Terrys had never grown rich; many of them were parsons; one of them made wooden clocks, now prized by collectors of Americana. My father's name was Luther; he had a brother who bore the name of Calvin, which shows which way the winds of doctrine blew in the family. Calvin and a third brother, James, were both Presbyterian ministers.

The young Luther had a certain talent, and above all a passion for art, and started forth on what must in those days have seemed a great adventure. The call came to a number of other American youths about the same time — Story, Rogers, Healy, Ives, Simmons, are a few of the names that come to mind. A group of voluntary exiles bringing up their families in a foreign land for love of its beauty. Pilgrim Fathers fleeing the "stern and rock-

bound coast," escaping from the narrow pattern of Puritan
communities, rediscovering the forgotten treasures of the
Old World, the significance of ruins, the romance of the
picturesque.

For all its ravishing beauty, Italy was perhaps not the
best place for their artistic education; the soil, for one
thing, was too alien, and they too entirely unprepared for
the lessons it had to teach.   But they were happy people
and lived in an innocent Bohemian Arcadia nestled in
a spur of Parnassus.

My father studied with Camuccini, President of the
Accademia di San Luca, who tried with all his might to
paint like Raphael.   My father also worked in the Life
Class at the Villa Medici — the French Academy.   He
was a good draughtsman and told me with modest satisfaction how Thackeray, when he once visited the school,
had stopped and looked at his drawing and exclaimed,
"By Jove, I wish I could draw like that!"

He painted many pictures — preferably large canvases
representing religious and allegorical subjects: Deborah
singing her song of victory; the vision of Ezekiel — God
the Father, with a white woolly beard, grasping a starry
thunderbolt over the prostrate form of the prophet;
Solomon visited in his sleep by Beauty, Riches, and
Wisdom, in guise of three smiling Græco-Roman goddesses; Jacob dreaming on his stone pillow under the sky-
propped ladder full of angels ascending and descending;
and many more.

My father's studio was in the Via Margutta under the
Pincian Hill.   My little brother, Arthur, and I were often
taken there to sit for our portraits.   For one big picture

MARGARET AND ARTHUR TERRY

A portrait by their father

we posed in our shifts sitting on the knees of Adelina, Arthur's pretty peasant nursemaid. She was dressed in the gay Roman costume long since discarded by all but models and wet-nurses and sat in a swing with a child on each knee.

The sitting still, even in a swing, was tiresome, but the place was full of compensating interest: the life-sized articulate manikins with their foolish faces and untidy human hair; the property chest full of treasures and mysteries; a white satin gown that had belonged to Napoleon's mother, Madama Letizia; a red velvet mantle trimmed with ermine that seemed very regal; flowered waistcoats; brocaded skirts; beribboned sleeves; laced coats; and then the tubes of paint that squeezed so pleasantly on to the palette. Sometimes when I had sat very still I was allowed to squeeze them myself, proudly and carefully.

Behind the studio was a shady, overgrown garden, smelling of roses and violets, with a great bitter-almond tree that blossomed in earliest spring.

My father achieved a modest success as a painter in the innocent '50s, '60s, and '70s. He sold pictures to his compatriots and often painted their portraits. In the '80s his clients became rarer. The public had become more sophisticated. The new manner had made the old seem obsolete; unknown visitors rarely rang the little jangling studio bell, and the studio became a hermitage. During the last twenty-five years of his life my father went on painting with unflagging ardor for the great pleasure that it gave him. He died in 1900, eighty-seven years old. The art world had gone by him, but I think his days passed very happily in the colorless studio light; for he lived in Rome, the city of his choice, and painting is of all the arts the one that seems to give most constant pleasure to the craftsman.

He was very gentle and conventional; he had left his own people and the land of his fathers for the sake of art; he had fallen in love with the Rome of the Popes, but he highly disapproved of anything that resembled artistic Bohemia, and he held unaltered his Calvinistic views on Catholicism and the Roman clergy.

In the year 1861 he married my mother, Louisa Cutler Ward, widow of Thomas Crawford, an Irish-American sculptor of some note. It was Crawford who decorated the dome of the Capitol in Washington with the bronze statue of an Indian. Its bronze doors and some of the marble bas-reliefs surrounding them are also by him; and when he died in 1857 he had just completed the sculptures which adorn the Washington Monument of Richmond, Virginia. My mother was left a widow with three daughters and one son — the youngest child, Francis Marion, who eventually wrote *Mr. Isaacs* and *Saracinesca* and many other novels.

Louisa Ward also came of old New England stock. The Wards and the Greenes, to whom the Wards were several times related, gave more than one Colonial Governor to Rhode Island. A Ward fell with Wolfe at Quebec. Colonel Ward, my mother's grandfather, fought in the Revolutionary War. His commission was signed by Washington. He married a daughter of Governor Greene, and his son, another Samuel Ward, was my mother's father.

Soon after the Revolutionary War the family moved to New York. They were there when the great inaugural ball was given in honor of the first President. Many years later, when I came to America as a young girl, I was taken to see Cousin Nancy Greene, ninety-seven years old. She lived on her Rhode Island farm with her two sons, both of whom were over seventy, but whom she continued to treat as thoughtless youngsters. She told me how she was staying with the family in New York when she was only fourteen; everyone was getting ready for the ball, and little else was talked about. Nothing had been said about her going to it and she knew they thought she was too young; nevertheless, she got her best India muslin embroidered frock ready, and, when the family came downstairs dressed in their finery, she too was there, hoping ardently to be taken along. "But Colonel Ward was a terrible man, and when he saw me come down with the rest of the family, all eager and ready, he sent me back to bed." "And you know," the old lady added with a tone of bitter regret still sharp after all those many years, "he might just as well have let me go."

My mother was beautiful and much beloved, a radiating centre of kindness and pleasantness. She could never cease from caring and providing for people: our clothes were given away just when we began to feel comfortable in them; she had a drawerful of candle ends for a poor boy who wanted to study at night; books were in perpetual circulation; jellies for the invalids; pumpkin pies for homesick American travelers. She had the gift of helpful understanding and was, I believe, wholly

charming to all who knew her; she was a little shy and
quite unworldly.   She really seemed to prefer the society
of those she could benefit to that of people who could
interest or amuse her, and was to a certain extent the
victim of her virtues; she could not and would not deny
her door to those who knocked.   Bores and importunates
were never discriminated against; she considered it a part
of Christian duty to suffer them gladly, and how they
flocked!   I think there must have been some sort of line
drawn, for they were never invited to meals, nor did
they come to the Wednesday-afternoon receptions.   They
generally arrived about eleven o'clock and stayed till
lunch was announced.   They came to pour out their
troubles; to ask for help, material or spiritual; to talk
about themselves.   They always found what they sought
and they went away comforted and assisted, but Mamma's morning had been laid waste and trampled by wild
asses.

I think I owe to these very early impressions a certain
hardness of heart.   Our parents influence us incalculably
by their example, but their influence sometimes results in
a reaction.   I often overheard people saying I should
never be like my mother, and I realized that this meant
I should be less beautiful and less charming; but in my
secret soul I hugged the assurance that I should never
spend long hours closeted with dreary suppliants.

I remember a foolish dream I once had: I dreamt I had
died and gone to heaven; an angel was showing me the
way and led me through a folding door.   To my surprise
and great disillusion I found myself in the *camera verde*,
our big green anteroom, and it was filled with Mamma's

LOUISA WARD TERRY

morning bores, sitting around the room complacently. Think of having taken so much trouble to get nothing but this!

My mother was a devout Episcopalian. Before the Italians took Rome, no Protestant churches were allowed within its walls. The English Church was a converted hay barn on the Via Flaminia just outside the Porta del Popolo. It was to this we were taken on Sunday mornings. The whitewashed walls, the dull hymn singing, the long service, were a great weariness to my childish soul. The Roman churches seemed so much more real, and more alive. I used to buy rosaries and holy pictures with my pennies. I cannot remember the time when Catholicism was not the true religion for me.

My younger brother, Arthur, — Arturo we called him, Italian being our nursery language, — was a pretty child, with a row of glossy curls hanging over his neck and one on top of his head which was curled over a stick with great care. When told he could not have a second or perhaps a third helping of his favorite pudding because he was already quite full, he would point to his *riccio,* his hollow topknot, and assure us that was still empty and could hold some more.

When we were quite small and Rome was ruled by Pio Nono there were French troops, a regiment from Antibes, quartered in the city. They were unpopular with the Romans, and "Antiboiano" was a current term of reproach synonymous with "blackguard." In the dining room stood a little corner cupboard where sugar and sweetmeats were stored; this was generally locked, but sometimes left open; we were not supposed to investigate,

let alone help ourselves to what it held.   But the dining
room was next to our ballroom-playroom, and the little
corner cupboard was just to the left of the door that led
into it; door and cupboard happened to be ajar one day,
and Arturo was caught in the forbidden act.   *"Brutto
Antiboiano!"* exclaimed the butler, who came in at that
very moment.   *"Io non sono Antiboiano,"* said Arturo
with great seriousness, as he drew his head out of the
cupboard and slapped his chest.   *"Sono galantuomo."*
He quite rightly felt the epithet was too strong.   I am
told the Bulgarians still use the term "Catalan" as one
of extreme opprobrium, in memory of the Almugavares,
a Catalonian regiment quartered on them by the Emperor
of Byzantium many centuries ago.   Perhaps the old
Catalans behaved worse or the Romans have shorter
memories; the Roman of to-day has dropped the word
"Antiboiano" out of his vocabulary.

Arthur had simple tastes and loved his watering cart,
which he was content to drag around for hours at a time
thinking of nothing, as it seemed to me, while my head
was full of fairy tales, kings and queens, knights and
enchanted princesses.   I was being fed on Grimm's
Märchen and Andersen's stories by my German nursery
governess.   I am perhaps the only American child that
heard Cooper's Leatherstocking tales in German, and
called them *Lederstrumpf*.   But what I loved best was
high romance, knights-errant undertaking perilous adventures for the sake of ladies in distress.   The only way
in which I could fit the good little Arthur into this
imaginary world was by pretending he was my liege
knight, faithful and true.   I coaxed him to kneel down

before me and put his two folded hands in mine and swear he would do everything I asked of him forever.

"Not forever," said Arthur prudently, though he had no idea of what it was all about.

"Well, for three months then." And I took charge of the situation. He was very good about keeping his promise and fetched and carried for me faithfully. Towards the end of the three months he grew weary of this servitude and resolved not to renew the contract, but by cajolery and guile I got the better of him and kept the poor little *galantuomo* as my vassal and slave for something like a year. Our mother knew of the arrangement and was only amused by it, so my rule cannot have been very harsh.

II

PALAZZO ODESCALCHI

WE lived on the second floor of the Palazzo Odescalchi, designed by Bernini, but not for the Odescalchi family, who acquired it in the eighteenth century. It is a sober specimen of Bernini's work, built in stone and brick around a handsome colonnaded court; its proportions very nobly Roman.[1] It had a broad white marble barrel-vaulted staircase and beautiful high-studded rooms with coffered ceilings. The hall, anteroom, and drawing-rooms formed a long *enfilade*.

First there was a *sala*, a big, nearly empty hall with benches for waiting messengers or footmen; then the *camera verde*, a large green anteroom-library furnished with old carved bookcases; the red room, which was used as a sitting room where the family assembled before dinner, and spent the evening when there was no party; then a stiff little square room hung with yellow damask, where the piano stood; and the so-called magenta room. Do not start at the name of the color. It recorded a French and Piedmontese victory and had not yet been associated with the ugly aniline tint it has come to suggest.

[1] The modern wing facing the Corso was built at the end of the nineteenth century.

This was the real drawing-room and much the most beautiful in the house. The walls were hung with panels of a deep oleander-pink brocade with silver-gray flowers; the vaulted ceiling painted with a heavy trellis of grape-vines on a burnished gold background. The centre of the vault flattened to a square picture of Bellerophon on Pegasus, slaying the Chimæra, painted in pale blue and white *camaïeu*, like Wedgwood pottery.

Beyond this was my mother's room, all painted in flowers and light colors, and smelling of orris root and violets. My father brought home a bunch of violets every day, bought on the Piazza di Spagna, as he walked from his studio in the Via Margutta; they were placed on her dressing table and I cannot think of the room without remembering their fragrance. The dressing table was hung about with pink silk under pleated flounces of lace-trimmed lawn; there was ample room for me to creep in and sit under it, in a lovely rosy solitude with a doll or a book, while Mamma was dressing or writing letters. Some friend or relative had sent me from America two picture books, one about Little Red Riding-Hood and the other about "Who Killed Cock Robin." This last I gloated over in a rapture of melancholy. Its doleful refrain seemed infinitely pathetic: —

> All the birds of the air fell sighing and sobbing
> When they heard the bell toll for poor Cock Robin,

and moved me to delicious tears, especially when I had the book all to myself under the curtained table. Every time I read it I could cry a little more, and one day Mamma was disturbed by the sound of convulsive sobs.

She raised the sheltering flounces and found me in a tempest of tears. The book was taken away from me, in spite of my protests and promises that I would never cry again; nor did I ever find another that moved me half so much.

My father's room was very handsome, with sober eighteenth-century landscapes painted on the walls, but less gay and inviting than Mamma's; at least I did not like it half so well.

I linger wistfully over the details of these rooms; their faded splendors were infinitely dear to me. How often do I visit them in my dreams, always with a glad sense of home-coming. They were swept by fire soon after we left the Odescalchi in 1878, so that gilded carvings, looking-glasses, brocades, and painted silks exist only in my memory of them, and when I try to put this into words I am describing a ghost seen only by myself.

But the best of all was our playroom, a very large ballroom left nearly unfurnished for our use. Its walls were covered with panels of India silk decorated with classic arabesque patterns painted in *gouache*, alternating with very tall mirrors made in sections — those dim, eighteenth-century mirrors which reflect the light very softly and seem to hold the shadows of things long past. The six doors were elaborately decorated with mirrors and gold carvings, with classic medallions on the lower panels. The door knobs were in the shape of incense boats, for the Odescalchi claimed descent from Balthazar, one of the three Kings who brought the frankincense to Bethlehem, following the Star. The whole decorative scheme was unusually rich, yet so delicate in its detail,

PALAZZO ODESCALCHI

and its colors so skillfully blended to a warm mother-of-pearl harmony, that all who saw it were in admiration of its beauty.

There were three French windows with iron railings, looking on to the Piazza and Church of the Holy Apostles; their embrasures so deep that by letting down the portières we obtained the cosy privacy of a small room. From these windows we watched the world go by. We could sit on the floor with our legs through the railings, dangling over the great wooden shield painted with the armorial bearings of the Odescalchi family, a double-headed eagle and gold incense boats, surrounded by the collar of the Golden Fleece.

Stare in finestra — to stay at the window — was a great feature of Roman life. There was always so much to see; the streets were so full of leisurely happenings; there were weddings and funerals in the church opposite which were always interesting. I remember a particularly magnificent occasion — the funeral of the last Grand Duke of Tuscany, Francis VI, with whom that line of the Hapsburgs became extinct. There were endless processions of monks, Knights of Malta, and diplomatic representatives. The Roman Senate sent three glass coaches with outriders and footmen — real footmen in the sense that four of them walked by each coach, holding long silken cords which were fastened to the top, presumably to steady the vehicle on bad roads. The Senatorial turnout was very gaudy — bright crimson and yellow, the footmen in knee breeches and white cotton stockings well padded with straw at the calf. To our great amusement we saw some street urchins dart out of the crowd and plant little pin flags in these while their owners walked on unconcerned.

Every evening the great bronze bell rang out the Ave Maria a quarter of an hour after sunset, and the Roman day began then. "One hour of night," "Three hours of night," were current expressions. Time was not regulated by clocks, but by the ringing of the Angelus. All opera-goers are familiar with the phrase in Leoncavallo's *Pagliacci*, *"alle ventitre ore"*; few know that twenty-three o'clock means an hour before sunset and Ave Maria.

Then the lamplighter would come with his long stick on his shoulder, at the end of which burned a little guarded flame. He opened a tiny iron shutter in the wall under the lantern that served as a street lamp, and let this down by a chain; the lamp burned some sort of oil, perhaps kerosene; it had to be filled and trimmed and lighted with the burning stick and then drawn up again to its place and the iron shutter locked. This was always interesting to watch in the twilight; it seemed so kind and faithful of the man to take all that trouble every evening.

The Roman fire brigade — *pompieri* — are fine showy fellows with brass helmets, but they came in, I think, with the Italian régime. When I was a child the fire engine was a sort of pushcart with a tub and a hose and a little hand pump attached to it. I think it was part of the chimney sweep's outfit. A fire started in the Palazzo Odescalchi and burned for three days without doing much damage. No one suggested our moving out. My mother woke up one morning hearing a child whimper in her room. She looked up and saw a sad little black face looking out of a hole in the wall, with tears streaking the soot-grimed cheeks. The poor sweep had lost his way in the labyrinth of black chimneys; he had been sent up to try to find out what the fire was doing. In the thick stone and brick walls, the great oak rafters could stand a few days' smouldering.

When night fell the place was full of terrors and darkness. For the drawing-rooms there were Carcel lamps, which had to be wound up from time to time with queer gurgling noises from the mechanism that pumped the oil up into the wick; but the halls and passageways, any rooms that were not being lived in, were lighted with tiny floating wicks, whose flickering flame merely outlined the darkness it could not dispel. The high ceilings were lost in blackness. The house was full of strange noises and unaccountable shadows. The carpets were laid over a thin layer of straw which rustled a little at every footfall. At night in my bed I heard footsteps and was sure of ghostly presences.

When nurses were succeeded by a governess and I was ten or twelve years old, it was thought proper to give me a room to myself. (Arthur and I had always shared a huge nursery which held our two beds and those of the two nurses with much room to spare.) I was put into a smaller one, very prettily decorated, but the terrors of the night were so great that it was decided to divide the big nursery by a partition that made two rooms of it but did not go all the way up to the ceiling, so that Arthur and I could talk to each other before going to sleep. "Good night" — "Good night" — "Sleep well"

— "Sleep well" — "We 'll see ourselves to-morrow morning if God wills" — "We 'll see ourselves to-morrow morning if God wills." This became a sort of magic formula and kept away evil spirits.

We seem to have been encouraged to believe in ghosts; the grown-ups believed in them and were sure of their visitations. Mr. Augustus Hare was a frequent guest. He came to Rome every winter for a few months, and I think he dined with us every Sunday night. He was a dapper little man with a narrow aquiline nose and rather beady penetrating eyes, with an extraordinary gift for story-telling.

Arthur and I had our supper with the nurses in the ballroom, but when Mr. Hare was expected I was allowed to sit up after supper and join the family in the drawing-room in order to listen to his wonderful tales. It was not a case of listening, but almost of actual experience. Mr. Hare was a master in the art, and exacted conditions which precluded any possible distraction or interruption among his listeners. The lights were turned low. No one was allowed to do fancywork. The doors were locked, no servant must come in to put wood on the fire or even to deliver a message. And in this crepuscular stillness he told us with nerve-racking vividness of the Secret of Glamis Castle, or the terrible story of the Vampire, or of Madame de Traffard's night journey with his sister. All his stories seemed to have happened to members of his own family or to intimate friends. He told them slowly in a curious, rather nasal voice which had an extraordinary variety of tone and pitch — as he neared the climax it would tremble, and break, and rise almost to a shriek while he writhed on his chair, twisting and wringing his hands, tortured, as it were, by the intolerable horror of what he was telling.

Some of these stories can be found in his *Story of My Life,* and they make excellent reading, but it is impossible to convey how much more thrilling they were as he told them. And when the dreadful thing had happened, and left us all shattered with mysterious terror, the lights were turned up and the fire was poked into a blaze, the servant came in with the mulled wine, and life resumed its reassuring reality. But I had been up long enough and must find my way through the outer darkness of the ballroom, the corridor, and many rooms and passageways, to my shadow-crowded bedroom, where I lay for hours quaking in an ecstasy of fear — Was the Vampire rattling the window lock? — Was it the werewolf, howling out in the storm?

Lord Houghton [2] was another English friend whom we all liked. He was a frequent visitor. I can only remember that he was charming in spite of a curious, but to me very fascinating, grimace. He wore false teeth which must have been uncomfortable to him, for every now and then in the course of conversation he would click them together and dart his tongue out above the upper row — to relieve, I suppose, the distress of the ill-fitted gums. It gave for a flashing instant an indescribably satanic look to the otherwise kindly face. This moment was so brief that one must not let one's eyes wander for an instant for fear of losing it. Perhaps I embarrassed him with my rapt and steadfast gaze.

[2] Monckton Milnes.

Some of our happiest hours were spent in Roman villas. Even as children we would be sent with our nurses to spend an afternoon in one or another of these beautiful places, to vary the monotony of going to the Pincio. There was the Villa Colonna on the Quirinal Hill. The gardens stretched all the way from the palace on the Piazza SS. Apostoli to the high wall opposite the fountain with the great horsemen, on the Square of the Palazzo del Quirinale. It had shady avenues of laurel and ilex. There were the remains of the great Temple of the Sun, Roman sarcophagi, statues of neglected gods, broad stairs of moss-covered marble. All silent and solitary, though it lay in the heart of Rome.

There was the Villa Ludovisi, perhaps the most beautiful of all, with its great collection of Greek and Roman sculptures, its immemorial grove of ilex trees, its shady avenues. One cannot think of it without a pang, for of all this glory nothing remains but a few small private gardens. The whole villa was cut up into lots and its site is now occupied by the wide Via Vittoria Veneto, on which stand the modern palace, built by the Boncompagni and bought by Queen Margherita after the death of King Humbert, and a row of "palace" hotels. Let us pass with averted face!

The exquisite Villa Chigi is still intact and cherished by its princely proprietor. The Villa Corsini on the Aventine has been vulgarized into a public park with a huge open square where an equestrian statue of Garibaldi stands — for the new order.

The Italian villa is as artificial a creation as a symphony. It is composed of evergreens, carved stone, and splashing water, as an orchestra is made up of strings, wood winds, and brasses. But with these few elements what wonders have been achieved, what variations of felicity!

The Quirinal Garden was among our favorites. That was when we were very small and when it still belonged to the Pope. We had a permit to go there from one of our friends at Court, a *Guardia Nobile*, for the public was never admitted. Its narrow avenues ran between high walls of clipped box, — they seemed as high as a house, — and years afterward, when I drove through them on the way to Court balls, I looked out of the carriage window to see if they were really as tall as I remembered them. In the dusky half-light they looked taller than ever. There in a secluded corner we buried our favorite canary bird. Arthur's yellow omnibus, drawn by two spanking bays with real harness that could all be taken off, was the hearse; Haroun-al-Rashid, a knitted Turk with turban, scimitar, and flowing beard, and Beatrice Bijou, my idolized French doll, were the chief mourners, and everything was done with such decent and appropriate pomp that the ceremony went far to console us for the loss of our darling songster.

On rainy days we were sent to St. Peter's for our walk; St. Peter's with its golden temperature seems warm in winter, cool in summer. I believe the thermometer does not vary more than ten degrees in the course of the year. We loved the immense Basilica, the colossal *putti* (cherubs) holding up the holy-water basins; the great monuments that lined its walls were full of interest: the lion, on one, whose mouth was open enough for us to put our hand in, always with some trepidation; the terrifying skeleton holding up the heavy marble draperies over the entrance of the tomb of a Pope; the impassable bronze statue of St. Peter, whose toe we rubbed and kissed as we saw others doing.

Pio Nono reigned over the Papal States. We used to see him driving about in his great glass coach with outriders and caparisoned horses. We all knelt on the sidewalk to receive his blessing as he went by. He often came to the Pincio, the public garden where our mornings and most of our afternoons were spent. He would get out and take a little walk attended by a group of ecclesiastics, chamberlains, and *Guardie Nobili;* and there was a flutter of excitement in the shady avenues which were our playgrounds when His Holiness's coach drew up on the *piazzale* and the kindly white figure alighted. We left our play and ran to surround him and receive his blessing. He would give us his ring to kiss; speak to this or that one. One day my brother and I were the favored ones; he took Arthur up in his arms and asked the nurses who we were. When told regretfully that we were Americans and Protestants, he patted our heads and promised to pray for us. This made a great impression on me.

Pio Nono was much beloved. He had a ready wit and a lovable personality. He was also supposed to have the evil eye; but this was his misfortune, not his fault, and it did not interfere with the affectionate veneration in which he was held.

Many of those who knelt as he passed would furtively *fare le corna* — make the horns — to avoid the bad luck he might bring them. The horns are made by folding the second and third fingers over the thumb and extending the first and fourth. The hand thus casts a shadow that vaguely resembles a devil's head and is believed to avert satanic influence. All Romans believed in the evil eye and avoided contact with those who were said to have it; they were carriers of bad luck. It was a cruel rumor to start about anyone, and was sometimes used as a hidden weapon. In Pio Nono's case it did not interfere with his popularity. Many considered him to be a saint; there were even rumors of minor miracles. A man suffering cruelly from the gout begged for a pair of His Holiness's stockings that they might relieve him of his pain. The *Guardia Nobile* who carried the message told us the story, and how the Pontiff gladly gave the stockings with his blessing, but said he had never found they did his own gout any good.

Things that had belonged to him were treasured. We had a white slipper, elaborately embroidered with a gold cross where the faithful should kiss it, obtained for us by a friend at Court, Marchese Cavalletti, stepfather of the beautiful Lily Conrad, of whom more anon. This hieratic slipper was enthroned on the mahogany *étagère* among choice bits of old china and articles of virtu.

So we grew up in several creeds and several languages. I cannot remember learning to speak German, French, or Italian. English was taken for granted. We spoke it with a foreign accent, but it was the mother tongue. To this day I cannot quite refrain from a sense of pity for those who grow up with only one language. What pleasure do I not owe to this freedom of the Western world!

III

VILLEGGIATURA

In midsummer Rome became unbearably hot, and July, August, and September were spent either in the mountains or by the sea, generally in a villa hired by the family after endless debate. My father never felt the heat; he would stay behind and write us of afternoon breezes which cooled the atmosphere. We knew that it was his great love of Rome which made him prefer almost any temperature to absence from its precincts.

It was nice to be in a railway carriage — "in the travel," we called it — and to arrive in strange places which always seemed cool and full of novelty. A Swiss chalet, a Tuscan villa, the Cocumella at Sant' Agnello di Sorrento, each had its own flavors and delights; but I, for one, was always happy to return in October to the spacious Odescalchi; the marble stairs seemed to welcome me home to a more stately existence.

One summer we spent in the Poggiarello, a charming eighteenth-century villa near Siena. It must have been the summer of 1869. My brother Marion Crawford had been sent to St. Paul's School, Concord, New Hampshire, three years before, in an effort to make a "good American" of him. How often my father used that term to us! And how unconvincingly, for did we not know that he had fled his native land in early youth to live in a country he liked better? I cannot remember Marion's going away, but of his return for the summer holidays, and of the elaborate *festa* we children prepared for his arrival, I have a vivid recollection. We gathered innumerable snails, empty shells of the *escargot* variety, which must have abounded in the grounds of the Poggiarello. Each of these was filled with oil and held a little floating wick; they were placed in the grass on either side of the drive, through the part that surrounded the house. The nurses must have done most of the work, but we children had collected the empty snail shells and were much elated by the double row of twinkling lights that marked the windings of the drive as our hero came home that summer night. Marion was fifteen, tall and handsome; the apple of my mother's eye. Mimoli was eighteen; Annie twenty-one; Jennie, the older sister, had died when I was a baby.

We had staying with us that summer Lily Conrad, an American girl of rare beauty. Her mother, widow, I think, of a Confederate officer, had married the Marchese Cavalletti of the Pope's Noble Guard. Lily had been educated at the Sacred Heart Convent of the Trinità dei Monti. (Later she married Marchese Theodoli and lived in a handsome palace on the Corso.) She was considered one of the most beautiful girls of her day; very tall and slight, with hazel eyes and an abundance of wavy golden hair.

Marion was dazzled and bewitched! He persuaded my mother that St. Paul's was no place for him and never

went back to school.   He worked with a tutor in Rome;
not very hard, I fancy, for he managed to attend all
the balls and parties where his particular star was likely
to shine.   He passed for older than he was.   This school-
boy passion for the golden Lily ripened into an unalter-
able, lifelong devotion.   I do not think there was ever
any scandal about them; it was recognized as part of the
order of things.   She was three or four years older than
he.   We all knew about it.   Marion, or rather Frank, —
"Franchino," as we then called him, — used to hum
"Annie Laurie" to himself and I knew he was thinking
of Lily Conrad.

> Her brow is like the snowdrift,
>   Her throat is like the swan,
>   Her face it is the fairest
>   That e'er the sun shone on.

Sunshine and snows of yesteryear!

The Crawfords were different from us; I always knew
it, but not till many years later did I understand what
the difference was.   It was a streak of genius in them,
combined with their Irish blood, and perhaps conditioned
by it.   All three were handsome, proud, and brilliant.
Annie, the oldest, was gifted with many talents and
showed great taste and ability in whatever she undertook, but she was bad-tempered, dangerous to family
peace.   My mother's gentleness was no match for her
violence; there were unpleasant scenes; we feared and
avoided her, but greatly admired her skill.   She painted
flowers; she modeled in wax; I have now two little silver
pomegranates beautifully wrought by her.   She wrote

stories. She was an omnivorous reader. Her room was full of French books and flowers and interesting things. Théophile Gautier was a great favorite with her, and I read and loved all his poetry long before making schoolroom acquaintance with the French classics.

Mimoli, the other Crawford sister, was pleasanter to live with, easier to love. She had grace and charm, she had a delicately outlined face with very blue eyes; she was kind and gay and generous with us children, while Annie hardly noticed us. Mimoli too was gifted, she wrote verses, she painted in water colors, but her work had not the uncanny mastery that Annie showed in whatever she put her hand to. Eventually Mimoli's talent proved the more available. She married Hugh Fraser, in the English diplomatic service; he died as Minister to Japan, leaving her with two sons to educate and very little money. She eked out her widow's pension by writing. *A Diplomat's Wife in Japan, Roman Yesterdays,* and many other volumes flowed from her facile pen and found favor with the public, while Annie's finer talent came to nought.

Marion, the youngest, was a darling of the gods, exceedingly handsome, tall, well-built, with blazing blue eyes and very regular features, an excellent brain and universal facility. He modeled and drew easily and well; he sang; he knew an indefinite number of languages; he even studied Sanskrit. He took up novel writing almost accidentally after he had spent a couple of years in India. It was the sudden success obtained by *Mr. Isaacs* that determined his career as a writer. He always had a leaning for the occult, and Bulwer-Lytton's

Zanoni was long his favorite novel.   He believed he had seen and braved the terrible *figure on the threshold*.

The summer of 1870 we spent in the mountains south of Turin.   Our hotel, La Certosa del Pesio, was formerly a Carthusian monastery and was in a fold of the Maritime Alps, surrounded by great forests of chestnut trees that shed such soft green light through their translucent foliage.   There were endless cloisters and ruined chapels, which we used as our playgrounds.   Some hundred miles north of us the Franco-Prussian War was raging.   Mars-la-Tour, Gravelotte, Sedan, were being fought.

We children, a little group of polyglots such as are always to be found in European summer hotels, divided into a French and a German camp and fought with such determination, such successful strategy, that France with us was completely victorious.   The Germans were cruelly beaten.   We must have been rather hard on them, for I remember an irate Italian father complaining of the punishment inflicted on his daughter, who was a German soldier, and a bad one at that.   I remember her as a golden-haired, blue-eyed, very gentle little creature, with no taste for soldiering.

That summer was memorable to me for my first experience in hero worship.   Those were the days of the table d'hôte.   The guests assembled and sat together at long tables; one talked with one's neighbor; occasionally the chance acquaintance ripened to friendship.   Perhaps the traveling public was more homogeneous then than it is now, people were less on the defensive against fellow travelers, and we never dreamed of asking for separate tables in the dining room; there were none.

A PAGE FROM THE LEAR ALPHABET

C —"The Comfortable Cow, who sate in her arm-chair, and toasted her own
bread at the parlour fire"

One day there appeared at luncheon sitting opposite to us a rosy, gray-bearded, bald-headed, gold-spectacled little old gentleman who captivated my attention. My mother must have met him before, for they greeted each other as friendly acquaintances. Something seemed to bubble and sparkle in his talk and his eyes twinkled benignly behind the shining glasses. I had heard of uncles; mine were in America and I had never seen them. I whispered to my mother that I should like to have that gentleman opposite for an uncle. She smiled and did not keep my secret. The delighted old gentleman, who was no other than Edward Lear, glowed, bubbled, and twinkled more than ever; he seemed bathed in kindly effulgence. The adoption took place there and then; he became my sworn relative and devoted friend. He took me for walks in the chestnut forests; we kicked the chestnut burrs before us, the "yonghy bonghy bos," as we called them; he sang to me "The Owl and the Pussy-cat" to a funny little crooning tune of his own composition; he drew pictures for me.

I still have a complete nonsense alphabet, beautifully drawn in pen and ink and delicately tinted in water colors, done on odd scraps of paper, backs of letters, and discarded manuscript. Every day Arthur and I found a letter of it on our plate at luncheon, and finally a title-page for the collection, with a dedication and a portrait of himself, with his smile and his spectacles, as the "Adopty Duncle." The drawing is much finer, more masterly, than would appear in the rough reproductions in the published copies of his work, for he was a professional painter. He had been drawing master to

Queen Victoria and her children. His health had suffered from the English climate and he had come to Italy
for the sunshine. He published some delightful books
of travels in Italy, with very carefully drawn illustrations.
These have been forgotten and overlooked. His immortal nonsense is part of English literature — some of it,
indeed, part of English poetry. I never saw him again,
but he has never faded from my memory — a fixed star
twinkling across the waste of years.

On our journey back to Rome we found all the stations
guarded by *Garibaldini* — red shirts. (Red shirts, black
shirts, *bianchi*, *neri*, and now the red of Soviet Russia and
the brown-shirted Nazis — uprisings and revolutions have
always expressed themselves in a color.) We reached
home that October to find the Italians had marched in
by the Porta Pia; Rome had fallen after a very short
resistance; Pio Nono was a prisoner in the Vatican; there
was a plebiscite. I can remember some of our friends
with tricolor badges, voting for United Italy. My people
were so instinctively conservative that they disapproved
of the new order and regretted the papal supremacy, not
very logically, it seems, for they disapproved of the Pope,
but enjoyed the picturesqueness of papal functions and
mediæval survivals. Eventually they were all presented
at Court and my mother became much attached to the
first Queen of Italy.

IV

THEATRICALS AND WEDDINGS

ONE winter (it must have been soon after the fall of Rome), the older sisters, Annie and Mimoli Crawford, organized some private theatricals, and a real stage was built in the ballroom; this added a great new interest to life. Madame Linard, our French visiting governess, trained us and our friends to act some of Madame de Genlis's plays (Madame de Genlis was the royal *gouvernante* of Louis Philippe's children).

This was only moderately interesting, as the plays were dull; the real excitement lay in getting up plays of our own. I had been reading Schiller's *Jungfrau von Orleans*, and was fired with the ambition to play the part of Joan of Arc. I arranged a simplified version of the piece and the family was invited to attend the performance. When the curtain went up I saw in the dark across the footlights a crowd of people whom the treacherous grown-ups had invited without telling us about it.

I remember the evening as one of great anxiety and sense of defeat, before insuperable difficulties. I naturally took the part of Joan: a shiny cuirass and helmet that Arturo had been given at Christmas were just the

thing, but why the white satin skirt that had belonged to
Madama Letizia, borrowed from our father's studio
property chest, should have seemed appropriate to wear
with it seems less clear; but with a shield on one arm
and a lance in the other I had no misgivings as to the
correctness of my costume.   My troubles were far graver.
There were only three of us to play: myself, Arthur, and
Sofia (the daughter of Mario, the footman, and his wife
Palmira, who was a dressmaker and made our frocks).
They lived upstairs and Sofia was allowed to come down
and play with us.   She was most anxious to do her part;
I had her as my *confidante*, which enabled me to describe
complicated happenings we could not possibly simplify
enough to act ourselves.   But the scene of the Maid's
capture by the English, of her trial and her death, had
to be gone through with.   Arturo was to be the English
Army, a very straggling army; it came on the stage one
soldier at a time, always the same soldier.   There was
no open passage behind the stage, which was just high
enough for a child to go under it crawling, between the
trestles that supported it.   Arturo was urged to crawl as
quickly as possible to appear again as the next soldier,
but on the second or third passage there was a sub-
terranean disturbance, a muffled cry, and sounds of broken
crockery.   It was pitch-black under the stage, and there
was not room for a grown-up to go to the rescue.   However, someone at last managed to draw the poor child out.
He had upset some paint pots and was covered with red
and brown smears, and I all the time on the stage, alone
with the faithful Confidante, making conversation while
waiting to be captured.   But the capturing warrior had

to be wiped off before he could appear again, so the capture was omitted and the curtain rung down. I told Sofia about it in the next scene, in my prison cell. The last scene was the burning. We had a pyre of real firewood. I stood behind it on a high stool, glorious in my armor and voluminous white satin skirt. We had been allowed to pour alcohol on the logs and set fire to it, but Madame Linard, who was stage manager and had no business on the stage, insisted that she must light the fire herself and stand over it to make sure that no harm came of it. My historic sense was deeply outraged at having a governess in a black silk dress for an executioner and I realized that it had all been most disappointing. To my surprise the grown-up audience seemed to have enjoyed the performance.

By this time I was about nine or ten years old. Ernesto Rossi, the popular tragedian, gave a performance of *Hamlet*, and to my unspeakable joy I was taken to see it. It went to my head like strong wine. For days I carried the Prince of Denmark in my soul, and if anyone asked me what I was thinking about, I would answer, holding out my empty hand with Rossi's expressive gesture: *"Parole — parole — parole."* Later in life I saw Sir Henry Irving, Edwin Booth, Salvini, John Barrymore, and many more in the part, in performances that I know must have been far better, but none ever gave me quite the same ecstasy.

My mother, seeing my enthusiasm, gave me the copy of Bowdler's Shakespeare she had owned as a child, six or eight faded green volumes with all improprieties eliminated from the text. These I pored over con-

tentedly for some years, but when my own children
wanted to read Shakespeare I let them have the un-
bowdlerized edition.

Miss Fanny Kemble, the famous actress, was a friend
of my mother's. She and her daughter, Mrs. Wister,
and her grandson, Owen, passed a winter in Rome at
about this time. Miss Kemble had long since left the
stage; she had married Mr. Butler, a Southern land-
owner, and had published a still fascinating book describing her life on a plantation. Owen Wister, who was a
few years older than I, came to a little French class
Madame Linard held in our apartment. I was charmed
but not a little shocked by him, he seemed so emancipated
from our unquestioning obedience; and when he showed
me, in the back of his copy book, a malicious caricature
of Madame Linard, who was short and fat and wore
spectacles, he seemed little better than one of the wicked.
Such irreverence I had never imagined.

The Wisters gave us children a wonderful Twelfth
Night party; there was a cake with a bean in it found by
Ernesto Tilton, another child of American parents who
had long since made their home in Rome, and the youngest of three brothers with whom we often played. Having found the bean, he became king of the party and
was asked to choose his queen. His choice fell on me
and we were ceremoniously crowned by the great Fanny
Kemble. Ernesto was too young to appreciate the importance of the occasion and acted more like a careless
Dauphin than a ruling sovereign, not taking the thing at
all seriously, while I was thrilled to the core, which
evidently pleased the old queen of tragedy. She put a

wide-flowing purple silk scarf about my shoulders as a royal mantle and showed me how I must hold my head high and walk regally. I asked for nothing better, and glowed with enthusiasm as she drew herself up to her full height, "like this" (I remember her as immensely tall), and walked across the room as if she owned the whole world. Then was brought in a huge ball of white yarn that had to be unwound by us and was found to contain presents for everyone; on me as queen regent fell the task of distributing the gifts. Our revels ended with a supper and we each had a tiny bottle of champagne, holding, I suppose, three or four thimblefuls of the gay liquid. We went home blissfully exhilarated.

Miss Fanny Kemble appeared in public in Rome that winter at a great benefit performance given for I know not what Roman charity. She gave the sleepwalking scene from *Macbeth*. It was an afternoon performance and I was allowed to go with the grown-ups, and was duly impressed by her bloodcurdling "Out, damned spot!" but it was not quite so thrilling as her lesson in how to be a queen. Years later, when I was in Boston as a young girl, I saw Owen Wister take the part of the Messenger in a performance of *Œdipus Tyrannus* given by the Harvard undergraduates. They recited the Greek text, of which the greater part of the audience understood not one word, nor did the tone and gesture of the actors convey much meaning until the Messenger rushed in, all breathless with the horror of Jocasta's death. He told it all in Greek, but we all understood; did not the blood of the great Mrs. Siddons and Fanny Kemble flow in his veins?

In 1873 we went to the Bagni di Lucca for the midsummer months. The Crawford family had spent a
summer there nineteen years before; Marion was born
there. It is a famous old watering place in the province
of Pistoia, on a spur of the Apennines, surrounded by old
chestnut forests, a favorite Italian resort. I remember
much coming and going in our hotel salon; an abundance
of what we called B.Y.M.'s (beautiful young men), besides a number of friends old and new of both sexes and
many nationalities. Annie and Mimoli Crawford must
have had a good time. Mimoli, the younger of the
sisters, was undoubtedly the more attractive; she was very
pretty and had great charm, with a sentimental audacity
which plunged her into successive romantic complications.
An officer in the British Navy, a Captain of Zouaves, a
Roman Prince, and a good many more figured in her
adventures in the *pays du tendre*. She was impulsive,
imprudent, and exceedingly attractive; I loved and wor-
shiped her and called her my *plus quam perfecta*, having
just begun Latin.

Annie was more gifted, less agreeable to live with;
she could be cruel, a disturber of the peace; she believed
that good hating was as necessary as good loving for the
development of human relations. She was tall and
slender and carried her small shapely head very high,
with a look of intelligent defiance on her proud face.
The Crawfords were very Irish, taking after their handsome father, with their blue eyes, dark hair, and well-
cut features. They were distinguished-looking and proud
of their race, in spite of the fact that they knew nothing
of their father's antecedents; his oldest sister had de-

stroyed all their family papers before she died and the secret was buried with her. Annie was old enough to remember her father and had never forgiven our mother for marrying again. She detested her stepfather, the kindest and most long-suffering of men, and did not hesitate to show it on every occasion. She made scenes; one never knew when the lightning might strike, and we were all afraid of her. Yet we all admired her, for she was, as I have said, unusually intelligent; her talk was brilliant; she could be delightful when she chose, even kind and generous upon occasion, but never wholly reassuring.

This *sæva virgo* met her fate that summer in the person of Erich von Rabe, a lame Prussian officer, wounded in the Franco-Prussian War of 1870. His leg was supported by a flexible steel splint that enabled him to walk, with the further help of a cane. He was tall and rather handsome in a wooden sort of way, with stiff, ceremonious manners. Educated at the Prussian *Ritterakademie* and *Kadettenkorps*, the military training schools for officers to which only members of the noble or *Junker* class were admitted, he had little knowledge of or interest in anything that lay outside the closed horizon of Prussian militarism.

Like all Germans he loved Italy, music, and wine. He played the piano by ear with a certain fluency, stringing together odds and ends of more or less familiar melodies with interludes of *arpeggios* and trills when the mood was gay, or solemn chords when it was tragic. This was called *phantasieren*, giving the fancy free rein, and was much practised in the musical world of the mid-nineteenth century. We read of Chopin's improv-

isations and of Liszt's; it was probably an expression of
the romantic movement, a reaction against academic form.
I never heard really good improvisation.   I can imagine
that with a great artist at the keyboard fire might descend
from heaven, but in the hands of amateurs it never does.
All the hearer gets is a stringing together of trite phrases
over an accompaniment as commonplace as a photogra-
pher's landscape background.

At the Bagni di Lucca there were little carriages available for drives and excursions in which two could sit
behind the driver, with a rumble for a third passenger.
It was out of the question that Annie should go out alone
with Erich, and it fell on me, a child of eleven, to chaperon
their drives from the rumble.   Fully aware that romance
was in the wind, I could hardly help listening to their
conversation.   Erich did all the talking in an execrable
Teutonic French, for Annie spoke no word of German,
while her French was correctly fluent.   He told her all
the story of his life, his war adventures, which ended so
sadly for him with his being wounded, shot through the
leg by a sharpshooter while reconnoitring before the battle
of Gravelotte; his weary stations in various hospitals, and
endless regimental anecdotes, to all of which Annie
listened with rapt attention.   Truly love endureth all
things.   By the end of the summer they announced their
engagement and a silent gladness pervaded the family
circle.

We returned to Rome as usual about the first of
October, and great preparations were made for the
wedding.   Annie was not cross with anyone; she tingled
with joy; she had found her mate or master.   They were

A ROMAN PICNIC

Luther Terry is the bearded gentleman in the back row. The lady in the foreground in the dark dress is Annie Crawford. Her sister Mimoli is the second figure from the right

married in January with much pomp and circumstance. An elaborate trousseau was produced with many dozens of everything and all of the best. I find it described in a long letter from my mother to one of her American nieces, and can just remember the piles and piles of snowy, lacy things tied together in dozens with pink ribbons, covering an immense table when the trousseau was exhibited to admiring friends.

In the same letter my mother describes the dresses of all the bridal party: Annie wore a pale tea-rose satin *princesse* gown with sweeping train and long tulle veil; Mamma was in purple velvet trimmed with Brussels lace; the bridesmaids in pale blue faille with tea-rose-colored feathers in their bonnets. "Daisy," she writes, "was radiant in faille *vert d'eau*, polonaise of white cashmere bordered with swansdown; hat *vert d'eau* with a swansdown edge and the prevailing *rose-thé* feather." I forgot to say that Mamma had one in her purple velvet bonnet. I can well remember feeling very grand in my pale green silk, white cashmere, swansdown, and pink feather combination.

My other sister, Mimoli Crawford, married Hugh Fraser, a secretary of the British Embassy, the following spring, and after the family exchequer had paid for two trousseaux and two elaborate weddings within a few months of each other, the American remittances suddenly stopped coming. A banker cousin of my mother's had been entrusted with the charge of her property. It was at the time of the great gold speculation on the New York Stock Exchange which ended in the "Black Friday" crash. The cousin had speculated with the money he

had in trust, had lost heavily, throwing good money
after bad. My parents were faced with the necessity
of a complete change in their way of living. Horses and
carriages were sold, the household was reduced, and a
régime of strictest economy enforced.

There were to be no more grandeurs, but I was growing fast and urgently needed new underclothes; these
were ordered of stout "unwearable" cambric without the
least scrap of edging or adornment. I hated their penitential simplicity, and, grudging the older sisters their
superabundance of finery, I felt like a Cinderella forgotten by her fairy godmother. I think this was the
only time I ever truly resented the pinch of poverty.
I had a good cry over it and really never thought of it
again. There were too many better things than clothes
crowding in on life.

V

WEST PRUSSIA IN THE SEVENTIES

WE spent the following June in Venice, to be with the Hugh Frasers before they sailed for China, where Hugh was appointed secretary of the British Legation, to be gone for five years.

Venice was all enchantment. The delicious silence of the gondola after the rattle of the train; the fabulous beauty of the city rising out of the lagoons; the palaces and churches, the Piazza di San Marco, where we fed grain to the pigeons in the morning, and in the afternoons sat at little tables eating ices and listening to music from Florian's, then as now the fashionable confectioner. We made long gondola expeditions to the Lido, to San Giorgio, where we visited the Armenian monastery, and found a young monk happily ensconced in a corner of the garden, reading a forbidden book. We knew it was forbidden, because he hastily hid it under his seat and turned very red and fled away. One of our party had the curiosity to examine the volume, which was no other than *I Promessi Sposi*, Manzoni's classic novel. An all-day expedition to Torcello, to see its wonderful mosaics and remnants of long-ruined splendors. Another to Murano, where we saw the glass factory and watched the making

of beads and the blowing of liquid glass into great magical
bubbles to be fashioned into vases and bottles and
chandeliers.   Every day brought forth new marvels.
But the happiest hours of all were those I was allowed
to spend alone in the Accademia, the incomparable picture
gallery.   It lay near our hotel and it was miraculously
decreed that I might go there alone, since I seemed to
enjoy it so much, and fill my eyes with loveliness.   Titian,
the two Bellinis, and Carpaccio were my favorites; I was
particularly charmed by Giovanni Bellini's little allegories,
not that I very well understood their meaning, but they
seemed exquisitely to belong to the world of fairy tales
and wonderland in which I still lived.

It was many years before I saw them again and with
the eyes of an experienced sight-seer.   I was glad to find
them as intimately pleasing as ever; and I was also glad
to have my childish preference so well confirmed.

After seeing the Frasers sail away in their P. & O. liner
to brave the Far-Eastern adventure, my mother, two
brothers, and I went to Germany to pass the rest of the
summer with the Rabes on their West Prussian estates,
while my father went to New York to see what he could
recover of my mother's shattered fortune.   He managed
to save a small remnant of capital, enough to yield a
very modest income, enough for us to live on in the Rome
of those days, which, besides being the place that we
loved best in the world, had the solid merit of being
cheap.

We reached Lesnian in the late Northern spring, and
the great lilac hedge around the lawn was still in bloom
when we arrived.   Old Frau von Rabe, Erich's mother,

welcomed us with every hospitality. She was a tall stately woman in bandeaux and wore a black lace cap whose purple ribbons and lace hung over her ears and neck. She lived in the big house that had been left her for her lifetime.

Annie and Erich occupied the so-called "Pavillon," connected with it by a greenhouse. This had been built by a Neapolitan general, a Frenchman who had served, fought, and commanded under the Neapolitan Bourbons, and who had, when retired, attached himself to the Rabe family. They invited him to spend the rest of his days with them and he built himself this pleasant little house next to theirs, and lived in it till he died. I am sorry to remember so little of what I must have been told about this romantic old gentleman, who left the beauties of the Bay of Naples to live in a flat Northern country of fir forest and potato fields for the sake of ending his days near the family of his choice. He introduced tomatoes to the Lesnian vegetable garden, to bring perhaps a note of the warm South into his dietary exile; they did well there and were much appreciated as an exotic delicacy. His last years were spent in a wheel chair, which, long after his death, was still to be heard rolling in the attic of the Pavillon, where it had been stored. Frightened housemaids heard it in the middle of the night, rumbling over their heads.

We were comfortably lodged in the big house. It was a roomy, mid-nineteenth-century structure with a handsome *perron;* it was surrounded by a *parc à l'anglaise,* that is, by lawns and shrubberies merging into woods, with a winding driveway and paths and arbors. To re-

lieve the featureless flatness of the prospect a pond had
been dug in the middle of a little wood, and the earth
that came out had been piled into a small hillock, the
only protuberance the landscape boasted as far as the
eye could reach; it was always referred to as "the hill."

To me the greatest charm of Lesnian lay in the
Gemüsegarten, a big walled garden where fruits and
vegetables abounded and flowers were grown for the
house. Brink, the tidy German gardener, was very
kind to me and allowed me to cut all the flowers I wanted;
armfuls of them, from the long beds of tulips and narcissi,
forget-me-nots, mignonette, stocks, and all the old garden
favorites. It was my first acquaintance with a real
garden; Italian villas have no flowers to speak of, and
I had never dreamed of picking all the tulips I wanted;
it gave me a sort of rapture. From that time on I have
loved gardens with an abiding love, but it was to be many
years before I was to have one of my own.

The house was run on a generous scale. There was
the old gray-whiskered butler who had been with the
family since Erich and his younger brother, Oskar, were
children, and who was supposed to be peculiarly sympathetic to young men who had taken too much the night
before. He had, they said, a most tactful manner of
rousing them out of their morning slumbers, asking,
*"Will Herr Baronchen ein Glas Selterwasserchen, oder
vielleicht ein Heringchen geniessen?"* ("Would the little
baron take a wee glass of soda water or perhaps a little
herring to make him feel better?") — but the caressing
German diminutives are untranslatable. The upper house
servants were all German; there was a German "Mam-

sell" housekeeper in charge of the establishment, and a great number of Polish *Mariellen*, a word halfway between "wench" and "slut," working in the kitchen, dairy, and stillroom. The coachman, grooms, and farm hands were all Polish, lived squalidly, were all illiterate, and were treated as serfs. Their Prussian masters did not hesitate to handle them roughly upon occasion; they seemed abject and brutish; at all events they were treated so.

In every Polish village there was a little shop run by a Jew. He sold everything from farm implements to *schnapps*; he lent money at high interest and was so much more intelligent than the simple folk of the glebe that he could do what he liked with them. He was often justice of the peace. I think the office was elective and that Erich succeeded in ousting him and holding it for a while, but the peasants, who were all the Jew's debtors, eventually fell back into his toils. At the harvest festival they all came to do a sort of homage; the family and any guests who might be staying in the house stood on the steps of the porch and watched the parade of farm wagons, horses, and cattle, and peasants. Men, women, and children came up, some bringing flowers and fruits of the field and orchard, and all embraced our knees and kissed our hands. They were a people conquered and oppressed.

Erich had a sister and brother younger than himself. Adelheid, the sister, was very kind to us children, and we grew fond of her; not so Annie, who disliked her heartily, and soon concentrated her power of hating upon her.

Fortunately for Adelheid she had an admirer, Charles

Robertson, the son of a famous English preacher; he and his sister came to Lesnian for a long visit at the end of which Adelheid and Robertson became engaged. I do not know if marriage was his purpose in coming or if love was developed by the long colloquies in the shady arbor; in any case his presence must have given her pleasanter things to think about than Annie's obvious antipathy to her.

Robertson was tall and handsome; rather soft-looking, though perhaps only by contrast with the martial bearing of the Rabe brothers and cousins. He read aloud very well, and those of us who understood English would gather about him on rainy mornings and listen with delight to his reading of Edgar Allan Poe's stories and poems. His rendering of "The Gold-Bug," his almost chanting of "The Bells" and "The Raven," were unforgettable. It was my first introduction to Poe's weird magic of sonorities that has never lost its spell for me.

Old Frau von Rabe, *née* von Schenck, had grown up in friendly intimacy with the Bismarck family; she and the Iron Chancellor were on terms of "thee" and "thou," having played together as children and seen much of one another during their youth in Berlin, when Frau von Rabe was lady in waiting to the Queen of Prussia.

When Annie and Erich were in Berlin as a newly married couple they were entertained by the Bismarcks. Annie described the party to us, and a certain bourgeois simplicity that reigned in the princely household. The table was handsomely spread for supper, but the sausages were not the kind the Iron Chancellor preferred, and he called to his wife that he wanted the other kind, and she dutifully left the room and returned with a platter of the *Leibwurst* in her hand. He carried Annie off to a sofa for a quiet chat, much interested in the fact that she was an American. He began to talk American slang and then to sing American college songs in a low voice. Annie, who knew little or no American slang, and had, I suppose, never heard an American college song, showed her great surprise and asked him where he had learned it all. "Oh, from my good friend Motley, when we were students together in Bonn." The intimacy between the American historian-ambassador and the great German statesman lasted through life. Annie and Erich never returned to Berlin, and left Lesnian only to take a through train to Rome when they could get away; so they saw no more of the Bismarcks after that first meeting.

We spent another summer at Lesnian two years later, when I was a *Backfisch* of fourteen and took more part in the family life. The house was again full of relatives: Frau von Rabe's brother, General von Schenck, and his two daughters, Lily, who later married the great historian von Willamovitz, and Theresa; Thekla von Brauchitsch, another cousin; and a number of good-looking officers, cousins, all in Guard regiments. We danced, played games, we waxed sentimental.

The prestige of a German officer in those days is hard to exaggerate. He was the centre of all attraction. In his smart uniform he had the brilliance of a tropical bird, of a rare orchid. He belonged to an all-powerful organization. He represented youth and power in gorgeous panoply. The girl or woman who fell in love with him was carried along by all her loyalties.   How could she do otherwise than place him on a high pedestal and burn incense before him?   He was to her the *Vaterland*-made man; and such a smart, good-looking man!

Their fathers, uncles, and grandfathers were all generals.   I asked them once if they had any male relatives not in the army.   They looked surprised, and thought very hard for a moment before remembering a distant cousin who, being a cripple, had become a lawyer.   Oskar von Rabe, Erich's younger brother, Captain in the *Garde-Cuirassiers*, was the life of the party.   He sang and I played his accompaniments; he danced beautifully.   We were told he was the best dancer in Berlin, and much run after by the great ladies.   We girls were all a little sentimental about him, and felt it could not be otherwise, he was so gay and so human.

That second summer we spent at Lesnian, my aunt, Julia Ward Howe, brought Maud, her youngest daughter, to Europe.   They were in London for the season; Aunt Julia had many friends there.   Those were the days of professional beauties, a group that seems to have comprised every class of society — great ladies, lesser ladies, actresses, and so forth.   Their photographs were for sale, and when one of them entered a ballroom, it was said that people stood on chairs to see them over the heads of other onlookers.   Maud Howe was very handsome, and much admired in the beauty-loving London of the '70s.   Frau von Rabe heard that the Howes were coming to Germany and invited them to Lesnian.   My mother had not seen her sister for many years and was delighted when they wrote their acceptance.

Aunt Julia was a personage; I have never met any-one in the least like her. A small woman of no particular shape or carriage, her clothes never taken care of, her bonnets never quite straight on her head; and yet there was about her presence an unforgettable distinction and importance. Her voice in speaking was very beautiful, her face had a sensitive gravity, a look of compassionate wisdom, until a twinkle of fun rippled over it and a naughty imp laughed in her eyes. She had none of my mother's holy meekness; she could upon occasion show temper (her hair had been red, although I knew her only when it was gray). She was an intellectual, a student of philosophy, a writer of serious essays, a Greek scholar, an early and ardent champion of woman's rights; but all this seriousness was leavened by a flashing wit and a capacity for excellent fooling.

Her husband, Dr. Samuel Gridley Howe, had died the winter before she and Maud came abroad. He was much older than she, had been a great philanthropist, an abettor of revolutions and champion of all who suffered oppression. As a young man he had gone to Greece to fight for its liberation from the Turkish yoke. He arrived there just as Byron died, attended his funeral, and brought his helmet home to Boston as a treasured relic. He tried to help the Poles in their struggle for liberty, and had been arrested in Berlin, when carrying important and incriminating papers, during the revolutionary days that sent so many distinguished German liberals to this country in perpetual exile. The Prussian police had come to his hotel early one morning and knocked at the door of his room, bidding him open in the name of the law. He had slept with the papers under his pillow, and in the few seconds that elapsed before he unlocked the door, he had the presence of mind to stuff them into the hollow bust of the King of Prussia that adorned the mantelpiece; the police came in, searched everything but the sacrosanct replica of their royal sovereign, and found nothing. Nevertheless they bade Dr. Howe pack his valises forthwith while they looked on, and marched him off to prison. He spent six weeks there and was released by the intervention of the United States Minister. Some years later a reliable friend was sent to Berlin to occupy that same room and retrieve the papers.

After he married Aunt Julia they both became enthusiastic abolitionists. They were friends of Charles Sumner, Wendell Phillips, and of all that group, so frowned upon by Boston's more conservative element. Besides his political and revolutionary philanthropy, Dr. Howe was very active in other fields — in teaching the dumb to speak with their hands, the blind to read with their fingers. He was instrumental in founding schools for their education, and was for many years at the head of the great Perkins Institute in South Boston, where the blind were trained to useful trades. His must have been a romantic figure — a bold rider, a fearless partisan in the cause of the weak and the oppressed. He could not have approved of his wife and daughter consorting on friendly terms with Prussian generals and their officer sons. All the glitter of military rule had no glamour for him.

Nor, indeed, did it for his widow, who was at first amused and then perhaps a little bored by the elaborate

German formality that prevailed at Lesnian. The house party consisted of some fifteen or sixteen people of all ages, all closely related, and at the end of every meal, every man present, from the oldest general to the youngest lieutenant, went around the room and solemnly kissed the hand of every woman, be she dowager or *Backfisch*, saying, *"Gesegnete Mahlzeit"* (blessed meal). Aunt Julia thought she would introduce a little diversion into the rite: in the midst of all the ceremonious hand kissing she tripped across the room to where I stood and solemnly pulled my nose. There was a moment of consternation, nobody even smiled; the only thing to do was to pretend it had not happened. It would certainly never happen again; and, "Oh," she said to me later when we were alone together, "it was not funny at all!" It was perhaps in half-conscious tribute to Dr. Howe's fiery liberalism that the odd little demonstration was made.

When the Crawford sisters were married my mother had agreed to make them handsome allowances. It was a verbal promise not ratified by legal contract or marriage settlements. The change in her circumstances made it quite impossible to keep this promise; she gave them what she could, depriving herself of all superfluities; had the full allowances been continued, there would have been less than nothing left for the rest of the family. It was towards the end of our second summer at Lesnian when the situation which had been going on for over two years became acute. Most of the summer guests had departed, the officers having gone back to their regiments, and everything seemed very peaceful and friendly with those that remained, when Annie suddenly unmasked her batteries. She came into my mother's sitting room late one evening after what company there was had parted for the night, and made one of her great terrifying scenes, declaring she was being defrauded, that she must and would have the money that had been promised, that Mamma must give, though the rest of the family starve, and many other cruel and outrageous things. Poor Mamma was in tears; she had no kind of retort; she could only say how deeply grieved she was and exhort the furious Annie to patience. These dreadful visitations of Hecate repeated themselves night after night, while by day everyone seemed as pleasant and friendly as possible. On one occasion Annie brought Madame Mère, as she called her mother-in-law, and her daughter Adelheid, now Mrs. Robertson, to strengthen the attack; they came to add their comments and corroborate Annie's claim that the sum promised at the time of her marriage must be paid in full. My poor mother could only weep and protest and finally went on her knees, imploring them as Christian gentlewomen to cease from their recriminations. Aunt Julia came in on one of these painful colloquies and was magnificent. She was not afraid of Annie nor of the corporate nobility of Prussia; they seemed to her a mere "pack of cards." She told Annie that she remembered her a naughty, bad-hearted little girl, and what she thought of her present behavior, in plain terms.

The Howes left Lesnian for further travels; Aunt Julia strongly urged us to accompany them, but it seemed to be out of the question, however much we longed to leave the house where the laws of hospitality were being so flagrantly violated. We had not the wherewithal and, besides, Mamma fondly hoped to placate the fury with tender words, when only hard and unobtainable cash would have served. So we stayed on into late September, harassed and humiliated, till the time came for us to go back to Rome and peace. I could never see how my mother endured those dreadful weeks.

Annie insisted that we should travel second class, in what turned out to be a crowded compartment, on the long night journey to Berlin. It was before the days of sleeping cars. We sat up all through the comfortless night, chewing the bitter cud of experience. The train drew into the station about five o'clock on that dismal autumn morning. We could not have felt more forlorn, when there in the drizzling dawn on the wet platform stood Oskar von Rabe, all glorious to behold in his white and blue and silver uniform, looking like St. Michael or Lohengrin. He had come to meet us and did everything to make us enjoy our two days in Berlin — took us to lunch at a gay restaurant, showed us the sights, and sent me the first box of bonbons I had ever received from a man. I never doubted that he was really charming.

Erich died in 1883, leaving Annie a disconsolate widow with two small children, Louise and Fritz. Erich had died suddenly. He had gone upstairs for the night; she was about to follow him when she heard a heavy fall, rushed up to see what had happened, and found him dead. He was buried in the family vault not far from the house, and Annie spent long hours lying prone on the cold ground to be as near him as possible. She was terribly alone; a stranger among strangers. Eventually she found doubtful comfort in mediumistic communications,

and became more and more absorbed by that dangerous
shadowland.   Fritz grew into a most attractive boy; he
was sent to a preparatory school for the *Kadettenkorps,*
and died there at fourteen.   It was a cruel blow to
Annie, who, through his death, lost her right to live at
Lesnian.   Erich left no will, and a German widow has no
claim on her husband's estate.   As long as old Frau von
Rabe lived, Annie was allowed to occupy her Pavillon,
but with her mother-in-law's death the place went to
Oskar.

This left Annie homeless and practically childless, for
she and Louise, her sixteen-year-old daughter, could not
get on together.   She had very little money and a great
deal of unavailable talent.   She wrote two short stories
which Macmillan published under the name of von
Degen.   (The Rabes would have felt it a disgrace to
have their name appear on the cover of a book.)

The writing was so good that the publishers begged
for more, but she could not bring herself to the discipline
of work.   She had a charming creative fancy and was
full of original ideas that she would begin to put down
but could never finish; suggestive titles for stories that
were never told.   One of these I remember was "The
Little Paper City of Hope."   Marion was so pleased
with this name for a book that he bought it from her,
seeing that she would never use it.   He wrote a novel
around the name, quite different and not half as original
as the tale she had in mind but could not bring to birth.
Her talent had a finer edge than his.   She drifted back
to Italy and finally settled in Rome, where she fell more
and more into the clutches of a medium, a spiritistic

padrona with whom she lived and by whom she was exploited. She became bedridden and lay for years in sordid surroundings of her own choosing, with no solace beyond remembering the past, her loves and hates, her great gifts, her keen sense of beauty, all brought low. I was in America when I heard of her death; it brought a great sense of pity and relief. I put on no mourning.

VI

FLORENCE AND FREE THOUGHT

THE year after they were married Annie and her husband came to stay at the Palazzo Odescalchi. Annie was to have her baby there and it was thought expedient to get me out of the way. So I was sent to a very small boarding school in Florence. It was hardly a school; Fräulein Johanna Müller took a few pupils to live with her in a sunny apartment with a pretty walled garden in the Via del Mandorlo. She had been a governess, the old-fashioned type of really cultivated teacher and educator to whom work was a vocation; ardent to communicate her knowledge and contented with her lot if she succeeded in forming and guiding a few young minds and morals.

Fräulein Müller had been warmly recommended to my mother by her friend the Countess Gigliucci, the once-famous Clara Novello, whose sons and daughters were intimate with my Crawford sisters and had been most successfully educated by Fräulein Müller. The latter had begun her career in England with the Primrose family; Archie Primrose, later Lord Rosebery, had been one of her first charges. She did not live to see him Prime Minister, but had much to say about him as a brilliant

and attractive boy. She had brought up another family
of English boys and girls, whose name I forget; she was
fond of all and proud of many of her pupils; several
had made a name for themselves. She had liked England
well, but had come to love Italy so much that at thirty-
five she had decided to leave off being a governess and
start her little school in the Via del Mandorlo.

Nowadays a woman of Fräulein Müller's attainments
would be at the head of some college, organizing liberal
education for the many, a great deal busier and better
paid; but missing perhaps the intimate satisfaction of
kindling the love of learning and thinking in this or that
well-disposed child, in establishing a close, often lasting
and almost parental relation with the girl or boy whose
mind she had brought to bud. The born teacher is a
living torch and cannot but pass the flame to all who are
capable of fire.

There were, of course, innumerable dull, unhappy, and
maladjusted governesses who led pitiful lives in families
not their own, with a daily realization of Dante's "How
salty tastes the bread of others and how steep the climbing up and down of others' stairs"; feeding on their own
hungry hearts; perpetually longing for what was perpetually beyond their reach, though they lived in the
midst of it. Many of these women are better off to-day
earning their living as stenographers, school-teachers, or
whatever; their circumstances may be narrow but they
are their own, whereas the governess is shown by those
about her how pleasant it is to be richer, idler, freer. If
she falls in love with her charges' older brother (this happened twice with us) or any attractive intimate of the

family she happens to be with, and snatches at a hope
born of desire, it generally ends in disaster; hers is for
the most part an unenviable lot.   But there were admirable exceptions, and thank God there always are —
women of courage, intelligence, and zest for whatever
they undertake.   Fräulein Müller was foremost among
these.

Under her guidance I became passionately interested
in my lessons: history, languages, literature, music — all
it was then thought necessary for a young girl to know.
Science and mathematics were left aside, but languages
were taught very carefully.   Literature was the corner
stone; we read a great deal of Dante, Shakespeare, and
Goethe.

I was only allowed to stay with Fräulein Müller for
seven months.   Then my mother learned that she was
an "atheist," that her friends were all freethinkers, that
my soul was imperiled.

There was some truth in this.   Professor Schiff was
our near neighbor and friend, his wife was also a friend
of Fräulein Müller's, and he had a daughter of my age;
we saw a good deal of them.   They were Hebrews.
The Professor was the one I liked best.   He had a great
deal of white hair, a long white beard, and very living,
searching brown eyes.   We often went to his laboratory,
just around the corner, where he gave me my first
thrilling glimpses into the wonderland of the microscope: the jeweled texture of a geranium petal, the delicate feathery dust that colors the butterfly's wings, the
spider's claw that carries a dainty tortoise-shell comb,
and the fairy toys all carved in purest ivory revealed in

a pinch of chalk.   I had no idea the world was so beautiful all the way through.

Professor Schiff was a then-famous physiologist and
kept a yard full of dogs for experiments in vivisection.
The thrills of the laboratory were not all æsthetic.   On
one occasion some gruesome gobbets of raw meat lay on
the table near the microscope.   "Oh, those are nothing,"
said the Professor; "the muscles of a man who died of
typhus; I was just examining them."

Fräulein Müller had another great friend in Professor
Moleschott, a noted doctor and physicist, who published
a much-talked-of book in which he stated that without
phosphorus there could be no thought.   *Ohne Phosphor
kein Gedanke* became a kind of catchword in discussions
on the immortality of the soul.   It discarded the *anima
cogitativa* of the schools into the limbo of the negligibly
improbable.

Materialism and rationalism were in the air, though
they had never reached the second floor of the Palazzo
Odescalchi, and my mother was shocked at the thought
that I was being exposed to the dangers of this new way
of thinking.   My salvation was at stake; I was impera-
tively ordered home, just as I was going to learn about
everything.   Fräulein Müller and I wept in each other's
arms; and we were both sure I should never be educated;
we felt we were the victims of cruel obscurantism.   But
there was no disobeying orders and I went home for
Christmas terribly disappointed and downcast.   I was
thirteen.   My life would be a failure!

In my mother's sense the harm was done; bringing
me home did not mend it; Fräulein Müller knew noth-

ing of religious practice or experience; she represented
the intelligentsia of her day, for whom faith was a cast-
off shackle of the mind.   She did not disparage religion
but completely ignored it; yet I remember her reading
me Faust's words to Gretchen in the famous garden
scene: —

> *Wer darf ihn nennen*
> *Und wer bekennen*
> *Ich glaub ihn?*
> *Wer empfinden*
> *Und sich unterwinden*
> *Zu sagen: ich glaub ihn nicht?*
> *Der Allumfasser,*
> *Der Allerhalter,*
> *Fasst und erhält er nicht*
> *Dich, mich, sich selbst?*

> (Who may name Him and profess belief?
>   Who can feel and cheat himself to say,
>   I do not believe Him?
> The all-embracer, the all-preserver,
>   Does He not hold us,
>   Does He not preserve
>   You, me, Himself?)

She read the lines reverently, with deep sense of their
meaning.

Fräulein Müller would twenty years later have been
called an agnostic.   She was a born teacher and awakener
of the mind, and kindled an ardent thirst for knowledge
in her willing pupils.   She aroused intellectual curiosity.
It seemed there was nothing one could not learn about
and master — "languages, history, art, all the natural
sciences at my fingers' ends," I wrote in a letter of reso-

lutions in which I outlined my ambitions with pitiful fatuity.   I am sure she conscientiously abstained from trying to shake my childish faith in religion as it had been taught me, but the admiration she inspired convinced me that whatever she thought and did was right, and there was no concealing the fact that she never went to church. And she did do fancywork on Sundays; something my mother never allowed.

I came home more than ever estranged from Anglican observance.   The services in the church outside the walls were jejune, uninspiring; their only hold on the imagination lay in the beauty of the language, and this I admit was a strong one.   The Book of Common Prayer, and above all the King James version of the Bible, are incomparable; these I never ceased to love, nor can I forget the impression made on me by the last chapter of Ecclesiastes, when I heard it for the first time beautifully read by some visiting English Bishop — I was still a child and did not in the least understand what it was all about, the silver cord, the golden bowl, the daughters of music, or the voice of the bird, but the high magic of the words caught me up in a golden rapture.

On the other hand the Anglican catechism seemed infinitely tedious and the English hymns very four-square and dull, when all about us the Roman bells rang out the splendid braided rhythm of the liturgical cycles.   The joyful, the sorrowful, the glorious mysteries; these were the heart throbs of Rome.

In Holy Week we always attended the Office of Tenebræ.   I particularly liked to hear it at St. John Lateran.   The lamentations of Jeremiah are sung to ancient melodies whose origin is lost in the many centuries through which they have been handed down.   Perhaps they were Hebrew threnodies; they are the immemorial cry of human sorrow and desolation, answered by the beautiful responsory: *"Jerusalem, Jerusalem, convertere ad Dominum Deum tuum."*   Then the singing of the Miserere in the gathering dusk when all the candles had been extinguished save the one which was hidden behind the altar, and the crowd knelt in silent recollection till the final *strepitus* (the banging of books and benches) broke the spell and sent us out into the tender twilight of the Roman spring, back to the present realities of our little human lives.   Marion and I often walked home together; our way lay by all the great Roman monuments — Constantine's Basilica, the Colosseum, the Forum, the Capitol; and the pageant of Roman history seemed to have a sharper outline than the happenings of our own existence.   The great Past is not dead in Rome — rather does it at times make the Present seem shadowy and ephemeral; we become a part of the stream of life that has flowed for so many centuries past those same temples, arches of triumph, porticoes, and palaces.

The other day I heard a talk by an intelligent American schoolmaster about a new school he was opening in New Mexico.   He gave us his very enlightened ideas on education and told us that he laid particular stress on the teaching of history, avoiding the use of textbooks, rather letting the boys browse at will through a number of books on the subject in hand.   Then he showed us pictures of the school.   It was very healthily situated between a

sandy desert and snow-capped mountains — and I wondered what historic images could shape themselves in the
brains of boys who had nothing to look at but sand and
snow.   Rome tells us her story without reference to textbooks.   It sinks into our sense of things and becomes
part of our consciousness, as it never can to a child brought
up in a new country lacking all concrete images of the
past.

My mother had me prepared for confirmation, hoping
to waken my languid interest in the Protestant Episcopal
branch of the true Church.   She maintained that Protestantism and Catholicism were both equally true; that
Almighty God held the two in His two hands without
preference for either; but she did not like people to change
from one to the other.   Not that she liked the word
"Protestant."   She had leanings to the Tractarians, who
revived so much that was Catholic in the ritual and
practice of the English Church, and preferred to call it
Anglo-Catholic.   She was sorry that Newman, whom she
so greatly admired, should have gone over to Rome.

I can remember little about my confirmation and first
communion; I went through with them because my
mother wanted me to, without unction or conviction,
feeling all the while that if I belonged to any church it
was not to this one.   But I cannot say that my thoughts
ran much on religion at this time.

Our pew in the English Church was on the aisle at
right angles to the nave, where the first pew was occupied by Sir Augustus Paget, the English Minister, afterwards Ambassador to the King of Italy.   With him were

Lady Paget, two sons, who only appeared during the Christmas and Easter holidays in their smart Eton suits and top hats, and a daughter of my own age. This daughter, Gay (now the Dowager Lady Plymouth), captivated my listless attention away from services and sermons. She was enchantingly pretty and her mother dressed her with a certain æsthetic eccentricity. She had stepped out of a Walter Crane picture book. Those were the days of Morris, Burne-Jones, the Pre-Raphaelites, and "High Art" in England. We had seen nothing like it in Rome. I gazed at her through several Sunday services, then to my great delight was invited to meet her by a common friend of my mother's and Lady Paget's, who thought it would be nice for the two little girls to play together. I well remember the occasion; we were both a little shy.

Lady Paget took a fancy to me, and I was often asked to come to nursery tea at the Embassy near the Porta Pia. The ice was soon broken. Gay, with her real beauty and her odd English picturesqueness, seemed a creature of another world. She was intelligent besides, and as she grew older developed a talent for drawing and a charming voice. We became friends. In time she married and had children, and so indeed did I. I see her only at rare intervals, but never without some of the old delight; she was my first choice.

We had the same music master, old Mr. Ravnkilde, and he also loved. "*Ach*," he would say, "Miss Gay, she has the eyes of the wife of the deer!" This was in the intermission, while he sipped the glass of Marsala and ate the lady finger my mother always put on the

piano for him.   Poor Mr. Ravnkilde!   He was one of
the many called by the Muse and then not chosen.   He
was a Dane, and as a young man he went to Leipzig in
1847, hoping to study with Felix Mendelssohn-Bar-
tholdy, who unfortunately died the day Ravnkilde arrived
there — so he returned to Copenhagen and studied with
Gade instead.   Gade had been Mendelssohn's favorite
pupil.   Someone said on hearing one of Gade's compositions, "That sounds so like Mendelssohn that it must
have been written by Gade."   Ravnkilde wrote very
square, correct, and lifeless pieces for the piano, and gave
lessons for his living, to pupils who did not take music
too seriously.   Everybody had to take piano lessons in
those days.

My education did not come to the complete standstill
foreseen by Fräulein Müller when I was taken away from
her school.   It became more desultory, less scientifically
planned; I was allowed to study the things I liked and
had interesting teachers to humor me in my choice.   One
of these was a very learned German governess, Fräulein
Hoepfner, who wrote articles for the *Deutsche Rund-
schau,* and knew more history than anyone I ever met.
She had some degree of literary reputation, for when the
Dowager Empress Friedrich Karl (mother of Emperor
William) came to Rome she sent for Fräulein Hoepfner
to come and see her.   She wrote an excellent little
handbook for travelers about the saints in Christian art,
giving a short outline of their lives and the attributes by
which they may be identified; and she could write out the
genealogies of every reigning house in Europe, including
those that had long ceased to reign.   She was not at all

good-looking, but had a vague likeness to Botticelli's portrait of the Tornabuoni lady that made her face interesting. She fell in love with my handsome brother Marion and wrote a good deal of melancholy verse on the subject of her unrequited affection, speaking of herself as the poor, pale flower left to wither by the roadside. Marion liked her well enough and enjoyed talking to her; she was a brilliant woman in her way but doomed to dimness in the field of romance.

Jean Paul Richter, who later made a name for himself as an art critic and collector, first came to Rome as tutor to some little German princes, children of the Grand Duke of Nassau, which was still an independent principality. He became so interested in art and archæology that he gave up his position and remained in Rome to study these, supporting himself by giving private lessons. He used to take me and my governess sight-seeing once a week, and the history of art was diligently studied under his direction. Germans have a sense of "high seriousness" in this field and a happy combination of spiritual enthusiasm (*Begeisterung*) with intellectual thoroughness.

Burckhardt, Lessing, and above all Winckelmann were our textbooks, and we were taught to be very pure and classic in our tastes. Only Greek art and that of the Renaissance were thought worthy of our attention. Art critics had not then learned to appreciate the splendors of *Roma barocca;* the broken pediment, invented, I think, by Michelangelo for the Medicean tombs, was an abomination to them. Bernini's genius was held to be wholly decadent and misdirected, although even then it could

not be denied that some of his architecture was magnificent. Our whole attention was taken up by a remoter
past; but it did not go back of the fifteenth century.
The Romanesque was left for future generations to
appreciate, it was thought rude and quaint; little or no
attention was paid to the wealth of mosaics that have
adorned the Roman basilicas since the time of Constantine. But there was much to see and admire that lay
safely within the limits of Greek and Renaissance Italian
art. Michelangelo was as far as we went — he was the
heaven-storming Titan who left no successor. Any
early acquaintance with these incontestable masterpieces
breeds, I think, a constancy of the æsthetic sense. We
may later learn to appreciate other schools and widely
different ones, but the great masters of Greece and Italy
have taught us to look for what is essential to all art;
its imperishable message that the world is full of beauty
for those who have eyes to see. True art must be life-
enhancing, quickening and intensifying the spirit to a
sense of things immortal. It should in happy moments
reveal to us the Splendor of Truth and make us feel the
Eternal Present behind the shadow dance of fashion and
experience.

The great arts of the past have for the most part been
religious and hieratic; those of the present show a tendency to choose the purely material, the ugly, and the
vulgar for their subjects. We of the older school find
it hard to keep pace with their vagaries, but let us not
be too sure of ourselves. Scripture tells us that St.
Peter went up upon the housetop to pray, and became
very hungry and fell into a trance, "and saw heaven

opened, and a certain vessel descending unto him . . .
wherein were all manner of fourfooted beasts of the
earth, and wild beasts, and creeping things, and fowls of
the air. And there came a voice to him, Rise, Peter, kill,
and eat. But Peter said, Not so, Lord; for I have never
eaten any thing that is common or unclean. And the
voice spake unto him again the second time, What God
hath cleansed, that call not thou common." With the
same assurance and perhaps some justification the modern
artist bids us cast away our prejudices as to what is right
and seemly for art to represent.

Twice a week the learned Don Raffaelle Pagliari
came to read Dante with us; my mother always shared
these lessons and they were delightful. Don Raffaelle
seemed to have stepped out of a Longhi picture, in his
buckled knee breeches and shoes with larger buckles,
his broad-skirted coat and *tricorne* hat: the eighteenth-
century abbé. His clean-shaven face had a Socratic nose
which he liked one to notice. He was profoundly learned
and owned one of the most important collections of
Dante publications. He was chaplain to the Prince Gabrieli, who had married one of the Bonaparte Princesses. We sometimes went to see him in his rooms in
the Palazzo Gabrieli, literally stacked with books; par-
titions made of bookcases dividing and subdividing the
by no means spacious apartment till there was barely
room for Don Raffaelle to sleep there in a little corner
behind a bookcase.

He had the heart of a child, with great but entirely
specialized learning of that infinitely painstaking, accumu-
lative, unproductive variety to which Italian scholarship

often tends. He was over sixty when he came to give us lessons, and had spent his whole laborious life studying the *Divina Commedia*, making endless notes, following up every allusion. He knew where and how all the people mentioned had lived and all their private feuds and happenings. He intended some day to write a book about it, but was, I suspect, incapable of synthesis and lost in the great forest of which he so faithfully studied the trees.

It took us three years to read the *Divine Comedy* through with him, giving two or three lessons to each of the hundred cantos. I suppose no human work takes in more human experience, no poet has combined such eagle flights of the imagination with such deep sense of the ultimate, inexorable order of divine justice. Dante's poetry, his philosophy, his faith, sank very deep into my soul, and I am always grateful to Don Raffaelle for his painstaking initiation.

Outside of Dante he knew little. He was asked once to make out a catalogue of all foreign translations and adaptations of the *Commedia*. He knew no English and asked me to revise and correct a list he had compiled. I found among the translations mentioned Milton's *Paradise Lost*. "But, dear Don Raffaelle, this is an original work and no translation." "Perhaps not an exact translation, but it must have been inspired by Dante."

I always wondered why St. Augustine tells us to fear the man of one book. Is it because the one book has a tendency to build a Chinese Wall about the mind? It gives a sense of security and fosters intellectual dogmatism and incuriosity; eventually the stream of life passes over it, or finds a way round.

Some years later a friend of mine and I took lessons in Thomistic philosophy with a Monsignor Binzecker, who taught it at a seminary. He was profoundly learned and knew all St. Thomas by heart. If you asked him what he thought of Kant or Schopenhauer or John Stuart Mill, he would say with perfect simplicity, "Dear ladies, what is the use of reading these false philosophies; if what they say is true you will find it in St. Thomas, if it is not true you do not find it there. *Chi non dice così, dice spropositi.*" (Who does not speak thus speaks nonsense — only it is impossible to translate the pithy popular idiom, with the Italian pejorative prefix changing "proposition" into "absurdity.")

VII

ENTER MUSIC

WHILE I was with Fräulein Müller music suddenly became more important to me than all else; I suppose it was part of my general awakening; it came upon me with the intensity of a conversion. I happened to read a life of Beethoven in a German periodical for the young. Not unlike Michelangelo, Beethoven, that other Promethean Titan, completed and transcended a great cycle of classic art. His tragic story seemed to kindle my spirit with some of the fire he had brought down from heaven; it was another initiation. We are told that reading Beethoven's life had the same effect on Richard Wagner when he was a boy and was the spark that kindled that mighty beacon. The same torch may set fire to a palace or a haycock.

From always having enjoyed music I found myself transported by it; from practising half-heartedly for an hour a day, I began to work seriously at scales and finger exercises; to study Czerny, Cramer, and Clementi. In a couple of years I began to feel the need of a more interesting teacher. Mr. Ravnkilde was very pathetic. I think I was the only pupil he ever had who worked hard and ambitiously. "I knew," he said, with tears in his eyes, "that you would have to go to Sgambati, but I thought I was good enough to teach you for another year." Youth is cruel; I was sorry for Ravnkilde but entirely happy when Sgambati consented to give me lessons.

Giovanni Sgambati was Liszt's pupil, an admirable pianist and composer of merit. From Liszt he had received the Chopin tradition at first hand.

He would not teach unless he felt sure there was something to be done with the pupil. His method of eliminating the undesirables was to go to them once and never again. This was said to happen very often, and it was for this reason that he never gave new pupils lessons in his own house. Once interested in a pupil he was the kindest and most stimulating of teachers. He was a classic perfectionist; there was a quality of a Greek gem about his playing. Those who did not like it called it cold; it was certainly not rhapsodic, but could rise to great heights of a sort of noble enthusiasm. To hear him play Beethoven's Emperor Concerto always gave one the sense of having been present at a very great event. And Bach's D Minor Concerto was an unfailing rapture. That passage in the first movement which takes the place of a cadenza, where the left hand plays over and into the right in one of those exquisite ice-crystal figures of which Bach alone has the secret, can never have been played with a more intimate sense of its beauty.

Where would Sgambati stand now, in the great mêlée of globe-trotting *virtuosi?* It is hard to say. His horror of travel, his lack of ambition and averseness to being managed and arranged for, coupled with a certain irresponsibility, would probably have put him out of the running. He seemed happy enough in his rather obscure existence, obscure, that is, for a man of his real attainment. He was by far the best in the little Roman world of his day. Five or six chamber-music concerts given by his Società del Quintetto and a couple of appearances with the orchestra conducted by Ettore Pinelli seemed to satisfy any desire he had for contact with the public. He wrote two quintettes, several *concertos,* many piano pieces, a symphony; of late years Fritz Kreisler plays his little *gondoliera* for violin. He enjoyed giving lessons, so he assured me, and we, his grateful and devoted pupils, must have given him that sense of being understood and appreciated which the stars of the concert halls get from thunderous applause and curtain calls.

Several attempts were made to thrust him out into the greater musical world. He actually went to London once and played there with so much success that a manager engaged him and arranged a string of concerts for the following season. When the time came to leave Rome and undertake the journey, his valises were on the cab and he in it on his way to the station, when a horror of the adventure overcame him, and the futility of fame. The *vetturino* was told to go back to the house in the Via della Croce, the valises were unpacked, the London manager was notified that the Maestro was unavoidably prevented from appearing in London, and he, the dear Maestro, since he remained in Rome, felt he had chosen the better part.

The enchanting Rome of early summer — all the foreigners gone, the air full of the sound of fountains and the scent of flowers; the streets deserted during the noon hours, coming to life in the cool of the evening; all the pleasant summer street life, leisurely and sentimental; little tables on the piazzas with ices and coffee where the girls sat beside their mothers and exchanged shy, amorous glances with young men they did not know, or well-chaperoned conversation with those who joined the family group.

The streets were full of love-making that floated in the air like pollen in a flower garden. Half the time the lovers never exchanged a word. They might belong to very different classes, and know that they could never meet but in the long, long look, or perhaps in a dream. The young princess would sit demurely by her mother's side in the open carriage, for the afternoon *trottata*, but who could prevent the young violinist who played in the orchestra from standing at the corner, where they were sure to pass, and sending out his whole heart to her through his love-lit eyes? These flirtations went on in every class of life; Rome was alive with them, as were other Italian cities. In most cases they went no further than these ardent glances.

A Roman lady met a Danish doctor at my house; he was an old friend of ours and was taking care of my husband. I was telling her who he was when she gave her pretty laugh and said, "Oh, but I know him! He is an old street flirt of mine." She was very beautiful; a famous serenade was written to her, set to music and sung all over Italy; Lenbach had painted her as a girl and called the picture "A Roman Beauty."

Do not let me, by this little Roman parenthesis, con-

vey the impression that my dear Sgambati was one to
loiter on the street corners indulging the lust of the eye.
He was happily married to the woman of his choice, the
good Signora Costanza, and was no philanderer. When
one saw him in the street (he always walked to his lessons) he would have a big cigar in his mouth, a soft
black hat pulled well down over his head, his long musical
hair hanging over his ears and neck, not very tidy, but
he himself entirely serious and respectable. He was an
inspiring and exacting teacher; nothing was ever quite
good enough for him, yet a word or a smile of approval
was beyond words exciting and exhilarating.

When I was about fourteen my mother took me one
afternoon to see the great Madame Helbig. I was
working hard at my music and Madame Helbig's house
was a centre of musical life. She was a Russian, *née*
Princess Schachowskoia, a gifted and unique figure. She
had studied with Clara Schumann and later with Liszt
and was a good pianist and excellent musician. She
married Professor Wolfgang Helbig, Director of the
German School of Archæology in Rome. They lived
on the Tarpeian Rock, in a roomy modern house built
for the Archæological Institute by the German Government, near the Palazzo Caffarelli, which was the German Embassy.

Madame Helbig was a huge woman — six feet tall
and very stout. I have seen her sit down to play at a
concert and draw the grand piano up to her seat rather
than adjust herself to its angle. She wore her hair cut
to her neck and a straight shapeless gown of a dark heavy

material which fell from her shoulders to her feet.   She
had great vitality and passionate artistic enthusiasm.   She
drew, she painted, she decorated her house, she embroidered, she was interested in everything.

I was frightened enough when she asked me to play
to her and motioned me to the Erard grand piano, which
she explained had belonged to Liszt and was full of
lovely musical ghosts.   I managed to get through a Bach
gavotte and a Scarlatti *scherzo* without offending them
too much, and she must have taken a fancy to me, for
when we rose to take our leave she told me to come
again; to come, in fact, every Thursday afternoon and
make music with her; and these Thursday afternoons
became for the next few years the great events of my
life.

Madame Helbig had a second piano, a Pleyel upright,
and we read together sometimes on one, and more
often on two, pianos.   We went through the whole
available repertoire of four-hand music.   Schumann was
one of our favorites; his symphonies and chamber music
go well on the piano.   Liszt's Poèmes Symphoniques,
the Preludes, the Dante Symphony, Mazeppa, the
Christus Oratorio, the Tasso.

Madame Helbig read with great facility and was
patient with my shortcomings.   There is a delightful
excitement perhaps not wholly musical about reading
with a good musician.   It partakes a little of the tense
pleasure of a good run to hounds; you see a big obstacle
ahead and you gallop as fast as you can, without losing
control, over the good going, and finish panting, ecstatic,

hardly knowing how it was done. If she was satisfied with me and said, "Very good, my little Daisy," my cup was full.

Sometimes there were others to make music — famous artists would turn up, or young musicians seeking encouragement; and sometimes there was no music, but just conversation round the Helbig samovar. All sorts of interesting and amusing people, the literary and the artistic, the fashionable and the learned, ambassadors, travelers of distinction — that motley gathering which every season shapes itself into a new pattern in the kaleidoscope of Cosmopolis. The two noted historians, Mommsen and Gregorovius, met there one day; and Mommsen, willfully ignoring Gregorovius's fame, asked him, who had eight well-known volumes of Roman mediæval history to his credit, "Have you also been in Rome before, Herr Gregorovius?"

Eleonora Duse was an intimate friend. I saw her there for the first time off the stage, infinitely captivating, and surprisingly cheerful and healthy-looking. She never used rouge behind the footlights, and seeing her delicate and rosy skin in broad daylight, one understood why she did not wish to ruin it with grease paint, but to her audiences she always looked pale and a little tragic. I remember once the talk ran on money, and Madame Helbig, who was not at all rich but never allowed herself to feel poor, exclaimed, "Money, money, one must not think about it!"

"Eh, *cara mia*," said Duse, "one must have a great deal of it in order not to think about it!" *Per non*

pensarci bisogna averne assai. Poor Duse. It was not
for herself she needed so much money, but to satisfy the
demands of her rapacious, implacable poet lover.

There I first met the delightful Abbé Duchesne,
one of the wittiest and most learned men of his day.
The charming Prince Teano, later Duke of Sermoneta,
was musical and liked to play on two pianos; rather
to my dismay, I found myself one afternoon reading
a Liszt Poème Symphonique with him at sight before
a roomful of people. He was head of the Caetani family that always had glamour and interest for me. The
history of mediæval Rome is full of their doings —
Dante's Pope Boniface VIII, whom St. Peter so roundly
abuses in the *Paradiso,* and an earlier Pope, Gelasius II,
were both Caetani. They have been great people for
many centuries and have maintained a tradition for learning and accomplishment that put them in a class by themselves. The one who played the piano with me was just
a very handsome, cultivated, and most agreeable man
(he was old enough to be my father, there was no personal
emotion in my admiration for him), but his father, the
old Duke, was a renowned archæologist and Dante
scholar. It was he who made those excellent reference
maps of Hell, Purgatory, and Paradise, with all the
personages of the *Divine Comedy* marked in their appointed places, with the canto and verse where they are
mentioned: they are of great help to students. And his
oldest son, Leone, the present Duke, is well known to
Orientalists for his *Annali dell' Islam,* a monumental
work of great learning. Another son, Gelasio, studied
engineering, graduated brilliantly from Columbia Uni-

versity, and during the Great War won fame by blowing the top off the Carso: he was later sent as Ambassador to Washington and is now Senator. I cannot mention the Caetani without stopping to talk about them. I came to know them well in after years, and there is so much to say.

But to return to Madame Helbig's circle: there was the Russian Ambassadress, Madame Uxkull. She had the smallest waist and the largest eyes in the world, and great braids of blue-black hair which hung in double loops halfway down her back. She had a troop of adorers and always arrived with four or five of them in her train. Madame Helbig painted the portraits of all these admirers on white plates in delft blue. The Russian Embassy was redecorating its dining room and a portrait plate was destined to each compartment of the coffered ceiling in place of the conventional *rosace*. Nobody knew if the brown circles round Madame Uxkull's eyes were due to nature or art, and detractors said she wore false hair mixed with her own. Having heard of this, she came to Madame Helbig's tea one day and, taking off her hat, she lay down on the floor and ordered one of her young men to drag her round the room by the luxuriant tresses. She seemed to my simple eyes splendidly free, dangerous, and irresistible.

In those days we were all interested in fortune telling. There was an English painter, Mr. King-Salter, who was very successful in deciphering the mysteries of the hand. Madame Uxkull was anxious to meet him, but as she and her story were well known, an incognito had to be devised. A friend of ours took her to one of his studio teas, and, after all the more obviously important guests had been attended to, presented her as a young Russian governess in whom she was especially interested and begged him as a favor to look at her hand.   Mr. King-Salter fell into the trap.   He took the delicate hand in his, soon became absorbed, and eventually embarrassed, by what the lines revealed.   Presently he looked up into her face, covered with a thick spotty veil as the fashion of those days permitted, and said rather solemnly, "Mademoiselle, should you ever marry I advise you to choose a husband of the highest rank, for you are capable of leaving an attaché for an ambassador, or a secretary for a Prime Minister." The friend responsible for the interview, Mrs. W. W. Story, wife of the American sculptor, was horrified and did her best to clatter the teacups and provide a distraction to cover the unfortunate *gaffe.*   Madame Uxkull had been the wife of a Secretary of Embassy whom she left to marry Baron Uxkull, Ambassador.   During the Great War she was head of the Russian Red Cross, founded a strict religious order of nursing sisters, and died a holy woman.

After the first great performance of Wagner's *Ring* at Bayreuth, which was also the opening of the *Festspielhaus* and the first of the Bayreuth summer festivals, Joseph Rubinstein came to Rome.   He had been at the piano during all the rehearsals of the great tetralogy, had trained the choruses, and had made the first piano scores and piano transcriptions of the operas.   He undertook to initiate us, some dozen lovers of music, into the glories of the great cycle; the meetings took place at Madame Helbig's.   Donna Laura Minghetti had, so to speak, the principal rôle among the listeners, and would occasionally help by singing a snatch of a soprano part in a rather faded voice; she was a grandmother, but truly musical and intelligent.

Donna Laura was one of the most interesting figures in Rome of those days. She was an Acton of Naples, granddaughter of the Anglo-Neapolitan admiral. The gifted Princess Bülow, wife of the German Chancellor, was her daughter by her first marriage to Prince Camporeale. When I first saw her, at Madame Helbig's, she had married Marco Minghetti, the Italian patriot of the *Risorgimento* and at that time Prime Minister. Donna Laura was immensely sympathetic to artists; she had great enthusiasm and was an inspiration to many. She showed me a copy of *Tristan and Isolde* with a long dedication to her in Wagner's own handwriting, referring to her as the first interpreter of the rôle of Isolde. She had read the part over with him, evidently to his liking.

It was a strange, exciting world for me to see and come in contact with, in the guise of friendly music lessons, and I saw it with beglamoured eyes. I always came away from those Thursday afternoons exhilarated, treading on air. Sometimes my brother Marion would come to fetch me and we would walk home together by way of the long, easy steps of the Capitol, pausing at the top between the great statues of the Dioscuri; on our right the steeper flight of the Aracœli, where Gibbon sat and pondered on the Decline and Fall, with Rome at our feet in twinkling dusk, our heads in the clouds, feeling curiously elated. Was it Youth? Art? Rome? All three, perhaps.

After one of these entrancing afternoons, when Marion
had fetched me from Madame Helbig's and we had
walked home together in the gathering dusk, we reached
the Odescalchi later than usual. The family were
already at dinner when we came in, and, seated among
them, who but Annie von Rabe. She had arrived from
Berlin unannounced late that afternoon. Seeing her so
frightened me that my knees gave way and I collapsed
on the floor; she laughed and thought to reassure me by
saying: "Don't be frightened, Daisy, it is really I and
no ghost," but a ghost would have terrified me less than
the living Annie.

This was the only time it ever happened to me to "fall
through the floor" from frightened surprise, nor have I
ever seen anyone else do it, but, having experienced the
sensation, I know it is hardly a figure of speech.

Some years after I first knew them the Helbigs were
dispossessed of their house on the Rocca Tarpeia and
moved out to the beautiful Villino Lante on the Aventine, a very perfect specimen of late Renaissance domestic
architecture. There I saw Madame Helbig for the last
time in 1922, after the war and the Russian Revolution.
She was old and had lost her mind. She greeted me
affectionately, but took me for another old friend she
had not seen for many years. She went to the piano
and tinkled a few discordant notes — it was heartbreaking.
She seemed a symbol of Holy Russia, with its glory
departed, huge and helpless. She died soon after that
sad visit and is survived by her son, Demetrio, who, half
Russian prince, half German archæologist, has become an
Italian citizen and is a distinguished Professor of Chem-
istry at the Roman University.

But to go back to the golden age: I think it was in the autumn of 1877 that Madame Helbig took me to congratulate Liszt on his sixty-sixth birthday. I had not met him before and felt as though I were being taken into a supernatural presence. Pictures of him as an old man are familiar to all, but I never saw one that was not something of a caricature, a portrait of his warts; none gave the exalted distinction of his personality, the look of penetrating intelligence combined with kindly gayety. He wore a Roman collar and a long black coat of clerical cut. He received us with great cordiality in his shabby little furnished apartment, whither all Rome was flocking on the same errand, everyone glowing with the same enthusiastic homage.

When we left he whispered to Madame Helbig that he was going to give lessons to a group of young pianists and that she must be sure to come and bring the "little one," meaning me. I was not particularly little, but under Madame Helbig's huge protecting wing I seemed a very small chicken. This seemed too good to be true; to be admitted even as a listener to these famous classes was an unhoped-for privilege. Liszt in those days occupied with infinitely more prestige the position later held by Leschetizky. All young pianists vied for the honor of being his pupils. He had held his classes in Rome at Santa Francesca Romana for some years. That is where Sgambati had studied with him, and the young Princess Schachowskoia, and many others. I think in the last years of his life he did very little teaching; this class we attended was the last I know of. After this, Cardinal Hohenlohe put the many-fountained Villa d'Este in Tivoli at the master's disposal and he lived there when

he came to Italy. The *Jeux d'Eau de la Villa d'Este*
bears witness to his love of the place.

Liszt was sincerely religious. It was often said he
became an abbé (that is, took the first orders, for he never
was a Mass priest) so as to escape from marrying the
Princess Caroline Sayn Wittgenstein. Be this as it may,
there was sincere piety in his spirit. There are passages
throughout his work that have deep religious feeling.
The Magnificat in the Dante Symphony, the Christus
Oratorio with the beautiful chorus about the Magi, *"Et
invenerunt puerum,"* show a kind of mystic contempla-
tion. We used to see him at Mass at the Anima, the
Austrian Church near the Piazza Navona where the
singing was conducted by the Padre Müller, an excellent
musician who gave us Polyphonic and Gregorian Masses
on alternate Sundays. Liszt was there to pray; he was
generally alone, kneeling a little apart from the congregation, a reverend and majestic figure wrapped in his
own thoughts.

There was no price on his teachings; he was a great
prince or prophet of music and literally gave — he never
sold — his lessons, to whom he chose. There never was
anyone more generous in recognizing young talent, in
doing all he could to develop it and help the obscure
virtuoso to make his way to fame.

On the appointed day we found our way to the Sala
Dante, Rome's only music hall. It was part of the big
Palazzo Poli whose east wall supports the rocky back-
ground of the Fontana di Trevi and holds the niches of
Bernini's allegorical figures.

When we arrived the great Abbé met us at the door

and asked at once for *la petite,* who was completely hidden
behind Madame Helbig's towering bulk.   The class met
in a smaller room not connected with the concert hall,
a shabby unfurnished apartment that had been used as a
storeroom after seeing better days, for it had traces of
eighteenth-century decorations on its doors and window
frames.   It was dimly lighted by a few guttering candles
stuck into bottles.   We sat on rickety straw chairs, but
the sordid accessories took nothing from the prestige of
the occasion; rather they added to it a flavor of adventure.
It was like seeing a great commander issuing orders from
a wayside tavern or a baggage car.

Besides the four or five young pianists who formed the
class there were perhaps half a dozen of us who had
come to listen, Donna Laura Minghetti, Baroness Meyen-
dorff, and one or two others.   The pupils played what
they had prepared and Liszt corrected, blamed, encouraged their work.

It was interesting to notice the varied degrees of tension
that he brought to the different composers.   When
Chopin was being played, only the most delicate precision
would satisfy him.   The *rubatos* had to be done with
exquisite restraint and only when Chopin had marked
them, never *ad libitum.*   Nothing was quite good enough
to interpret such perfection.   A student played one of
Liszt's own rhapsodies; it had been practised conscientiously, but did not satisfy the master.   There were splashy
arpeggios and rockets of rapidly ascending chromatic
diminished sevenths.   "Why don't you play it this way?"
asked Liszt, sitting at his second piano and playing the
passage with more careless bravura.   "It was not written

so in my copy," objected the youth. *"Ja, das dürfen Sie
nicht so genau nehmen"* (Oh, you need not take that so
literally), answered the composer. He intended his
rhapsodies to be played rhapsodically, with a certain character of improvisation.

One of these lessons, the most memorable, was given
to a young man who had prepared Beethoven's *Sonate
für das Hammerklavier,* an arduous work alike for listeners and performer. The boy had worked hard and
played all the notes in all their harshness. Liszt was
not happy about the performance. He corrected and discussed; the boy had in no wise reached the soul of the
matter. When it came to the divine *Adagio* Liszt took
the pupil by the shoulders, gently shoved him out of his
seat, and sat down to play it himself, pouring out his soul
to us in the dusk of that room, turning it into a space
between stars, with the distant splash of the Fountain of
Trevi as bourdon to the heavenly melody. I do not think
that movement can ever have been played better or have
moved any group of people so deeply before or since.
It was the end of the lesson. Donna Laura and Madame
Helbig had tears streaming down their faces. We had
been in the Great Presence.

Liszt dismissed the pupils and offered to walk home
with Madame Helbig and me. *"Je prends la petite sous
le bras." La petite* was rapt to the seventh heaven. He
asked me to play to him, but at that time my wrist, from
too much practising, had developed a bad sinew and so
I could not, and on the whole I was not sorry. I wanted
him to think I played better than I did.

VIII

AMERICANS IN ROME

AUNT JULIA HOWE and her beautiful daughter Maud
came to stay with us in Rome the winter following their
visit to Lesnian. Aunt Julia drew many friends about her
wherever she happened to be, and Maud's admirers
flocked like moths about the candle. I was fourteen,
neither child nor woman, and at that time too much
taken up with music and study to give much thought to
the things of life. Aunt Julia called me her Goethe
and said she was my Schiller. I never knew why, unless
it be she found some German impress left on me by my
various German teachers and governesses — perhaps
a trace of pedantry combined with sincerest enthusiasm.
She continued to use these two names to the end of her
days, and I have many letters from her all beginning
"Dear Goethe" and signed "your Schiller." She made
Maud and me read Burton's *Anatomy of Melancholy*
with her for half an hour every day after breakfast.

That winter I was promoted to take charge of the
tea table at the Wednesday-afternoon receptions, and
sat up for the informal parties that generally succeeded
the Sunday-evening dinner. A number of American
friends were in Rome that year and often came to these

little entertainments, where they liked to meet our
Roman-cosmopolitan circle made up of as many nation-
alities as the group that witnessed the coming of the
Holy Ghost.

This was my first contact with Americans of America.
There was no question that they differed from us Americans of Rome; their speech was slightly different from
ours, and they were sadly handicapped in their intercourse
with our foreign friends by the fact that they could only
express themselves freely in English.   I liked some of
them well enough, some of them more than others.
Several of my surviving friendships date from that long-
ago Roman winter.   When I came to live in the United
States, many of them were very kind to me, remembering
the old Roman days.

Often they baffled me by a certain mistrust they showed
toward one another, a mistrust derived from a sense of
social sets and hierarchies in Boston, Philadelphia, or New
York.   I recall one vivid instance of this.   Two not
very young, but intelligent and well-bred girls were in
Rome with their mother, an old friend of Aunt Julia's.
Their father had been Governor of Massachusetts during
the Civil War; nothing could have been more unimpeach-
ably respectable.   They often came to the house; so
did a very smart young scion of one of Boston's first families, who was learning to paint in Paris.   One evening
it happened that the two girls did not seem to know any
of the twenty or thirty people gathered in the room.   I
was sitting at the table pouring tea, and seeing them
rather isolated, I asked the young Bostonian, who was at
my side, if he would not go and speak to them.   He told

me he did not know them, and when I offered to present
him to them, he appeared embarrassed, and answered that
he would rather not, since they did not move in the same
society in their native Boston.   I was, as it still seems to
me quite justly, outraged and told him with some asperity
that anyone he met in my mother's house was good enough
for him to know.   It would have been better had he had
the tact or the presence of mind to say he would rather
sit and talk to me, but it would not have given me the
glimpse of this curious social consciousness, common, as
I was later to find, to so many Anglo-Saxons.   The
young Boston aristocrat was perhaps an extreme instance
of the thing, but his unfortunate utterance expressed a
feeling that was new to me.   Romans take people at
their face value, and like them for their looks, their manners, their talents, and their ways; trusting to their instinct
to discriminate between the right and the wrong stranger.

Among those who were often at the house were Mr.
and Mrs. Charles Dorr and their son George.   Mrs.
Dorr had been a friend of my mother and Aunt Julia
since their early girlhood.   She had been engaged to
marry their brother, Henry Ward, and wore widow's
weeds for him when his death broke their engagement.
She was an interesting, masterful woman with much feeling and talent for painting.   While in Rome she studied
with Giovanni Costa and was highly thought of by that
delicate and accomplished artist.   We were all a little
afraid of her, but she was very kind to me and won my
heart by inviting me to go with them to Naples on a
sight-seeing trip.   The party consisted of her and her
gentle husband and devoted son George — both ruled

by her; she seemed born to command, and they fondly
obeyed.   Aunt Julia and Maud came along, adding a
great deal to the pleasure and interest of the expedition.

Our slender family budget did not admit of random
pleasure trips; we never left Rome before it was too hot
to travel with comfort, and we would stay in the cooler
place until it was time to go back to Rome.   Nothing
could have pleased me better than to be given this golden
opportunity.   Naples was enchanting in the early soft-
ness of spring.   We went to Capri, of course, and to
Pompeii; and to Sorrento, where I was later to spend
happy summers and where my brother Marion Crawford
eventually made his home; and to lovely Ravello with
its magic Rufalo gardens.   There in the visitors' book
I found Richard Wagner's signature, and he had written over it: *"Klingsor's Zaubergarten ist gefunden!"*
(Klingsor's magic garden has been found!)

All these had their enchantment; who that has seen
them has not felt it?   But the culminating experience
was our visit to Pæstum, never to be forgotten.   In those
days the ancient temples stood in a wilderness of aspho-
del carpeted with violets, the fragrant European violet.
The country for miles around them was said to be infested
by brigands and malaria.   The shrines had been deserted
since the days of Cæsar; there was no sign of human habitation in the land.   Since then archæologists have started
excavations; they have put a fence about the ruins and
established a service of guards and an office for the sale
of entrance tickets and postcards.   The modern traveler
can see the beauty of the temples, but he misses the spell
that twenty centuries of silence and solitude had cast

about them at the time of my first visit. They were a revelation of Greek beauty, pure and more austere than that of Italy; I went a little mad over their perfection and in my rapture poured wine from our picnic basket on the altar of the forgotten gods.

Soon after this we rented our apartment in the Odescalchi to the Austrian Ambassador and moved into a small furnished flat in the Palazzo Zuccari on the Via Sistina. The following year our Odescalchi lease expired and we took up our abode in the Palazzo Altemps, where there were no coffered ceilings, no mirrored wall nor silken hangings. I missed them very much.

About this time the Princess Caroline Sayn Wittgenstein sent word to my mother that she would like to make her acquaintance because she heard that she had borne her losses with such noble fortitude. On the appointed day the eccentric old lady came to see us; she was small, bright-eyed, and very intelligent-looking, with a masterful manner. One had heard a great deal about her. She had lived with Liszt in a romantic castle, they were engaged to be married, but the ceremony had to be postponed, owing to the difficulty of obtaining the annulment to her previous marriage to Wittgenstein. When this was overcome and she was ready to become his bride, Liszt astonished the world by taking holy orders. She was very pious and consoled herself by writing many books on theological subjects. She led a retired life in Rome, choosing her friends among learned ecclesiastics and different individuals whom she found interesting. In Lent she was sometimes seen extended face down in the shape of a cross on the floor of a church, doing penance perhaps for unforgotten joys. She and my mother had little in common, and the meeting was unsatisfactory. Mamma felt that there was something patronizing about her coming at all; she knew next to nothing about us, and what we knew about her was not of a nature to provide us with conversation. The strain was somewhat relieved when she asked me to play to her. I chose a Liszt arrangement of the Schubert Ave Maria. She patted me on the back and said pleasant things; but the acquaintance never ripened to intimacy and did not as far as I can remember go beyond the exchange of a few formal visits.

Our apartment in the Palazzo Altemps was on the second floor. On the first lived the Duke and Duchess di Gallese, with whose daughter, Maria, I soon struck up a pleasant friendship. She was about my own age (eighteen or nineteen), intelligent and companionable, and extremely pretty. She went out a great deal more than I, and would tell me about the balls and parties she attended, and show me the piles of favors she had reaped at the last cotillon. Her mother's sister was the Princess Bandini, who had at that time the most fashionable salon in Rome. Maria was not happy at home and often told me how glad she would be to marry anyone who might come her way; she had plenty of admirers, but suitors seem to have been scarce. Her mother had a difficult disposition and no one was ever asked to the house; it was rumored that the Duke had lost or squandered most of the property; this may have put difficulties in the way of arranging a suitable marriage.

Some years later, while we were spending the summer at the Villa Cesarini in Genzano, the Roman papers announced in glaring headlines that Donna Maria Gallese had eloped with the poet Gabriele d'Annunzio, and told how the pair had been captured and brought back to the Palazzo Altemps, where the Duke and Duchess had consented to their marriage. We were much shocked.

Soon after we had returned to Rome, Marion and I were walking in the Corso one morning, when a *carrozzella*, a little open one-horse cab, drove by with Maria and her poet lover. Maria saw me first, and waved and kissed her hand to me, looking radiantly happy and prettier than I had ever seen her; but before I had time to make an answering sign Marion clutched my arm and said very quickly in a tone I dared not disobey: "You must not recognize her." I never saw her again. The Roman world closed its doors to her; her tardy wedding did not condone her offense. Her own aunt, the Princess Bandini, did not invite her to her parties. She had little lasting joy of her marriage, for the poet was not a faithful husband and had a succession of more or less notorious love affairs; the romance with Eleonora Duse, described in his famous novel *Il Fuoco* (Fire), came several years later. I used to hear of Maria from some of her men friends, who were also mine, and who continued to see her. One told me she had confessed to him that she longed to look out of the window of a Roman *palazzo* again before she died. To *stare in finestra*; a very Roman wish.

These lines will never meet her eye; she will never know how badly I still feel that I was not allowed to return her greeting.

IX

THE WESTERN WORLD

In the spring of 1879 my mother decided to take me to America. Her Crawford daughters were both married, Marion was in India, studying Sanskrit, Parsee, and other Oriental languages, my brother Arthur was at school in Germany and was under the care of some very old family friends; there was no reason we should not go, but it seemed a tremendous adventure and it must have taken a great deal of persuasion to obtain my father's consent to such an undertaking. We planned to visit Mamma's sister Annie, Mrs. Adolphe Mailliard, who lived on a ranch in California with her husband and family; the two sisters had not seen each other for twenty-five years. My mother had not been to America in all that time nor had the Mailliards come to Europe. The two sisters kept up a faithful correspondence in their fine steel-pen handwriting, their letters very sweet and a little flowery in their effusive affection: Aunt Annie's to Mamma began, "Dear Beata," while the answers were indited to "Dear Benedetta," and the four, five, six thin sheets of closely written paper carried the household chronicles across the many thousand miles that divided the Palazzo Odescalchi from the San Geronimo Ranch. My father reluctantly consented to go with us as far as New York.

So we left Rome for Paris, stopping there for a few days on our way to England. I am ashamed to find how little impression my first visit to Paris made on me. The stuffy hotel with heavy dark curtains draped about the beds, the angry cab drivers, a visit to the Bon Marché, the Louvre, where I was duly ecstatic over the Venus of Milo, who looked very like a young Roman *principessa* I knew and admired, the Galerie d'Apollon with all its costly magnificence, and Notre-Dame, the first great Gothic cathedral I had ever seen, and still for me one of the most beautiful in the world — these are all that left pictures in my memory.

We dined one evening with General de Charette and his handsome American wife, Antoinette Polk. A halo of romance hung about this couple; both had fought and risked their lives bravely in defense of lost causes. She was a Southerner — niece, I think, of President Polk. She must have been unusually beautiful, with large dark eyes and penciled eyebrows, regular features, a mass of ash-blonde hair, tall and distinguished; she was a bold rider and used to carry dispatches across the Yankee lines in the last dark years of the War of the Rebellion, and had some narrow and adventurous escapes — helped perhaps by her fearless youth and great beauty. She and her brother and sister came to live in Rome after the last surrender, and something must have been saved out of the wreck of their estates, for they kept a fine establishment, and when I was a child the beautiful Antoinette was much admired in Roman society. The Crown Princess Margherita took a fancy to her and she was a great favorite in court circles.

We had at that time the same visiting French governess, Madame Linard, who spent her mornings with the Polks (Antoinette's brother and sister were still of schoolroom age) and her afternoons with us, and always conveyed to me the sense of how much grander they were than we. On their table an elaborate dessert was served every day at luncheon, though none of the Polks ever touched it; this seemed splendidly lavish. It was probably served to please Madame Linard, who had a sweet tooth.

General de Charette had commanded the Papal Zouaves when they made their brave stand against Garibaldi's troops in the breach of Porta Pia on September 20, 1870. They were prepared to fall to the last man, but Pio Nono sent word to stop the fighting. The Italians marched in and Rome became the capital of United Italy. The Charettes were married a few years after this and Rome saw them no more.

It was thrilling to spend an evening *en famille* with this legendary couple who had so comfortably survived their lost causes and were leading a pleasant life in the pleasantest of capitals. Madame Linard happened to be in Paris and was also at dinner. Afterwards the General took her and me to the Circus.

General de Charette gave me a copy of the Papal March, played by the famous silver trumpets of which we used to hear so much. These were silenced when the Pope became a prisoner in the Vatican; Leo XIII revived them many years later on the occasion of his being carried for the first time in the *Sedia Gestatoria*, to receive and bless an innumerable pilgrimage assembled in the Basilica of St. Peter's. I was there with some of my children and shall never forget the great spectacle of truly Byzantine splendor, nor the sad contrast of those silver trumpets playing the mawkish, character-less *Marcia Papale*, which I had known, from the copy given me by General de Charette, to be a worthless composition. Nevertheless the crowd cheered vigorously and many were duly thrilled by the silver trumpets.

In Paris I was also taken to see a very old lady, the Duchess de Fitz James, whose mother, if I remember rightly, had been lady in waiting to Marie Antoinette. She was all silver gray and old lace, very grand and gracious, and showed me miniatures and souvenirs of the royal family.

Then we went to England and stayed in a country house in Surrey and on the Isle of Wight. It seemed to me exactly like Alice in Wonderland — the country all marked off in little squares, and also, like the novels I had read in the Tauchnitz edition, with good-looking young men in flannels, and picnics on the river, cricket matches, and young curates about the tea tables — all the stage setting of English fiction considered safe read-ing for the *jeune fille*. I had been brought up on Charlotte M. Yonge, that bulwark of innocence, and on my first visit to England what I saw of people and places seemed conjured out of her pages. I was not convinced of their reality, nor of their interest.

We did very little sight-seeing. In those days I
was so passionately Roman that I had small curiosity
for other countries. Like the American sight-seer who,
on entering a gallery, asks to see the best thing in it,
and feels it idle to look at anything else, I was sure
I had seen what was best worth seeing, and lived in the
only place where life was worth living. The National
Gallery, however, delighted me; it seemed to hold, as
it were, in a golden solution the sunshine and genius of
Italy. This and the Elgin marbles were all that I knew
how to look at in England.

We sailed on the *Gallia*, a very long narrow Cunarder,
considered the best available, being new and larger than
others, but soon condemned as a passenger ship and used
for laying transatlantic cables. She rolled unmercifully
and hooted her way across the Atlantic through heavy
fogs. The hoot of the foghorn was a terror to me, and
another sinister note was added by the fact that a passenger died on board and was packed in ice in one of the
lifeboats. We had seen him carried on board at Liver-
pool in dying condition, accompanied by his wife. He
must have died a few days after, and as a widow she sat
draped in black under the icy lifeboat with no one near
her.

In New York we were welcomed by Uncle Sam Ward,
my mother's oldest and only surviving brother. Another
radiant uncle, and my true uncle this time, though all
the world called him Uncle Sam. He had visited us in
Rome when I was a child; but there I had seen little
of him and our real friendship and mutual devotion began with this second meeting.

Here I should like to make a digression and speak the praises of delightful people. They are generally so much better than famous ones. There have been so many ignored by history and the biographical dictionary. Like the golden threads in a precious tapestry we catch a glimpse of them here and there, on the emperor's cloak, on the warrior's helmet, on the girdle of a great dame, on the dagger of a page, a few bright stitches — and they disappear into the duller background. They do not make the picture or have any importance in the action represented, but they incomparably enhance its beauty and its worth. This of mine is but a poor image. Charming people are the light and the joy of the world.

For some we loved, the loveliest and the best —

and some we know only from what we have heard: Madame de Sévigné's Abbé "*le tout bon*," W. B. Yeats's "beautiful Mary Hines," only a name in a shining mist; and girls like Clara Middleton in *The Egoist* and Natacha in *War and Peace*, and so many others. Delightfulness was the essence of their being. They have not made history, but their presence in the world made causes worth fighting for, made life worth living, turned the valley of tears into a place of smiles and laughter. It is good to know that such people have always enriched the world with their presence, without trumpet blasts of fame, leaving no tangible masterpieces to testify to their worth. Their masterpiece was their life.

Uncle Sam was one of these favored ones. His life had been varied and checkered; oldest son of a rich New

York banker, well endowed and well connected, he had been sent abroad with an unlimited letter of credit after he had graduated from Columbia University. We are not told whether he abused this paternal trustfulness. On his return he married Emily Astor, oldest daughter of William B. Astor, granddaughter of the original John Jacob. The marriage was happy while it lasted, but the young wife died in giving birth to a daughter, Margaret. The young widower grieved and then consoled himself by marrying a showy and fascinating Creole, the beautiful Medora Grimes. This was not at all to the taste of the staunchly respectable Astors, who had carefully selected their wives among the best families; and the grandparents took little "Maddie," who was not much younger than the youngest of their own large brood, and brought her up with the rest of their children. The marriage with Medora Grimes turned out badly; perhaps the Astors were right in their disapproval.

Sam Ward went West in the '49 gold rush. He had lost a great deal of money. The bankruptcy of his father's firm was attributed to him. He was not fortunate, or perhaps not skillful, in money matters; he lost three fortunes in the course of his life. But he never lost his zest for living and giving, and in California he found no gold but much adventure. At one time he bought a canal boat and fitted it up as a hotel and restaurant where food and drink were of the best.

There were legends about these years, romantic tales of which the family knew only whispered fragments; there were young women — one lived with him disguised as a boy; wild doings for those prim Victorian

UNCLE SAM WARD

A cartoon by Spy, drawn in 1880

days — startling, considering the sober old New York background from which he sprang. One does not wonder the Astor family was shocked. Then he came East again without a fortune, but always living sumptuously. He went to Washington, where he made himself useful to Senators and Congressmen in bringing them together, always with the help of excellent food and rare wine; he was everybody's friend and was proclaimed King of the Lobby.

When we arrived in New York he had left Washington and was living in an apartment on the ground floor of the old Brevoort House on Eighth Street and Fifth Avenue, speculating, and at that time very successfully, on the stock market. He was, as I have said, a real connoisseur of wines, and, to keep his palate delicate, he never drank spirits or seasoned his food with pepper or mustard. The only liqueur he approved was yellow Chartreuse, and he invented a drink called a "Sam Ward," concocted with this and the peel of a lemon laid around the inside of a glass filled with cracked ice. He told me he was satisfied to have given his name to this as a claim to remembrance, pointing out that only a very few names were permanently associated with food and drink.

He took my mother and me to Newport on the Fall River Line. On the way he gave us our first taste of soft-shell crabs, among what seemed to me curious surroundings. The dining saloon of those days was surrounded by bunks over which hung green baize curtains like those with which we are so unpleasantly familiar in Pullman cars. It was very hot and stuffy, and negro waiters fanned us with palm-leaf fans. Nevertheless, Uncle Sam managed to convey the sense of a banquet. Whenever he was host it was a dinner with Mæcenas.

He had another passion which I should perhaps have mentioned first. He was not quite so successful in it as in the giving of little dinners, but poetry was very dear to his heart and he wrote many verses which fluttered a little in the breeze of friendly intercourse and then took their way down the stream of forgetfulness.

He was something of a scholar and Horace was his favorite. He was never without a copy of the *Odes* in his pocket; his next choice was Omar Khayyám.

In Newport we stayed with Aunt Julia and the lovely Maud, who was at that time being courted by a handsome young English painter, John Elliott, whom she later married. They lived in a pleasant house about seven miles from Newport, not far from Portsmouth, Rhode Island. There I came to know and love another of Aunt Julia's daughters, dear Laura Richards, who had already written a number of happy children's books and delightful nursery nonsense giving joy to her many little readers — and herself an exquisite joy to all who know her. Uncle Sam had given them a telephone, a comparatively new invention, and one evening we were called up and told that President Garfield had been assassinated.

I learned to appreciate my Aunt Julia more than ever. She was the best of company, witty and wise, merry and many-sided. I have spoken before of her beautiful voice, unlike any I ever heard; low in tone and pitch, but penetrating, with a delicate edge to her words. There was poetry in her, and laughter, and wise compassion. Her pronunciation was very distinct and exquisitely correct, without a sign of preciosity or affectation; difficult to describe, impossible to forget. You could not find anything more removed from the careless, loose-lipped American speech of to-day.

For a couple of hours every morning she enjoyed what she called her "P. T." (Precious Time), digging at the classics when she was not writing a poem or preparing a lecture. Her door was locked and no one was allowed to disturb her. In espousing the cause of Woman's Rights, in going on the lecture platform, she had broken with the pattern of good society. My father always spoke of her with reserved approval. She was too talented to fit into the mould of convention which in those days held the American World to such firm monotony.

X

CALIFORNIAN EXILE

Mamma and I started from New York on our long journey to California early in October. My father had bought our tickets and secured a drawing-room for us; he and Uncle Sam saw us off at the station in New York — the dear uncle with all sorts of goodies for the trip, and a handsome silver tea caddy filled with an especially delicate brand of tea. This caddy is still in daily use on my tea table, a constant reminder of that long-ago departure. In 1879 it took, if I remember rightly, some eight days to cross the continent. Before we had settled down for the night, the conductor discovered that our railway tickets were for another line, the Canadian Pacific. We had no idea that two lines existed; neither had my father. We were much distressed by the discovery. I cannot say enough about the kindness of that conductor. He was a gray-whiskered fatherly angel, and assured us that he would arrange things for us and that we must go to bed and not worry. But we were not at the end of our troubles. I climbed into the upper berth and a few hours later was taken with a violent seasick colic; I had a most miserable night. Early in the morning the good conductor (his name was

Henry Joy — it was engraved on the globe of the lantern he carried on his arm) came to see how we were getting on. It was evident that I was not fit to travel any further, and it was decided that we should stop off at Chicago. Henry Joy was leaving the train there and knew of a good hotel, and its manager, to whom he recommended us. There I spent a week in bed; we attributed my distemper to the upper berth, and it was many years before I dared to sleep in one again. While I was recovering my mother went to a bank to get some money. She had no papers of identification, nor even a check book (she never had one in her life), but told the gentlemen behind the bars who she was and that she banked with Drexel and Morgan in New York; she looked so lovely and convincingly innocent that they handed her out the required sum.

As soon as I was on my feet again we proceeded on our journey, forgoing the privacy of the drawing-room and occupying two sections to avoid the dangers of the upper berth. There were no dining cars in those days; for breakfast, lunch, and dinner, the passengers were herded into station restaurants, where unappetizing meals were dealt out to them in countless little bird-bath dishes containing dabs of this and that. One must hurry lest one be left behind; the train departed with little notice. We were told it happened not infrequently that those who lingered over their meals would come out on the platform to see the train disappearing towards the horizon. One angry passenger, who had been thus left behind, asked the station master if it was not customary to give a signal before the train started. "Well," drawled the indifferent chief, "sometimes we rings, but mostly we hollers." The "hollering" outside on the platform could not possibly be heard in the clatter of the noisy dining room, and passengers must look out for themselves.

In due time we reached San Francisco and found our way to the Mailliard ranch in Northern California, a couple of hours' drive from San Rafael, along rough roads.

Adolphe Mailliard's father was the illegitimate but acknowledged son of one of Napoleon's brothers, and Adolphe, tall, handsome, and accomplished, had been brought up in the imperial family. When King Joseph lived in exile at Bordentown he had been with him as part of his household. It was at this time that he married Annie Ward, and soon after took her and their first child, Louise, to California, where he bought a tract of land, settled, and raised a family; there were two daughters and two sons. He was at heart a republican, and very deliberately turned his back on what remained of the royalty created by his great-uncle. Uncle Adolphe was in New York that winter we were in California.

The Mailliard house was roomy and comfortable enough, but bare of ornament. Bedrooms and living rooms were all whitewashed, all carpeted alike, in stern protest against decorative frivolity. On the mantelpiece in the dining room stood a bronze clock that had been in Napoleon's room at St. Helena; and there were a number of other Napoleonic relics: the Emperor's camp dinner service in silver gilt, beautifully wrought; the manuscript diary of O'Meara, the doctor who took care of Napoleon during his captivity, and kept a daily record of his moods and symptoms; and many of the great man's little personal belongings.   I remember some large fine handkerchiefs marked with a very small "N" surmounted by an imperial crown, which gave a sense of pathos.   The furniture of the house was austerely simple, without grace or seduction.   The house itself lay in a fold of the hills; the view from the broad covered verandah that surrounded it was of sequoia forests and branching valleys.   It seemed to be all they had to make them happy, and "the beautiful shadows on the canyons" were commented on after every meal.

But my Rome-sick spirit found it hard to live on mere landscape, and life on the ranch seemed stripped of all interest.   "This dreadful country," I wrote to my learned old German governess, Fräulein Hoepfner, "where nobody knows anything about anything!"   One experience I remember with pleasure — it was learning to ride.   Our Italian summers had included endless *asinate*, rides on donkey back, through vine-clad hills and up steep mountain paths to ancient monasteries built on the sites of older temples; but I always knew that it was not real riding, and the joy of being on a horse first came to me that winter in California, and has stayed with me for the rest of my life.   I rode a rough but willing nag that my cousin Jack would fetch up from the corral, and I forgot St. Peter and princes and palaces in happy canters among the hills and streams and lovely valleys.   There were no neighbors; occasionally a few visitors from San Francisco.

I remember a charming old geologist, Professor Joseph Le Conte, who told us about rocks and glacial epochs, and gave us his spiritualized version of Darwin's theories. They were later published in a book called *Religion and Science*, which I liked very much and still have in my possession.

There were also younger men who came to stay. One, I remember, fell in love with my mother, who was still beautiful. Tennyson's "Tithonus" was read aloud one evening and the ardent youth had to leave the room, he was so moved by the line,

> Immortal age beside immortal youth.

It seemed to apply so poignantly to his own case, as he explained to me the next day, that he could not endure it.

My poor aunt perpetually struggled to maintain civilized standards in the wilderness; to inculcate table manners — to prevent her children from passing the cream with their right hand to their left-hand neighbor. Details of family etiquette had to be punctually observed, lest life should lose all grace and amenity. She was a sweet and loving tyrant; the traditions, religious and social, which she had brought with her into the strange country were of a rather conventional kind, but she did her best to uphold them. There was no church anywhere in the neighborhood, — there was in fact no neighborhood, — but Sundays were observed by collecting the family for prayers, and by the reading of a sermon out of a book, a dreary form of worship unlikely to waken any spark of enthusiasm, a feeble faithful effort to hand on the torch. How many women throughout the ages have tried to do likewise! How hard and often how hopeless the task! There is a Greek bas-relief representing a young man, naked, on a spirited, forward-leaping horse, followed by a woman in flowing garments, who carries a covered vessel draped so that her hands do not touch it. A friend suggested to me that it was a symbol of humanity: the man leading the way into the future by his inventions, his achievements in war and peace, his enterprises of every kind, while the woman follows him preserving as best she may the treasures and toys of the past, lest they be lost to the race. She gathers up what she can in her haste to hurry after, not to be left behind, and odd trifles she happens to value are taken along with precious heirlooms.

The long uneventful winter on the ranch was pleasantly broken by visits to the McAlisters in San Francisco. Hall McAlister was my mother's first cousin and a brilliant lawyer; he and his wife and family received us with warm hospitality. There were three handsome daughters and a son, and innumerable cousins swarming in and out of the house. There were parties with music and dancing. Mrs. McAlister and her daughters were good musicians and sang well. San Francisco society seemed more alive, more cosmopolitan than what I had seen in the East.

But I was unfeignedly glad when the time came for us to leave California, and could not help showing a "shining morning face" as the day of our departure drew near. This troubled my gentle mother, who felt I should make a decent show of regret, in acknowledgment of all the kindness shown us during our eight months' visit. But even the mitigated taste of frontier life had been wholly distasteful to me, and I sang with joy that it was over.

A childhood and youth passed happily in Rome had

quite unfitted me for appreciating the merits of America;
I saw the United States with foreign and unfriendly eyes.
This is common to all or nearly all children of American
parents brought up in Europe; it is the penalty they pay
for the many advantages they have received; their own
country will never be quite their home, they will be guests
and strangers, if they eventually come to live in it; they
will eat their daily bread with ashes of nostalgia for a while
— and acute nostalgia is no imaginary trouble.   It is a
painful inhibition that prevents you from finding normal
pleasure in your surroundings, your whole soul perpetually
longing for the other place.   It leaves you helpless and
miserable, "an abscess on the universe," as Marcus Aurelius
puts it.   But Time, the great comforter, eventually brings
relief and you learn to live where you have to live, and to
enrich the Here and Now with memories that have woven
themselves into a tapestry for the walls of the inner chamber; they are like the little familiar household gods that
Rachel took away with her secretly when she left her
father's house to follow Jacob into a foreign land.

Time and distance are the great destroyers of tradition; the Greek woman on the bas-relief may be thought
of as carrying what she most prizes of the past into the
future, Rachel as taking the pieties of home into her exile.

XI

AMERICANA

WE recrossed the continent in the late spring and spent the rest of the summer paying visits. We stayed in country houses, with parks and gardens that have now become city lots, in the neighborhood of Boston; with kind, very refined old ladies in lace caps and black silk dresses, who had been girlhood friends of my mother's. Their houses smelt of lavender and straw matting, and I called them "Aunt this and that."

The poet Longfellow invited us to dine with him in Cambridge; he had been an old intimate of the family. He was a charming old gentleman and received us with affectionate cordiality. He was short, but his abundant white hair and beard, and fine gray eyes, gave him a look of poetical dignity. He talked with my mother of old times, and, with me, of Rome and Dante and the things I was hungering for, and gave us a delightful evening in his handsome old house. It had been Washington's Headquarters during the Revolutionary War and was, as I remember, well furnished, with fine old mahogany and family portraits; it had a look of good tradition and well-ordered comfort. As a little girl I had loved his poems, and used to learn them by heart while my nurse was brushing and braiding my hair for the night; but at seventeen I had put away the taste with childish things, and was rather nervous before meeting him, lest I should show the lack of real enthusiasm required by the occasion; it would have been so nice to have good smoky incense to burn, and I had none left.   But the benign old gentleman was far too wise and kind to make it seem necessary, or even fitting.   He had great fame and many honors in his day, and accepted their decline with philosophic detachment, even amusement.   He told me of a couple of English globe-trotters, who brought no letter of introduction, and who had excused themselves for calling on him by saying that as there were no ruins to see in this country they had thought it would be a good idea to visit Mr. Longfellow.

We went to Bar Harbor to stay with Mr. and Mrs. Dorr, in the fine house they had just built in the approved, many-gabled Queen Anne style that then prevailed, and which in the simplicity of those days was thought quaint and attractive.   I had grateful memories of my happy trip to Naples that I owed to Mrs. Dorr's kindness, and found her as friendly and interesting as ever.   She was noted for her hospitality and liked to collect interesting people.   Everyone was glad to be invited to her dinners. These had an element of adventure.   She seated the guests as she thought best, but if conversation flagged and things did not go quite to her taste, she would order her guests to change places.   This was considered a manner of rebuke, for it meant that one had either talked too much or too little.   We are told of one courageous guest, a Peabody, if I remember rightly, who once refused to

MARGARET CHANLER AT SEVENTEEN

A picture taken at the time of her first visit to America

leave his place; and when his hostess repeated her order in a tone that could not be ignored, he bowed and said: "Madam, I was taught that resistance to tyrants was obedience to God." But this only happened once; the company was generally docile, and each one carried his napkin, glass, and broken bread to the new place assigned him, and relieved his feelings by grumbling about it afterwards. I enjoyed Mrs. Dorr's dinners very much, and was only once admonished across the table that I had talked long enough to Mr. A on my right, and must turn my attention to Mr. B on my left.

Mrs. Dorr was one of the pioneers of Mt. Desert; when she first went there Bar Harbor was a small fishing village. Her property is now the centre of the Mt. Desert National Park. After her death her son George made it over to the country, and was tireless in his efforts to have the government appropriate more land and take the proper measure to save as much as possible of the beautiful island from the desecration of summer cottages scattered over the landscape. With patience and great perseverance he built this tribute to his mother's memory, for the joy of his fellow man.

While staying with the Dorrs I had a strange experience. In those days we all dabbled in psychic mysteries — theosophy, spiritism, Ouija board, and table-rapping. Mrs. Dorr was an ardent believer. She had lost a son before I knew her, and received messages from him. Paper-and-pencil miracles were in the air. Uncle Sam received notes, scribbled in pencil on blue paper, from a lama in Thibet, Kout Houmi Lal Sing. They would flutter down from the ceiling while he was taking a shower or turn up on his desk when no one had put them there. Madame Blavatsky had published her *Isis Unveiled;* Sinnett, his *Occult World.* We all read the Upanishads and Edwin Arnold's *Light of Asia.* Astral fluid, Karma, "the jewel is in the lotus — om," were familiar expressions. My mother particularly enjoyed table-rapping; she did not believe in spiritism, but loved the unexplained.

I do not know how much Mrs. Dorr had studied the spiritual borderland; she was certainly what would be called psychic in the vocabulary of the adepts.

One evening while we were staying with her it was proposed to try table-rapping. George wisely declined to take part, and left the room. I think there may have been one or two others present besides Mrs. Dorr, my mother, and myself. We chose a rather heavy black teakwood table. Mrs. Dorr sat next to me. My mother and I had done it very often, and the table had always moved, whether by our unconsciously pushing it, or by the tapping of some occult odic force, I was never sure; but this night it seemed fastened to the floor and would not stir. We sat silent for a long time, waiting. Presently Mrs. Dorr's hand — an old, terrifying hand — crept across the narrow black space that separated it from mine; she said, "My hand is moved," and laid it heavily on mine. It gave me a violent shock. I shrieked with horror and fell unconscious. When I came to I was lying on the floor, awakened out of my swoon by a strong dose of *sal volatile* being poured down my throat and spilled over my face. I have no idea what happened, but my mother hurried me off to bed.

We were to leave for Boston the next morning. When I awoke I felt very ill, and told my mother I could not possibly start; but she insisted: our parlor-car seats were engaged; we were expected at a friend's house; she wanted to get me away. We bade farewell to our kind hosts, took a little steamer to the mainland, and boarded our train. I felt more and more miserable.

Presently a middle-aged friendly face — Mr. James Gillespie Blaine, with whose family we had dined in Augusta not long before — greeted us; we were begged to sit with him in the drawing-room, which he had to himself. I was made comfortable on the sofa and began to feel better. Mr. Blaine possessed the high art of conversation; one subject led to another — books, history, travel; we browsed through many pleasant pastures of the mind. I forgot all about the black table and the occult forces. When I reached Boston I felt cured.

We went to the old Brunswick, still standing, but long since superseded by more fashionable hotels.

The next morning I was far, far worse. We sent for Aunt Julia's friend and favorite physician, Dr. Wessel-hoeft, an ardent homeopathist. I had a bad case of chicken pox — which prolonged itself into a curious nervous disorder which homeopathy seemed unable to cope with. I could not bear to see people, and was, I suppose, in a semi-hysterical condition. The doctor thought it might have been caused by some thwarted love affair; it was nothing of the sort! I was possessed by a cloudy terror.

After some months of seclusion, I got well, began to go about, saw my friends, and made new ones; but

I could not for several years bring myself to meet
Mrs. Dorr again. She was hurt by my complete estrangement; but to me the whole experience had an importance
which I may not have conveyed in this brief account of it.
It worked as a practical, pragmatic caveat to the whole
tendency of tampering with the dangerous approaches of
pseudo-spirituality, of forcing an entrance through what
someone has well called the back door of the soul, of trying to apprehend materially things that pertain to the
spirit. That Mr. Blaine, through the charm of his
conversation, had been able to ward off for a whole day
the imminent approaches of a serious illness was in its way
just as tangible a proof of the control of matter by mind
as were ever the informatory rappings of a table touched
by mediumistic fingers.

I stayed on in Boston with Aunt Julia Howe, in her
house in Mount Vernon Street, and there I gradually recovered and came back to life and found it pleasant.
I fell in with a group of congenial contemporaries, and
was asked to join a girls' Sewing-Circle lunch club. These
are founded every year by the débutantes of the season,
and continue to exist as separate entities as long as there
are any members left alive. They never mix their vintage and keep the succeeding generations in separate and
exclusive layers. I was amused and interested, and enjoyed my temporary membership. The girls were an
unusually attractive group and among them I made
some charming friends. One of them, Grace Minot,
stands out as a very radiant memory. She had great
beauty, a small neat head "smooth as a robin's," well set

upon her shapely neck; there was unusual grace and charm
in everything she said or did.   She was much admired and
had many adorers; but her social success only added to
her charm, she took it so gayly and naturally.   I feel
that I am trying to describe a particular rose that bloomed
and faded long ago; it had a poignant perfection, all its
own.

In those days, before a ball the men sent flowers to
the girls they expected to dance with, and these had to
be taken to the party.   Grace would enter a ballroom like
an army with banners.   Her bouquets were tied together
in chaplets on satin ribbons, and hung over her arm;
sometimes there would be two of these long and rather
cumbersome strings of trophies, and her partner would
have to carry one of them, and was proud to do it.   Innumerable Jacqueminot roses were part of the triumphal
pageant.   Jacqueminots were her favorites, the fashionable flower of the season, and very expensive.

Boston girls, and American girls in general, are brought
up to feel that "coming out" is the all-important event,
the great test of their capacity.   Marriage they come to
regard as something of an abdication, a settling down to
the hard facts of life, a play for safety rather than a gamble
for conquest.

Living with Aunt Julia, I saw something of the older
Boston world: wise and learned old gentlemen who had in
their youth been abolitionists, transcendentalists, idealists
of sorts, and had given Boston its intellectual reputation.
Dr. James Freeman Clarke, the Unitarian divine, was one
of my aunt's dearest friends; her voice melted with devout

admiration whenever she mentioned his name.   He wrote
a book called *Ten Great Religions,* in which he gave a
summary sketch of Buddhism, Confucianism, Mahom-
etanism, and the rest, winding up with Christianity,
from which he eliminated all that was dogmatic or miraculous, giving it his preference on purely ethical grounds;
yet Aunt Julia told me that he had spoken to her of his
belief in Christ's Resurrection, his feeling that some
strange thing had happened on the first Easter morning,
which could not rationally be explained away; but no
such surmise found its way into his book.   Unitarianism
officially excludes the supernatural.   In adapting itself to
the rationalism of the nineteenth century it would seem to
have discarded much that is essential to Christian faith;
nevertheless Aunt Julia was in her own way deeply religious, and Dr. James Freeman Clarke had about him
something of the real saint.

Dr. Oliver Wendell Holmes was another of her
friends, and much beloved, an altogether delectable man.
It was he who, at the party given to celebrate Aunt Julia's
seventieth birthday, said that Mrs. Howe could only be
called seventy years young.

Mrs. Gardner, the famous "Mrs. Jack," was already a
prominent figure in the Boston of 1880, which she
charmed, scandalized, and greatly preoccupied.   She had
not yet built the Fenway Palace or begun to collect its
many treasures.   She was talked about for her unscrupulous flirtations, her lavish extravagance, her seasons of re-
pentant piety.   On Ash Wednesday she would appear in
penitential black with a rosary hanging from her belt.
She was a member of the Church of the Advent, where

the Cowley Fathers were as nearly Catholic in their practice as their Protestant Episcopal bishop would allow;[1] but
they can scarcely have been responsible for the dangling
rosary. She stood out in vivid contrast to the people
among whom she lived, and seemed to belong to another
age and clime, where passions burned brighter, pleasures
were more sumptuous, and repentances more dramatic
than in sober Beacon Street. Some of the more conservative social groups looked askance at her; Grace
Minot was not allowed to go to her parties, nor were
several others of the Sewing Circle I belonged to. Aunt
Julia appreciated her charm and intelligence, and Maud
Howe was one of her best friends, always called in to
comfort and console, in the not infrequent emotional
crises that marked the episodes of her life.

I heard more than I saw of her in those days, though
I occasionally went to her house, which was not very
different from other rich houses in the Back Bay. I
came to know her better many years later when she lived
in her great Fenway Palace, surrounded by priceless
works of art, an almost legendary figure. After we left
America she had a much-talked-of flirtation with Marion
Crawford, from which he escaped by following us to
Rome. Maud was sent for and had to spend many days
in her house.

[1] The Cowley Fathers no longer have any connection with the
Church of the Advent. Their Boston church, St. John the Evangelist,
is on Bowdoin Street.

XII

RETURN TO ITALY

THE following summer Uncle Sam hired for us one of the so-called Cliff cottages in Newport. A row of these extended from the old Cliff Hotel, directly next to Cliff Lawn, the summer home of the Chanlers, which was eventually to be mine in later years. The Chanlers were Uncle Sam's grandchildren. Their mother had died some years before, leaving ten small children. The distracted widower, John Winthrop Chanler, had not long survived her. The two oldest boys, Armstrong and Winthrop, known always as Archie and Wintie, were just growing up; there were six younger ones — in all, five boys and three girls; two boys had died before I knew them. Archie and Wintie came to see us very often. We used to take them on catboat sails and picnics. Wintie was the most entirely charming boy I had ever seen, but it never for a moment occurred to me that he was for me and I for him. He was just back from Eton and preparing to enter Harvard College in September.

My father had joined us and so had my brother Marion, which made us all very happy. I went to a good many parties, dinners, luncheons, and dances — but never felt quite in step with the Newport world. I was too foreign;

I spoke with a strong Italian accent; I was too much interested in things that in no way pertained to the cogent business of youth. I was conscious for the first time of being picturesquely, but not at all fashionably, dressed. I used to think out my clothes very carefully with the intention of having them look Greek or *quattrocento*, but the little dressmakers I could afford were rarely successful in carrying out my ideas. The result may easily be imagined, and when in a room full of smartly dressed girls of my own age I was uncomfortably aware of irremédiable mistakes in my apparel. At balls I felt decidedly dim and never knew the tingling exhilaration of the ballroom rapture until much later. Far more than going to dances I used to enjoy making music with Mrs. Wolcott Gibbs, an excellent musician who had two grand pianos.

The fashionable world of Newport seemed dull, wholly taken up as it was with the externals of life, fine clothes, well-appointed houses, and smart turnouts; the few interesting people seemed to live apart in a sort of limbo of comfortable frumpiness and had on the whole a better time, in spite of smaller material resources. Either group could have added so much to the pleasure of the other had they but known how to mingle. Aunt Julia herself was no respecter of coteries and she had devoted friends and admirers in both camps, and with her one never failed to have a good time. She did not pretend to be "smart," but had a very true sense of social relations, and a fund of wit and wisdom that made everyone enjoy her company. She had a funny little song she had made up, which expressed her attitude to the Newport world: —

Non sumus fashionabiles
   But *sumus respectabiles*
And in a humble one-horse shay
   We rumble tumble as we may.
Then *gaudeamus igitur,*
   Our soul has not to fidget her.
Chorus
   So *gaudeamus igitur,* our soul has not to fidget her.

She had no end of songs both grave and gay, but mostly
gay, the music and the words her own; and would sing
them with much charm and expression, tinkling the accompaniment with her still youthful hands. She never
touched the pedals nor could she write out the music.
Her music was her little wild garden kept for her intimates, to whom it gave great pleasure. She had a delightful set of children's songs, composed for the grandchildren, of whom there were many: a musical friend
wrote them down for her; perhaps they exist somewhere.

It was in Newport that summer that my brother Marion
met Bessie Berdan, whom he was later to marry. She was
very handsome and attractive and had much social art.
She too was a stranger, but seemed to manage better
than I.

It was there that I met Edith Wharton, then "Pussy"
Jones, who was later so vastly to enrich my life with
her abounding gift of friendship. We were at a musi-
cale given by Mr. Edward Potter. I had played the
piano and accompanied my brother's singing. My father
came up to me and said, "I want you to make the acquaintance of Miss Jones, the daughter of one of my best

friends." We threaded our way through the crowded rooms to a cosy corner where Miss Jones was holding animated conversation with a young man. The presentation was made with much warmth on my father's part; Miss Jones did not look at all pleased or interested, and I, feeling I had interrupted an amusing, possibly important *tête-à-tête*, made my escape as soon as possible. Edith says she does not remember this at all, but remembers me as one whom she at once felt drawn to, and tells me flattering things about my music. To me she was then just one of the many well-dressed girls with plenty of admirers who made me feel slightly ill at ease.

After passing the summer in Newport we took leave of America and boarded the good ship *Washington* of the Florio Line, sailing for Genoa. I had, in the two years spent in the United States, become to some extent repatriated, and found myself, rather to my surprise, a little sorry to leave the country; but when we reached the port of our destination and saw *Genova la superba* rising out of the water in a glory of sunset I was all rapture at returning to the land of beauty. What joy to see the Apennines again, and olive trees and cypresses!

We soon settled down into the old grooves at the Palazzo Altemps. I again had lessons with Sgambati, who urged me to prepare myself to obtain the diploma of Santa Cecilia at the Roman Academy of Music. This took many hours of practising and left me neither leisure nor energy for other things.

For the summer of 1882 we hired the Villa Cesarini at Genzano, a village in the Alban Hills not far from Rome; a handsome seventeenth-century palace dominating the

rather squalid little town; it had a charming bosky garden terraced down to the Lake of Nemi.

The ancient Roman galleys were then lying there deep
under water only suspected by archæologists, but my
donkey boy told me a story that must have come down
through the ages about a splendid anchored ship in the
middle of the lake, where a great lord kept his only daughter to prevent her from running away with the pretty page
who had won her heart. He had destined her to a rich
and powerful suitor, but rather than marry him she bribed
the watchman to sink the ship the night before the wedding. I think there were remnants or traces of the great
iron stanchions to which the ship had been moored. It
was not thought possible in those days to drain the lake
sufficiently to reach the sunken vessel. When this was
finally done in recent years several ships were discovered
and salvaged: highly decorated pleasure boats, creations
of idle imperial fancy; too large to move in the narrow
blue waters of the volcanic lake.

The Hugh Frasers shared the Villa with us. My
brother-in-law was then Secretary at the British Embassy
in Rome; my sister and her two boys spent the summer
with us, while Fraser joined us when the Chancery did not
require his services.

The place had no resources; I filled my days as best
I could with reading and practising. Those Italian villa
summers gave wonderful leisure for reading books *de
longue haleine*. I read all of Browning's *Ring and the
Book* at Genzano, Lecky's *European Morals,* and I forget the many others.

We discovered a sad and sallow tutor living in the

house, left there by our landlords, the Duke and Duchess Sforza Cesarini, who had taken their two sons with them on a journey. Desimoni was an accomplished scholar and taught me a good deal of Latin in the few months I studied with him.

The Frasers had brought with them from Vienna, their last post, an excellent Viennese cook. This poor young woman soon fell ill at the Villa. The doctor was sent for and did not take long to diagnose the case — a *perniciosa* or black typhus, very serious and contagious. Everyone in the place seemed thoroughly familiar with the disease and the melancholy Desimoni assured me, in the intervals between Latin exercises, that it was always fatal; that someone died of it every summer. It had carried away the Duke's brother, the Conte di Santa Fiora, the year before, and another member of the family the year before that; and this was why the Sforzas had rented the Villa and gone elsewhere for their *villeggiatura*.

It never occurred to anyone that we had better move away from Genzano. We had paid our rent and must take our chances, with certain precautions: never exposing ourselves to the night air, leaving no windows open after sunset, never going into the garden except in the middle of the day. I need not remind you that malaria was supposed to be a poisonous exhalation; the secret of the mosquitoes had not yet been discovered.

Two nursing sisters were sent for from the Bon Secours Convent in Rome. Sœur Marius, a splendid French nun, came on the scene and made the summer memorable for me, a turning point in my life.

She and the other sister took turns at nursing the cook,

who eventually died, as Desimoni predicted from the first. But Sœur Marius became my great friend. She was a tall, spirited, commanding-looking woman with a lively wit and fine intellectual enthusiasm which monastic discipline had controlled and enhanced, never quenched. She took hold of me, I can think of no other expression, and carried me through the fog of spiritual uncertainty in which I was then floundering. My theological moorings had been cut seven years before in the months I spent with Fräulein Müller. During that time I had drifted through many waters. I had been dazzled and my reason captured by the writings of John Stuart Mill, Huxley, and Herbert Spencer, with a strong undertow of Pascal, Plato, the Bible, and the *Imitation of Christ*. I did not know what I believed. I did not like the Protestant Episcopal religion. The Roman Church had always been the only possible one for me, had always seemed beautiful and attractive, but inaccessible, irreconcilable with "Synthetic Philosophy" and the advance of modern thought.

I never doubted the existence of God and believed firmly in the human soul with its dark necessity of tending towards Him. Sœur Marius, when she could leave her patient, turned her attention to my case.

There was some sort of Novena going on in the village church and we would go together and listen to a sermon and assist at Benediction. The *curato* was eloquent in his way and I found myself interested in what he said; but Benediction has a peculiar attraction and wordless power of persuasion. In Italy, particularly in country parishes, the congregation sings the hymns, generally to old Grego-

rian melodies very roughly rendered; but the simplicity of
the ritual, the lights, the incense, the silence at the moment when the Host is raised in blessing over the kneeling crowd, are all profoundly moving.

Benediction is not a liturgical ceremony. It is almost
a popular creation grown out of devotion and desire to
behold and adore. There is no prescribed rite beyond
the singing of the *Tantum Ergo* and the reciting of the
collect, — *"Deus qui nobis,"* — both taken from the
Maundy Thursday and Corpus Christi Mass. Other
hymns can precede it, litanies and prayers, or the rosary
may be recited in Latin or the language of the country.
Benediction may follow vespers or compline or a sermon.
There is no obligation whatever to attend, but it should
not be given unless a certain number of worshipers can
be counted on. There must, however, be singing, candles
lighted (not less than twelve), incense burned, and, if
possible, flowers on the altar — all tokens of joy, earthly
images of spiritual things. It is perhaps an unconscious
form of sun worship, a reminiscence of spring festivals,
an awakening of the spirit through the senses.

The round, spotless wafer, whose circumference has
neither beginning nor end, surrounded by the converging
rays of the golden monstrance, is in itself an ancient
and deeply significant symbol. The One whom we can
neither describe nor define, in whom all qualities merge
to a white radiance, surrounded by unlimited direction of
Power — the rays are infinite, their lines, continued into
space, would reach every furthest star. It is meet and
right to kneel and bow our heads before this mystery, to
send up our prayers with the incense, to feel our hearts

burning with the tapers, our spirit rapt in the Cloud of Unknowing.

When all this was happening, my brother Marion was in America. He had become a Catholic a year or two before this, while he was in India. I wrote to consult him and received his answer. By a curious accident these two letters found their way to the Gardner Museum in Boston, whose curator kindly allowed me to copy them. Here in substance is mine, written from Genzano: —

GENZANO, 31 AUG. 1882

MY DEAREST MARION: —

If you were here I should take you out for a long walk and we could talk this matter over together, but as you are away I must try to put it into writing and I hope you will find time to answer very seriously and thoroughly. I have for a long time felt and argued out satisfactorily to myself, that Catholicism was the only form of organized religion logically and rationally possible — but I thought that this organization was perhaps after all a necessity more of the past than of the present, that the world was outgrowing the need of it and could read and interpret its Bible, say its prayers, right its wrong and do its right intuitively, each person being a law unto himself. Yet there is a great deal of seasickness on the waves of free doubt. Particularly if you try conscientiously to see the right and know the truth. But I need not go over these reflections; they have been made many times. Suppose then that we allow, as a fixed premise, that a religion is found necessary and prove that to me especially Catholicism would be the only possible form of it.

In the first place then, I dislike the English Church. That is certainly not logic — at least no rational proof that it may not be the best one for me. But I dislike it for the reason that it seems to me illogical and inconsistent. I need not name the discrepancies of its teachings to you I think — but what reason is there to believe St. Paul, St. John and all the first declarers of God's truths infallible, and yet to deny that in our present day God can reveal His truth to any man so as to make him pronounce right judgment upon it. If you tell me God, in point of fact, cannot, does not, or will not grant special revelations: "He has put His truth into the air, the stars, the woods, the character and eyes of man in the possibility of a man's saying 'love your enemies, do good to them that hate you' — and all these things are governed by iron laws — the results of forces at work for endless ages, which it would be unreasonable to suppose that He would for a moment suspend or counteract." Very well, my friend, your argument is sound so far as it goes — except that you have overlooked something in yourself which contradicts you; but while I take it for granted that something is there, you say it is not. We will not argue about it, agree to differ and part perfectly good friends. But now Anglicanism comes and says: God did reveal Himself once; but if anyone pretends to have a special revelation from Him now, that man is Antichrist and lies in his throat. I do not blame you if you do not believe in miracles at all — in the sick being healed, the dead raised, the five loaves made to feed five

thousand people. But if you believe these and that
St. Peter, St. Paul, and all the early saints could work
miracles, was no one after them to have the power?   Was
humanity ever to fall away after that, and the Church forever to look back?   There is no logical stopping place for
the mind between absolutism and rationalism.   This we
have talked over together often enough, have n't we?
Only then I felt satisfied with a sort of transcendentalized
rationalism which I have found to be chimeric, and like
a quicksand.   The truth is Isis and forever veiled, and we
feel the need of a symbol and figure which we can grasp
and which will represent it to us; it seems better to take
and believe in one which has been found and fashioned
by humanity's best and strongest powers for over eighteen
hundred years, than to make one for ourselves.

All this then I grant, but then come down to the smaller
personal matters.   I will take the bull by the horns and
speak to you of confession.   I grant that it is wise and
beautiful as a general rule, but I find it hard to face
being restricted in my reading by an ignorant confessor
who would not trust me to see the spiritual errors through
the material truths, and so denying me the knowledge of
the latter.   I fear I would end by breaking loose, used as
I am to entire liberty.   I would like you to write me, if,
reading as you do all the newest books and thinking as
you do all the most modern thoughts, you can still be a
good Catholic, and if you think I would be.   I write to
you because you and I have rather the same shape of
mind — that is, mine is like yours on a smaller scale.   We
are both quite cool and detached about these matters and
understand each other.   There is no sentimentalism at

all about my feeling — in fact, I wish I had more emotion, only that perhaps a cool deliberate choice is less likely to be repented of.

I know your time is very valuable and yet I do hope you will give me an hour or so of it. Here I talk to the archpriest, who is a good soul and very clever but used to dealing with the Genzanese, not with our rather more sophisticated type. Whom would you advise me to go to in Rome? I want a thoroughly broad-minded person.

Do not think I am acting or thinking on the sly. Mamma knows that I am preoccupied with the idea, and tells me she has deeply regretted that she prevented Mimo from taking the step when she was so anxious to, some years ago, and that should I feel a conviction in that direction she would put no obstacles in my way. But I shall wait for your answer and not do anything definite for at least six weeks. My greatest fear is that I should later change my mind and I want you to tell me if we can conscientiously carry out what we undertake. I had rather the Howes knew nothing of this yet, in fact that you did not talk of it to anyone just now.

Your most loving sister,

MARGARET

And here is my brother's answer: —

MY DEAREST MARGARET: —

I received last night your letter dated August 31st and I have read it most carefully and have it now before me. I need hardly tell you that it has given me more pleasure than anything I can remember for a long time.   Whatever you may decide to do, never change your mind again from the position you now hold in regard to religion in general, for it is the right one, whether you be Catholic, Brahman or Buddhist, remembering always that if religion is true, it was true before man was created, it would be true without his present existence, and it will continue true after he has passed away.   By religion, I mean primarily the being of one God, almighty, by the truth of religion, I mean the coincidence of that being with such definition thereof as the form of our belief presents to us.   The definition does not extend to the Whole, but covers such portions as are necessary for us to know.   The judgment, to use a convenient philosophic word (*das Urtheil*).   "God is good" is a definition of a portion of the Whole.   That it does not define the Whole is clear if we make the judgment converse and say: "Goodness is God," which is a manifest fallacy.   Upon this fallacy, however, rests the entire doctrine of Confucius, which is an attempt to deify the potential goodness of humanity, forgetting that such potential goodness must lack the elements of eternity and immutability, at least; and if imagined to be eternal or immutable, must rest on an *a priori* concept of the good, involving qualifying terms not found in the human nature upon which the whole system is based.   Similarly, then, if I say to you: "The Catholic Church is God," I am manifestly in error, but if I say: "The Catholic Church defines so much of God as it is necessary to know during this life, that we may attain to the next" — I am saying what is true, and what Christians of other denominations at the present day gen-

erally admit to be true. For if not, they would say that
Catholics cannot attain Heaven, a proposition now rel-
egated to a few prejudiced persons in Scotland and some
parts of Germany. Catholics, on the other hand, allow
that some Christians of other denominations may be
saved. This is shown in the fact that the baptism of a
non-Catholic, on admission into the Catholic Church, is
made invariably *conditional.* That is, it is performed for
greater certainty, in case the original baptism of the person
has been incomplete. Many persons are admitted to the
Catholic Church without rebaptism. Manifestly if such
persons had died after their first baptism without having
committed any mortal sin, good Catholics must admit
that they were saved. But what the Catholic Church
maintains in regard to other denominations of Christians
is this, that the Protestant Episcopal Church of England
(for instance, or any other) does *not* "define so much of
God" — that is, of His will and ordinance — "as it is
necessary to know, during this life, that *we* may attain to
the next"; and "we" means not those rare persons who
may be free from mortal sin, but "we sinners, we who con-
stitute the rank and file of a weak and sinning humanity."

You have come to me, my dear sister, in your present
situation, and I am sincerely grateful to you for having
done so. But you have come with certain questions which
require to be answered. That I would rejoice beyond
all others to see you become a Catholic like myself in
faith, I trust far better in deeds, you know. But none
would regret more than I to see you led by your heart
whither your intellect would not. First of all things,
therefore, it is necessary that in what I am going to say

you should consider not me, the Catholic, but the reasoning which you would admit in the discussion of other matters, neither of the soul nor of the heart, but of the head. I will endeavor to pass rapidly over the points you have granted.

1. You allow a religion to be necessary. By religion, I mean the being of one God, almighty. Whatever you mean can only be an extension of that simple expression. The attribute, almighty, contains the minor attribute, eternal, in itself. No finite being can be conceived possessed of the infinite Knowledge implied in the conception of infinite power. This Knowledge that religion is necessary you have arrived at by personal experience, as I know; you by the battle of thought, I by the battle of much wrongdoing. Having once arrived at this conclusion, it is yours, as it is mine, because one's own experience is worth that of all other men together, even if it differed from theirs; but it does not differ — it is substantially the same.

2. Lord Amberly, who wrote a famous book on the comparative characteristics of all known religions, distinguished between Faith and Belief. Faith is the term of larger signification, implying the experience that religion is necessary. Belief he limits to the form of individual creeds. Seeing you have Faith, the question of religion to you individually is reduced to a question of Belief. Admitting God, what do you know of Him?

3. You dislike the English Church, and you say it is not logic to dislike it. But a moment later you show a Knowledge of its manifest inconsistencies, not to use a stronger term. It is therefore not you who dislike the

English Church. Your mind, used to the procedure of pure reason, lucid and mathematic in its deductions, whether from a sound or an unsound basis, revolts against a system that does not argue correctly from the false premises it has itself laid down. It may not be rational for you to rise up and say: I dislike the English Church. But it is highly rational for any cultivated mind to rebel against the arbitrary attempt to inculcate false logic as a means of salvation. The cultivated mind, when it is right, finds it hard to distinguish between the impulses of the heart and the impulses of the brain. When it is wrong, there is no difficulty in making the distinction.

4. The imaginary person who says of God: "He has put His truth into the air, the stars, the woods, the character and eyes of man, in the possibility of a man saying 'love your enemies, do good to them that hate you' " — and says also "this is enough," is falling into the palpable error of confusing subject and object, the attribute with the divinity. If he goes further and becomes a nature worshipper, saying "nature is my God," I cannot see that he is any wiser than the savage who falls down and worships the white man's ticking watch, conceiving it to be a god, and who would, *a fortiori*, worship the watchmaker, seeing that to the savage he is the maker of gods. The nature worshipper is evidently a savage. The other, who considers the manifestation of God in nature sufficient for himself, overlooks, as you say, himself. God has made laws and courses for the stars and for the earth which, so far from being eternal and immutable, if we consider any one star as a whole, are constantly undergoing the modifications which even our short-lived as-

tronomers are able to observe.   Apart from the atom, no
laws are either eternal or immutable.   And as far as the
atom is concerned it is as purely imaginary — not fictitious,
but only construable through the power of the imagination
— as the soul itself.   That man, then, is imposed upon
by the revolving masses of the spheres.   If he would
reflect, as he probably knows, that the Pythagorean
proposition is practically untrue, and requires enormous
corrections, when applied to celestial measurements,
though it is quite possible that it may have been true once,
he would acquire a somewhat broader view of God's
activity in the Universe, than to speak with such satisfaction
of immutable and iron laws.   God's true immutability
is unseen, and if He has made laws for the unseen atom
which we may arrive at approximately, has he made no
laws for the unseen soul which we bear in us?   And can
we not know as much of these laws, whose workings we
can feel, as we do of others, whose effects we can only
observe at a distance?   I do not think this argument
falls beyond the bounds of pure reason.

    5.   Having thus briefly touched the objections to the
English Church and to the quietists and nature worshippers, and having found those objections overwhelming,
you turn with logic sequence to the Catholic Church.   You
find it to be modern and progressive, formal, and personal to the individual.

    Against the English Church you use with success two
arguments: the one "I dislike you," which is a true
argumentum ad hominem; second, "you are inconsistent,"
which you successfully supported.   Against the quietists
and nature worshippers you employed, or I have em-

ployed for you, the common analytical method. To these three arguments if brought (in your mind) against the Catholic Church, the three qualities you have found therein are sufficient reply. (1) Personally and individually you do not "dislike" the Catholic Church, though you find minor points of difficulty. (2) The Church is not inconsistent, for being modern and progressive her chief activity lies in the logical adaptation of herself to the requirements of mankind to-day and to the tenor of his thought and the steps of his advancements in non-theologic knowledge. (3) She is not open to attack from the common analysis because she is formal. Her form is built up from God — elaborate, indeed, but always immediately reducible to the first terms; whereas the quietist tries to build up to a God removed to an immeasurable distance, and the nature worshipper builds his God upon the forms that he sees.

You turn then to the Catholic Church, and your remarks come naturally under the three heads I have given. She is modern, formal, and personal.

1. Modern. She does not fall into the English error of denying the possibility of direct inspiration or of direct intervention in human affairs. Nevertheless she is very cautious about declaring miracles. The miracle of Lourdes, attested unwillingly enough by several Church of England clergymen, and by one at least in print, is not dogmatic — that is, neither you nor I are required to believe it to be good Catholics. For myself I do believe it. The English are constantly challenged to draw the line where divine intervention ceases. They cannot do so, and they answer, like Diogenes, *"solvitur ambulando"*

— "There are no miracles now, there must then be a line somewhere." This is poor logic as such, even were the conclusion approximately true.

In regard to the modern spirit of the Catholic Church, it has been noticed that a service in Westminster, or in York Minster, produces a far stronger impression of antiquity than a high Mass in a Roman basilica. And these outward expressions of a strong modern life should not be disregarded.

As for the relations of the Church to modern science, it need only be said that she adopts and authorizes the teachings of scientists so soon as they have stood the tests she brings to bear upon them. There have been enough theories set up and knocked down in the last two thousand years to justify her in waiting half a century before allowing the stability of Darwin's theory. But it is characteristic that one of the greatest astronomers of our time was a Jesuit — Padre Secchi, some of whose inventions are in use in all great observatories throughout the world.

Modern does not mean experimental, it means rather accepting the whole body of demonstrated scientific knowledge. The position of modern Catholics towards modern scientists is far more liberal than that assumed by scientific freethinkers toward the Catholic Church.

2. Formal. Upon this point it is hardly necessary for me to speak to one of your intelligence. The form is to the mass of mankind the definition of the thing, and in view of this it must often be necessary to make the form more elaborate than the thing, in order that to the uneducated mind of the mass, no portion of the thing may

remain undefined, that is, unsymbolized. The form is to most men what the signs of the fingers are to the deaf and dumb, the only means by which ideas are conveyed to them; and as deaf and dumb children are strictly forbidden to use abbreviations of an arbitrary nature, lest any confusion, misunderstanding, or loss of the power to express ensue, so with the mass of mankind, who are children as compared with intellectual man, it is necessary that the form, which is their only definition of what they believe, should be preserved entire and unchanged. On the score of antiquity and precedent most of the forms in use in the Catholic Church are unassailable, and their organization and sequence are such that the thing symbolized can always be found immediately in the symbol.

3. Personal. This point, I understand from your letter, is the one of most importance to you. I call the Church personal, because she proposes to follow the course of every individual from his birth to his death; not leaving him to think for himself, to live for himself, to save his soul for himself, but thinking for him in such matters as he is not able to master alone, teaching and exhorting him to live for others, and endeavoring to make him sure of the future. Her principal means of exerting this life-long personal influence over men lies in the institution of confession. It is the strongest argument in its favor, and in support of its divine origin, that its history is little short of miraculous. Nothing indeed would appear at first sight more improbable than that so large a body of mankind could be induced to confess truly and honestly their wrongdoings. Nothing is more certain than that

the majority of confessions are sincere, and that confession is a great practical benefit to mankind.

Now what you have previously granted you have
granted not for yourself only, but for mankind generally. It would require only the briefest synopsis to
show that you think, as I believe, that the Catholic Church
is the Church of the world — that is, you think that the
greatest practical good would be attained by the greatest
number of persons, if all the world were Catholic. No
end can be nobler than that which seeks the greatest good,
and no end is more worthy of sacrifice. Such an end cannot be reached without organization, and there is no
organization without rule. Confession is preëminently
the means by which the rule is made to act on the lives
of individuals. Remove it, and each man will at once
begin to separate himself, in small things at first, but soon
in greater according to his fancy. Think then that in
accepting it and conforming to it with exactness, although
your sins as compared with mine are no sins at all, you are
forming part of a whole; and by your own life are supporting and even strengthening those rules, ordinances
and principles which have for their object the good of
mankind. That when you kneel at the confessional and
say: "I confess to Almighty God," you are making a
confession of adherence to the soundest philosophy the
world has ever seen, as well as a confession of sin; and
that if people only confessed when their conscience became
unbearably active, a great many would never confess at
all, the means of enforcing the rule of good life would
be rapidly weakened, the bonds would crumble away, and
the Catholic and Apostolic Church would in a few years

present an even more deplorable spectacle of internecine schism to the world than that exhibited by the Protestant persuasions, in proportion as Catholics are more numerous and embrace a greater variety of races.

Thus accepting confession as a whole you will soon recognize that it is a real benefit to yourself, an assistance in the clear and unbiased judgment of right and wrong, a mighty purifier of small evils and an invaluable resource in trouble. All this you will learn by personal experience. There remains the important question, of tenfold importance to a person of your tastes, "How far will confession interfere with my freedom of choice in reading, with my freedom of speech in conversation?"

I need not tell you that you are right in asking the question. But first you ask whether I, who read the most modern books and think the most modern thoughts, am a good Catholic — in the sense of being a staunch adherent to the faith and a conscientious observer of prescribed duties, I answer: I am. I can find nothing in the Church at variance with the occasionally reliable results of modern science. The Church is not an encyclopædia of scientific facts, to be overthrown by the discovery of a new species of Univalve, by the propagation of a few truths among many fallacies at the hands of a J. J. Rousseau, a J. S. Mill, or a Herbert Spencer — a Giordano Bruno, a Leibnitz, or a Darwin. It is of course necessary to be careful in accepting what they state, for if you accept what one scientist says, wholly, you will not only quarrel with the Church; but with most other scientists. The most virulent enemy of the Church and of many of his fellow workers, the late Professor W. K. Clifford, obscures

the truths he sets forth with the most fierce blasphemy
of God and abuse of man, in works where any reference to
God or man at all is as clumsy as it is superfluous to
the matters in hand.   And yet Clifford made many discoveries in the field of mathematics against which the
Church has nothing to say, and he might have made
precisely the same discoveries had he been a Jesuit or a
Benedictine monk.   Be cautious therefore, and remember
that great men, as well as small, work in the half light
of very imperfect *a priori* knowledge.   The means of
inquiry, mind, education and industry, are all good; but
you have not read so much philosophy without perceiving
that we are very much at sea in regard to the fundamental
conception of all the things concerning which we inquire.
We do not even know what "being," which seems the
common basis of everything with which we have to do,
really *is*.

Above all, avoid confounding the impersonality of the
truth with the individuality of its expounders; the divine
nature of God with the humanity of His ministers, nor
seek to make the one responsible for the other.   You will
see many things you will not like in Rome, for the best
workers are put in the most important places, which are
the branches of the tree where the growth is, and the
worst are often kept at home that they may do no mischief.
Remember the principle; forget, if need be, its agents.

In view of all these matters, the choice of a confessor
is a very serious affair.   You are not, of course, bound to
any one confessor, and you may change as often as you
choose; but if possible avoid such changes as far as you
can.   I would hardly advise you to consult my old friend

Lily Theodoli. She is a good woman, few better; but her views are very different from ours. I mean, of course, about a confessor; you will find her armed at all points on matters of doctrine. If you go to the Jesuits, as she would advise you, you will find yourself amongst the most intelligent people, I allow, but I think that you will also find yourself in the midst of a party. I wish you could find my old friend Don Paolo Recanatesi — he is a man of the broadest intelligence and of perfectly phenomenal learning, though barely forty years old. He is to be heard of at San Filippo Neri, I believe, and he would know of some good men of broad views. You might write to him at "Osimo, *presso* Loreto Marche" — tell him you are my sister and ask him plainly to direct you to some good confessor of philosophic intelligence. The superior of the few monks left at San Giovanni in Laterano used to be a man of the same stamp. These are men unknown, but not the less large-minded for that.

On the other hand you might go to headquarters. Be presented to the Pope, tell him of your intention and ask him to advise you. He would not send you to a Jesuit. In all this I do not mean to say that if you are disposed toward the Jesuits you should avoid them. If you like the idea of a party, vigorous and active, but *always* a party, go to them. You will have no difficulty in finding a confessor of the most modern views. If you do this, go at once to the Theodoli, who will put you in the right way. Most of the "Blacks" now go to the Gesù, and many of them are in close relations with the Society.

And if possible, when you have decided upon a con-

fessor, abide by him; for changes only make life difficult.

I do not know how I can further advise you, my dear
sister, where a month must elapse between question and
answer. I can only say to you that I am glad of your
intention; that I trust you will persevere therein, and
not abandon it if you find a few narrow and bigoted people
in your path, and that I trust before long to hear you have
taken the final step. You can be intellectual, progressive,
inquiring, and yet be a most sincere Catholic, and I know
you will be. I have endeavored to answer your questions and to recapitulate the points on which you are
already assured. Read this letter aloud, with the dear
mother, when you have read it to yourself, for her advice
is better than mine, seeing she is more truly Catholic than
us all. And write to me again when you have time. I
began this letter on the 18th and to-day is the 21st, so you
see it has not been written in a hurry or thoughtlessly.
I have followed your instructions in regard to silence, and
I would advise you to be admitted to the Church privately,
or at least without any great publicity. It will be more
satisfactory to yourself.

And so, my dear Margaret, I beg God bless you and
keep you always —.

Your most loving brother,

MARION

The long melancholy summer at Genzano came to an
end at last. No one else in the family contracted typhus
and we thankfully went back to Rome as soon as the first
October rains had cooled the streets. I saw a great deal

of Sœur Marius and she asked Monseigneur Puyol, the Superior of the seminary of San Luigi dei Francesi, the French Church in Rome, to come to see me. He agreed to give me instructions and came once a week for several months. My mother was always present and my friend Blanche Broadwood, who was interested but not convinced by the conferences.

My mother's attitude was generously impartial. Herself profoundly religious, she had been troubled by my years of incredulity. When we were in Boston she had consulted with the Cowley Fathers of the Church of the Advent as to what had better be done to bring me back into the fold. Father Hall had come to see me and found me reading the *Dialogues* of Plato. He was a narrow, ascetic-looking man in a black cassock; he besought me to put away such pagan books. I hugged my volume of Jowett's translation and refused to consider myself in danger of hell-fire; he stood up and prayed over me, which embarrassed and annoyed me. Nothing came of the interview. My mother, on the contrary, found great comfort in his ministrations. I think she went to confession to him.

My sister, Mimoli Crawford, had several times in her life wanted to become a Catholic. My mother had always done her best to prevent it. I remember at one time Mimoli wrote her a long letter with a list of "plain reasons for joining the Church of Rome." My mother had an old friend, an English clergyman, Mr. Shadwell by name, who happened to be in Rome; a gentle, scholarly man to whom she showed this letter, asking him to answer the arguments with valid objections. All he could find to

say was, "Oh, my dear friend, let her go, do not try
to hold her back. They have all the Saints on their
side."

This had done a good deal to break down her defenses,
as also had the fact that Marion Crawford had become a
Catholic. Eventually she in no way opposed my being
received into the Church on the nineteenth day of March,
1883, in Monseigneur Puyol's private chapel at San Luigi
dei Francesi.

When the news of my becoming a Catholic reached
Dr. Nevin, the American pastor, he wrote my mother a
letter, half of condolence, half of reproach; saying, among
other things, that it was not possible that anyone of
Daisy's intelligence should long be satisfied with the
teaching and practice of the Roman Church. It was my
mother's fond belief that I would never have strayed from
the Protestant confession had it been more attractively
presented at St. Paul's within the Walls.

Dr. Nevin must have come to Rome when I was very
young. I cannot remember not knowing him. He had
been a cavalry officer in the Federal Army during the
Civil War, had a good record, and retired with the rank
of colonel. When I first remember him he told many
stories about camp life and battles and the negroes that
were being fought about. He was a sportsman, a horseman (though he did not like jumping, considering it an
"unnatural and unpleasant sensation"), fond of big-game
hunting, fine society, and good cheer; he developed a
great love and a certain expert knowledge of pictures
and curios and owned an interesting and valuable collection, many of its objects now scattered among the

museums of the world. He had an odd, nervous, or sentimental infirmity which caused him to break down and weep while preaching or reading the service. We never knew if he enjoyed this gift of tears; the congregation found it disturbing and quite out of keeping with their pastor's otherwise very masculine psychology. For some reason my mother and he had no great liking for one another. It was a trial to both that again and again they found themselves sitting side by side at dinner parties. They were considered appropriate *commensales;* he as head of the American Church, she as a prominent pillar of its congregation. They disliked the situation so much and it occurred so often that they would let the whole meal go by without uttering a word.

I came to know Dr. Nevin much better after I was married. He and my husband enjoyed one another's society and went off together on several hunting-camping parties, in the Campagna, in Sardinia, in Colorado. They were boon companions, and he was very friendly to me in spite of my defection. My mother had a pathetic yearning for more spiritual comfort than the good man could possibly administer. She blamed him for my estrangement from Protestantism.

Indeed no one was at fault. I like to think it was a case of predestination furthered by propitious accidents, that mine was an *anima naturaliter catholica.* These things are hard to account for and their germ lies hidden in the vital mysteries of our disposition. Environment and circumstances are the soil and the occasion of their springing to life and eventually bearing fruit.

When I married into a very Protestant family and

left Rome to live in the United States, my mother felt
sure that I would go back to the faith of my fathers,
"seeing all those nice people" were of that persuasion and
only the ignorant Irish of mine.   Nothing could have
been further from the eventual fact.   I was deeply
rooted in Catholic faith and practice.   America was a
foreign land to me, where for many years I felt like a
guest and a stranger, and where the Church was the
home of my soul.

I became a Catholic because I wanted to and I have
never for a moment had reason to regret it.   On the contrary, years and habit have deepened my convictions, have
strengthened my love for it; *"Dans cette foi je veux
vivre et mourir,"* as François Villon makes his mother say
in the ballad he wrote for her.

My father felt sure that I was the victim of mystifica-
tion, — lured by lies and blandishments, — that I should
wake up some day to find myself deluded and betrayed by
unscrupulous priests.

Had my conversion been more complete I suppose I
should have forsaken the world and become a nun, following the example of my dear Sœur Marius.   I considered doing this and thought about it a good deal,
wondering whether I should ever have the courage to
give up the world and follow the counsels of evangelical
perfection.   One morning I was awakened by a woman's
voice which said, in a high, clear tone, "Remember you
are not a wanderer upon a lonely road."   The voice
seemed to come from high above me; there was no one
in the room.   The words were to me a convincing message
and the sequel of my life proved it to be a true prophecy.

Only once more did I hear that same voice, many years later in Tuxedo when my then only son lay very ill. In the same way it wakened me out of my sleep in the early morning and uttered the one word "Bereavement." Johnny died that afternoon.

XIII

SORRENTO

THE next summer we all spent in Sant' Agnello di Sorrento at the Cocumella, an old-fashioned hotel established in what had once been a monastery. There were many terraces trellised with grapevine and paved with colored tiles; there was a flagged court with an old well-head in the middle of it, and a domed chapel decorated with pale green and blue tiles and a few ecstatic stucco saints. Here it was always cool and quiet, and Monsignor Maresca, the beautiful saintly old Bishop of Sorrento, used to come and say Mass there every morning.

We were surrounded on every side by orange and lemon gardens ever green and fragrant, and beyond them we could see from our terrace the Gulf of Naples and Vesuvius. The Piano (Plateau) di Sorrento lies about two hundred feet above sea level, stretches its fruitful acres from the mountains to the sea, ending abruptly in sheer brown cliffs that go straight down to the water.

Here and there along this unapproachable coast there are little narrow beaches, often only just wide enough to allow the fisher folk to draw up their boats and to dry and mend their nets as in Homeric or Biblical days. These are called *marine,* and each village has its own *marina* with a steep stony descent from the upper to the lower town, impracticable for any kind of vehicle, sometimes even for donkeys. These little places exist on all the rocky shores of the Mediterranean, Italy, Greece, and the Ægean islands. Where the coast shapes itself into a harbor the village grows into a town or a great city, sending its ships out to the seven seas, but the beach alone can support no more than a small fishing village, humble and poor through the centuries.

The Cocumella *calata,* or descent to the sea, was cut and hollowed out of the living rock, the brown, volcanic tufa; parts of it were dark steep corridors. Halfway down there was a landing with a big vaulted chamber open to the sea. It commanded the bluest view in the world, — Vesuvius and the sky and water, blue and blue and blue, — and was cool in the hottest weather.

This Marion had taken as his workroom, and here he spent his mornings writing in a cave like St. Jerome, minus the lion and the cardinal's hat, but, like St. Jerome, attended and adored by a little circle of fond ladies. Just then the circle was formed by his family.

Mr. Isaacs had come out the preceding year, had obtained immediate and world-wide success, and the publishers were clamoring for more copy. As *Mr. Isaacs* was the first book he had ever written or thought of writing, there was no unpublished manuscript to give them, and he went to work on his second novel, *Dr. Claudius,* followed by *To Leeward* and then by many others.

He wrote very fast, sometimes as much as a chapter a day, covering sheet after sheet of foolscap with his neat scholarly characters; never a blot or an erasure. He had none of the tormenting doubt of self-criticism. Working hard and conscientiously, he had confidence in his work and saw no reason to think that by doing it over he might do it better. This gave his pages a certain freshness. His books were extremely successful — to this the publishers' checks bore witness.

His pictures of Roman society in the mid-nineteenth century make pleasant reading even now. They are drawn from life as he saw it in those romantic years. The psychology is simple; there are good women and bad, always plainly labeled, and men of the highest courage and moral integrity opposed by unscrupulous villains.

The charm of his writing lay above all in his excellent gift of story-telling, and also in the great variety of settings and conditions in which his scenes were laid. Marion had seen life in so many different places, had tried his hand at so many trades, and knew about so many things. He could pass for an Italian, a Frenchman, a German (he was a member of the German Artist Club in Rome for six months before the other members found out he was not a German). He knew Russian and Norwegian and Spanish, Latin and Greek, of course, and Sanskrit and several modern Oriental languages. He kept his diary in Urdu while he was in India and for some years afterwards. He was interested in mathematics, philosophy, modern science, and ancient religions; he knew how to work in silver and understood the casting of horoscopes and could read characters and destinies from handwriting. He had a leaning to the occult

F. Marion Crawford

sciences; in those days there was much talk about "astral fluid," Mahatmas, unseen presences. Theosophy was in the air.

On the other hand, he was an experienced and bold sailor, had taken out a master's license, and was qualified to take command of a seagoing ship. And all this medley of knowledge and accomplishment was combined in him with a splendid vitality and a contagious zest in living. What astrologers would call a child of Jupiter, a real superman, before Nietzsche had invented the word. No wonder that his books never seemed to me as important as he himself!

He cared little for society and was at his most delightful best in the intimacy of the home circle — a shining, joyful creature in those days when we would come down the *calata* toward the end of the morning to carry him off for the noon swim.

No bathing has ever seemed half so enchanting as that in Sorrento, in the cool tideless rock-bound waters, very deep and clear and buoyant, of an indescribable blue that grows more vivid the deeper one plunges. Sorrento faces north, so that we were in the shadow of the high cliffs during the midday bathing hour.

Marion's boat, a lateen-sailed felucca with four sailors, was another of our joys. It happened sometimes that instead of two or three hours it would take eight or ten to reach our destination. An evening sail often prolonged itself to an all-night expedition and we saw the moonlight turn gray before the rose of dawn, and "the baths of all the western stars" before we got to bed. And many a lovely sail we took on these sapphire waters. When

the wind gave out, as it often did, the sailors rowed with
their big sweeps. We made many expeditions to neighboring islands and places along the shore — to Capri, to
Salerno, to Amalfi, and to the Isles of the Sirens.

One day — it was my birthday — Marion prepared a
special celebration. We were taken for a sail in the
morning and after rounding several jutting headlands
we landed in a beautiful great emerald grotto. On the
little beach at the back of the cave we found a picnic
spread — just such a picnic as Calypso might have arranged. We sat on the sand eating a delicious rustic
meal of fresh cheese and fruit, bread and wine, while we
watched the green waters rippling at our feet and casting
reflections up into the rocky vault which made it all look
a translucent jade. It is as fantastically green as the
famous Capri Grotto is blue, not nearly so large, but easier
of access.

At the Punta di Scutari (one of the many of that name
that dot the Mediterranean shore) the swimming was
superlatively good. There was a secluded ledge of rock
which served as dressing room for the girls; the boys
undressed in the boat. There were high overhanging
cliffs and the water was very deep and dark blue-green.
You could see fishes swimming far beneath the surface, but
the bottom you could not see, even with the sun striking
the water. There we disported ourselves like young
porpoises, diving off the rocks, playing ball, dancing
quadrilles. During one of these we terrified an American
cousin whom we had invited to join us on his assuring
us he knew how to swim. We were doing the figure
where one cavalier takes two ladies, one by each hand, and

advances and retreats before the single cavalier, finally joining him, forming a circle, and then separating into two couples. It took very vigorous swimming and his two ladies dragged him so hard through the water that they did not notice that his mouth and nose were submerged. He was sure we nearly drowned him.

Sometimes we went there in the late afternoon and sometimes even by moonlight. It was delightful to see the sunset from the water; the sun seemed very near when it dipped into the sea and disappeared in it a few hundred yards away. But the moonlight swimming was uncanny — the water was too black, we looked too white, and the sea seemed full of intangible, terrifying presences.

In the late summer of 1883 Uncle Sam Ward joined us at the Cocumella, a welcome addition to the family circle. He was now living in England, where he had many friends and many new adopted nephews and nieces. We have a picture of him by Spy which came out in the London *Vanity Fair;* it is called "Uncle Sam." Everyone loved him. He shared our life on land and water and brought with him a breath of the great world. We made expeditions with him to Capri, to Pompeii, to Amalfi and Pæstum. He was untiring in his enthusiasm to see sights; made Marion go up Vesuvius with him and spent long hours in the Naples Museum. Early in the autumn we all went back to Rome and he stayed on with us there, visiting museums and churches, meeting our friends and casting on all the kindly radiance which drew everyone to him. He liked my friend Blanche Broadwood and used to call us Black and White Magic. We lived very simply at the Palazzo Altemps, and the dear Sybarite found it hard, I dare say, to get used to the *Vino dei Castelli* which was served at our table, a rather sour little Roman wine.

One evening we had asked a few friends to meet him, Monseigneur Puyol among others. My father had a few bottles of rare old French claret saved from the wreck of our Odescalchi days. Some of this was served. I shall never forget the look of sudden rapture as Uncle Sam lifted his glass to his mouth and the delicate bouquet struck his unexpectant nostrils. "Château Lafitte '67," he murmured, as in prayer. Giuseppe, the old butler, had not announced it and the good uncle had no reason to expect anything but the usual table wine. I hardly think nose and palate can be more delicately sensitive than that — to name the Château and the vintage at a whiff.

That March, Lord and Lady Rosebery were on their way back from India and Uncle Sam had promised to join them in Malta for the last part of their homeward voyage. They were his very devoted friends; he had stayed with them, had in fact, after finally leaving America, made his headquarters at Delmeny, Lord Rosebery's country place. There Lady Rosebery begged him to write his memoirs, and as he was unwilling to take the trouble she made him dictate them to her. They never got beyond the first few chapters; these I have in a small volume of proof sheets bound together. They make pleasant reading; the account of his boyhood is charming and so is the description of his grandfather, Colonel Ward, who had fought in the Revolutionary War, and at its close retired to his farm on Long Island, where Uncle Sam used to stay with him. The old gentleman was a great stickler for Latin grammar and had introduced his grandson to Virgil and Horace at an early age. The memoirs did not take him beyond his student days; he graduated from Columbia very young, after a fabulously superficial examination by the Dean, in his private study. On one occasion he was taken down to West Point, and there showed such remarkable proficiency in mathematics that he was offered the post of Mathematical Instructor at a salary of a thousand dollars a year when only about sixteen (this sounds a little legendary; there is no way of verifying it; it is what he dictated to Lady Rosebery). Then he started for Europe on the Grand Tour; visited France and Germany; fell in with a romantic German baron, who invited him to his *Schloss*, and there the story ends.

He met the Roseberys in Malta and came back to us early in April. The journey had tired him and he had caught a cold which turned to bronchitis; other symptoms aggravated his condition, which was obviously serious. Sœur Marius nursed him. I could see that she felt little hope of his recovery. He lay in his bed with Omar Khayyám on the counterpane and Horace's *Odes* under his pillow. One night, which we all feared would be the last, he was very weak and could hardly make himself understood; I was with him and he evidently wanted something. I leaned over his pillow to catch the mumbled whispers; he wanted me to read "Come into the garden, Maud," aloud to him. His soul was young to the last.

He did not die that night, but rallied a little, and it was decided he should be taken to a better climate. Marion, Sœur Marius, and I went with him to Pegli — on the Italian Riviera.   He bore the journey well enough, but in a few days there was a turn for the worse and on the nineteenth of May it was all over.   Two hours before his death he dictated a letter to Lord Rosebery, his faithful "Sycophant."   Marion and I were heartbroken — we had lost our best friend.

Uncle Sam was a very high Mason and Marion feared the local Masons might turn out to do him honor.   The Masons in Italy are notoriously radical and anticlerical (Mussolini has seen fit to suppress them — if such a thing be possible).   Marion thought it best to have a very quiet funeral the next day and bury the dear uncle in the little Pegli cemetery.   There he lies on a sheltered hillside, under a marble tombstone ordered for him by Marion and Lord Rosebery, overgrown with ivy and climbing roses — just such a spot as his favorite Omar might have chosen for his final resting place.   (Uncle Sam liked to call himself Omar's successor.)

> Yon rising Moon that looks for us again —
> How oft hereafter will she wax and wane;
>   How oft hereafter rising look for us
> Through this same Garden — and for *one* in vain!
>
> And when like her, oh Sáki, you shall pass
> Among the Guests Star-scattered on the Grass,
>   And on your joyous errand reach the spot
> Where I made One — turn down an empty Glass!

We returned to Rome with heavy hearts.

XIV

A GAY COUSIN

IT was in June (1884) that Marion set out in quest of a wife. Some old friends of my mother's, Mrs. Randolph and Miss Goodrich, turned up in Rome on their way back from a visit to Constantinople. They had enjoyed it thoroughly, particularly the social side of life on the Bosphorus, and brought back enthusiastic accounts of the brilliant beauty and unusual attractiveness of Miss Bessie Berdan. The good ladies came to dinner and sang her praises all the evening. After dinner Marion and I sat up together talking life plans till late into the night. He wanted to get married; his books were bringing him a handsome income; he had vaguely flirted with one or two girls in Rome — none of whom seemed to me in the least suited to him. One of them had extraordinary charm, but I was convinced she would make a poor wife. I was anxious to get him away from her influence.

We had known and liked and seen a good deal of Bessie Berdan during the summer we spent in Newport. "Why don't you marry Bessie?" I asked with sudden inspiration.

"Bessie!" he answered, quite taken aback. "Do you think she would have me?"

Have him? Indeed, why not? He was young and

very handsome, *biondo era e bello e di gentile aspetto,*
already famous as one of the most popular writers of
his day. How could any girl ask for more? The idea
set him on fire.

We had an old green Venetian goblet with white
traceries (we called it the Luck of Edenhall). It was
always brought out on solemn family occasions, filled with
red wine, and passed around for the drinking of especial
health and fortune. Marion went and fetched this out
of its guarded hiding place, filled himself a bumper,
and drained it to the health of his Lady of the East.
Soon after this he left us to go to Constantinople. There
he wooed and won his *princesse lointaine.* His departure
left us very sad — all incentive seemed gone out of life.

Erich von Rabe died about this time. Our funds were
as low as our spirits. We were dressed in black bombazine
for the double mourning. Spring turned to summer with
the prevailing *scirocco* taking all life from the air. Joy
seemed forever banished. One day my mother saw in
the paper that Winthrop Chanler had landed in England.
As I have said before, he was her great-nephew, one of
the Chanler cousins we had known in Newport — Uncle
Sam's grandson. She wrote and asked him to come and
stay with us, mailing the letter before consulting the rest
of the family. When she told us we were amazed at her
enterprise — still more so by the prompt arrival of the
young guest on the twenty-ninth of June. He was twenty
years old and very good-looking; hazel eyes full of a
merry light, irrepressibly curly brown hair, an air of great
good breeding and courage in his handsome face, with a
constant ripple of fun playing over it. The tip of his

very straight nose had a way of contracting when a joke came into his head; it was always a good joke when the nose betrayed it — pointed to the laugh that must rise.

He still seemed a mere boy, as indeed he was, a charming embodiment of youth and high spirits — nothing like him had ever come into our lives before. We wondered why it should please him to stay on into the stuffy Roman summer; but he was amused by everything, and did not seem to mind the dullness of the dead season or the blazing heat.

Mamma and I wondered if he were aware of the fleas. Oh, the Roman fleas of those days! Like Horace's "pale death" they hopped "with equal foot in the Palaces of Kings and the hovels of the poor." All Roman houses harbored them irremediably; they lived in the interstices of the brick floors and in the straw which lay under the carpets. There were methods of fighting the enemy, never of evicting him. Wintie must be immune or else a stoic, we thought, till, after days of silent suffering, he betrayed the situation by scratching his arm, with a haggard look, and asked what might be done. Remedies and palliatives were administered and brought relief.

It grew daily hotter, but Wintie stayed on. He loved Rome and felt all the charm of its summer life.

We took him to Tivoli for a few days; it is always fresher there; the high waterfall dropping into the gorge under the Temple of the Sybil makes a little breeze and fills the air with the cool sound of splashing water. On the ninth of July I wrote in my diary: "Moonlight on the cypresses, nightingales in the laurels, soft summer night wind blowing the spray of waterfalls in our faces; all-

pervading music of fountain, brook, and cascade. Dear
Villa d'Este — crumbling temples, broken goddesses, ivy-
mantled nymphs, mossy old river gods, endless vistas of
fountains, grottoes, and ilex groves, with the broad
campagna beyond!   Two days of being utterly happy in
the moment — young and lazy — the sweet, warm sense
of being alive. . . ."

But youth and romance could not entirely compensate
for the discomforts of staying at the "antique hotel of
the Sybil," and on the fourth day we went back to Rome,
where it grew steadily hotter.   We were all too torpid
to make a move.   It was the young cousin who finally
carried off my mother and me; by sheer force of gay
persuasion he got us on to a train for Rimini, — a sea-
side resort on the Adriatic, — found a *villino* for us overlooking the beach, and helped us pay the rent.   My father
and brother Arthur soon joined us.   There we cooled
off and revived — we swam, we sailed, we made merry,
we were very happy.   I was so seriously romantic that
it never occurred to me that all this light-hearted fun
could turn into anything so important as love and
marriage; my twenty-second birthday was coming on and
I was preparing to bid farewell to youth.   I had long
gloated over Leopardi's beautiful

> . . . *E intanto passa*
> *Il caro tempo giovanil, piu caro*
>   *Che la fame e l'alloro, piu che la pura*
> *Luce del giorno e lo spirar.   Mi fugge*
>   *Senza un diletto*

and liked to think it described my case.

Wintie knew nothing of such sentiments. He was thoroughly pleased with life as it came — and, being full of sunshine, saw only the sunny side of things. He ignored occult forces, astral fluids, and obscure presentiments which so often troubled us. There was an old Scotch jingle he had picked up which seemed to express his relation to life — it ran something like this: —

> I'm a stout braw lad,
> I'll be serf to naebody;
> I've a good braid saird,
> I'll tak dints for naebody;
> I am merry and glad,
> I'll be sad for naebody.

He had other cousins in Europe whom he had promised to visit — he had indeed left America with no other intention, and after a month or more of Rome and Rimini he started for Bonn, where it was agreed he should join them. He spoke neither Italian nor German; the journey was rather complicated, Rimini not being on a main railroad line. The following letter came to tell us of his adventure. It was the first I ever received from him and gives the gay notes of his temper: —

4.45 A.M.

DEAR DAISY: —

As I have a small matter of 4 hours to wait in this blessed spot, I shall attempt to pass some of the time in amusing myself and I hope you, by writing a short sketch of my travels since I left you at 9 P.M. yesterday. To begin with that zealous cabman got me to the station a good 20 minutes before the train was due. He, the cabman, probably drove two or three more parties to the same train after he had left me. However, that's his business, as my old Irish friend on the *Gottardo* used to say. Well, to resume my tail (this is a specimen of my early morning impromptu spelling) — I succeeded in getting into a 1st class carriage without much difficulty. Luckily there was only one other component part, a very fat old man who let me smoke.

I smoked and dozed and dozed and smoked until 12, when we reached Bologna.

At Bologna I had to wait ¾ of an hour for my train. After getting my ticket and having made several attempts to board trains for Venice and other places to which I did not want to go, I finally succeeded in installing myself in a carriage for Verona or Mantua or Ala (whichever it is I want to go to) — with a bottle of wine and only two "companions." I seemed to be in a fair way towards an agreeable night. One of the "companions" was dressed in the most charming costume I have ever contemplated outside of a circus or theatre. It was a loose sort of blouse over a flannel shirt, trousers or rather tights of the same material buttoning tight to the leg from the knee to the ankle. Feet covered with a pair of huge soft yellow leather shoes with elastic sides. A natty traveling bag strapped across the shoulder and a small round skull-cap on the head. "A fellow feeling makes us wondrous kind." I immediately saw through the secret of the tight trousers (or felt through it, I should say). That man was impervious to the attacks of the enemy! There was not a place for them to get in! Oh how I longed to borrow the whole suit! The other "companion" was uninteresting and slept all the time. Unfortunately I followed his example; for at about 4.15 we reached this station, tickets were examined, and I found, by getting the man in armor to translate the wailings and protestations of some fifteen officials into French, that I ought to have left the train at some mythical place called Modena in order to get to Verona or Mantua or Ala or anywhere else except Turin, where I was going at the moment the Guard discovered my mistake or his mistake. At all events, "somebody blundered." The man in armor explained all with a fascinating smile by *"Vous avez dormi."* He also informed me that I would have to wait here until 9 A.M. for a train back to Modena — there I could catch the 1 o'clock for Munich. So here I am. (This elegant sheet of paper was procured after I had filled the first.) I believe the last sentence was "so here I am" — Well, as there is no manner of doubt about it there is no manner of reason why it should not be repeated *ad infinitum.* The name of the classic spot is, I believe, Piacenza. By consulting your map you can probably find out where I am. If you do you will know more than I do at this moment.

It seems to be more or less of a town; probably less, judging by my small experience of Italian towns. However, I have gained an hour on the four by writing this. The prospect of breakfast seems fair. So does the final attainment of the object of this most immemorial journey. My astral calm has been absolutely undisturbed through the whole performance. (I can find no other word sufficiently expressive.)

I am as dirty as a tramp, my once spotless shirt-collar is now a perfect specimen of fallen greatness.

The waiter in the station restaurant is a model of acuteness. He apparently speaks no known language, but comprehends my slightest gesture. For instance, when I ran my finger hurriedly up and down the marble table, and dipped it into a glass — he immediately brought pens, ink and paper. Clever, wasn't he? . . . I shall now leave for an hour, during that time I propose breakfasting, washing, and changing my shirt. Then a short walk about the town to improve my mind. By that time I hope to have consumed most of the remaining time. On second thoughts, however, I shall bring this to a close, as it is seven o'clock.

No! On third thoughts, and on looking again at the clock, I perceive it is only six; so you shall hear more from me after all. Au revoir!

HOTEL ST. MARC. *Time,* 7.25

Americanus sum! As I was starting out from the station to explore, an aged man rushed at me, seized my valise, or rather your valise, and muttering something about his being a *facchino,* started toward town. After following him for about 200 yards I bethought of finding out what he was up to. After sundry and manifold gestures, grimaces and good English oaths on my part, and many *issimos* etc., on his, he mentioned the magic word Hotel St. Marc. Immediately bright visions of breakfast, bath, change of clothes, etc., presented themselves in rapid succession. Bidding the aged man proceed and following him at a proper distance, I marched upon the town of Piacenza. After encircling the walls about twelve times like Joshua and Jericho we reached the palatial hotel. It really is very nice; I can hardly make up my mind to leave the place. Such a bath as I have had! And such a breakfast as I am going to have! And now that I am clean, brushed and polished the dignified waiter looks on me with a great deal more respect. This seems to be a very large and curious place. I see on a map of the town that there is a Palazzo Farnese here. Is that the wonderful one Aunt Loo was speaking of the other day? I must try and find time to see it. However, I don't wish to miss any more trains.

The waiter here is the image of Napoleon III and talks French about as well as I do — so that we get on capitally. Perhaps between us we can make out where I want to go.

This adventure has really turned out very well, considering the way things looked at four A.M. — Thank Heaven I never lost my astral calm! One always feels proud of one's own private little prowesses of that sort, especially if it turns out all right after all. Here's breakfast. Farewell.

8 o'clock. Just an hour before my train goes. Such a breakfast as I have had! Eggs in *tegamino,* a cutlet mysterious but toothsome withal, real white man's bread rolls, delicious yellow butter, capital *café au lait* with sugar in first.

Napoleon III tells me that the 9 o'clock train for Modena connects with my train. It is three hours from here. So you see I have lost about 18 hours in all, maybe more. It's all right, never mind!

Now good-bye — love to Aunt Loo and Toots.   Will
write you from Bonn if I ever get there.

Yours in a happier mood than I was 4 hours ago.

He returned to Rimini as he had promised and spent a
few more weeks with us, then went back to America,
Harvard College, the Porcellian Club, and "the boys."
Our correspondence languished. I did not understand
why, when it had begun so *allegro con brio*. Not till
long after did he explain why he stopped writing to me.
There was living in Cambridge at the time an older
woman, wife of a professor, who was very kind to Wintie
and some of his friends. They called her the "Old
Lady" and went often to her house. When asked for it
she gave them wise advice, not always taken, and had a
good deal of influence on them. A few months after
Wintie's departure from Rimini (we had exchanged half
a dozen gay, cousinly letters) he went to the "Old Lady"
and told her of his dilemma. He was corresponding with
two girls; one of them he had proposed to, but she had
laughed and told him he was too young; they had, however, parted on a semi-sentimental basis. Indeed, it was
for the sake of seeing her in Bonn that he had come to
Europe; the trip to Italy, resulting from my mother's
letter, had deflected him from his course. In the merry
weeks we spent together in Rome and Rimini there was
nothing of flirtation or courtship. But when it came to
correspondence he found himself embarrassed by the
fact that he preferred writing to me and receiving my
letters. He showed the "Old Lady" some of these and
some of the others; she saw that he liked mine best, and

her advice was to stop writing to either of us. He was only twenty-one; there was plenty of time ahead of him. Two years passed before he came back.

Marion Crawford was married to Bessie Berdan while we were at Rimini. He brought her back to Rome that autumn. They hired an apartment in the Palazzo Altemps. Bessie was much liked in the Roman world and was at once in the first flight of the younger married set.

XV

ROMAN FESTIVITIES

THE following winter I went out a great deal more and began to enjoy the way of the world as never before.

It was the great Orsini ball that first gave me a taste for it. Marion Crawford describes this ball in the first volume of *Saracinesca,* antedating it by some twenty years. The fine Orsini Palace (it now belongs to the Duchess Sermoneta, *née* Vittoria Colonna), built over the Savelli fortified castle, which in turn was built on the ruins of the ancient Theatre of Marcellus, had not been opened for years. The family had been absent; the Prince and Princess were leading separate lives, the Princess having the custody of the children. When the oldest daughter, Donna Clarice, was of age to be presented to society, the Prince prepared a sumptuous feast and invited all Rome to the party. The Princess would not relent and the Orsini débutante did not attend her own coming-out ball; but Roman society, Black and White, flocked to the summons. Nothing else had been talked of for weeks; Prince Orsini had done things magnificently and no one was disappointed. The garden courts were illuminated with torches and lanterns. One of these courts is particularly beautiful, planted with orange trees interspersed with many fountains which send up slender rods of crystal waters to break and fall with a tinkling splash into their marble basins. The grand staircase had footmen in the handsome blue and silver Orsini livery standing motionless on every step as the guests passed up. The great suites of apartments, some of which are decorated with charming seventeenth-century frescoes, were thrown open; the halls and reception rooms were lighted by thousands of candles disposed in every variety of chandelier and candelabra; all looked very grand and festive. A parquet floor had been laid in the great ballroom — a welcome innovation and infinite improvement on the old-fashioned linen-crash-covered brick pavement which prevailed in Roman palace ballrooms, while high in the gallery, O crowning bliss! a Viennese orchestra played the irresistible Viennese dance music of that day — the throbbing Strauss and Waldteufel waltzes.

The cotillon was in scale with the rest of the entertainment; it opened with a huge black bear rampant (the Orsini coat of arms) appearing on the floor, bearing on its extended paws a tray full of bouquets of Parma violets which were distributed to the men that they might present them to the ladies of their choice. This was followed by many other figures, the favors all on the heraldic leitmotif of the family escutcheon — scarlet and white scarves, white Pierrot caps with red cockades, little gilt bears on everything.

I do not know why it took all this elaborate setting to give me for the first time a certain heady rapture, compounded of youth, waltz music, flattered vanity, and the pride of life. I was a small frog in a large puddle; but

no one had a better time that night, and it was seven o'clock
in the morning when my mother finally took me home.
My poor mother!   She used to say that the cotillon was
the *Via Dolorosa* of mothers.   Modern society may have
its faults, but let us praise heaven that this cruel custom of
obligating mothers to sit up while their daughters danced
has been abolished or forgotten.

After this I became quite frivolous; I went to all the
parties I was invited to, and enjoyed them.   I look
through the pages of my old diary and find them full of
futilities.   A long procession of names to which memory
supplies no faces; young men who danced to perfection,
or with whom one had drifted into soul-stirring talk, any
one of whom might at any time prove to be "the not impossible he."   A few lifelong friends emerge from the
shadowy procession.

Don Giovanni Borghese, the Prince Charming of our
little world!   We were all flattered when he singled us
out, even though he never danced.   *"Les dames font la
roue quand Giovanni s'approche d'elles,"* as someone said.

He was slight, dark, and brilliant; he always reminded
me of de Musset's line: —

> *On l'avait fait petit, pour le faire avec soin.*

He was the youngest of Prince Borghese's seven sons.
His mother was a La Rochefoucauld and his French blood
showed in his clever talk and polished self-possession.
He was a sportsman too, had hunted big game in Africa,
was a bold rider across country, and wrote one or two
readable books.   He and I always talked French together.

Don Giovanni Borghese

There was Count Curzio Catucci, not good-looking, but *simpaticone*, as we used to say; one of the wittiest men I ever knew, with that savory Roman humor. Italian words can be funnier in themselves than the words of other languages. All the traditional figures of the *Commedia dell' Arte*, Harlequin, Pagliaccio, Brighella, Columbine, and Pantalone, play hide and seek in the vocabulary of a witty Italian.

There was a string of foreign secretaries and attachés — a Russian Prince so fascinating that I was afraid of him; a Turkish secretary who talked worldly wisdom in a clever, flattering way.

Roman entertainments were simple; the great houses were thrown open once a week in the evening; there was a tea table presided over by the daughter of the house, with *granita* (half-frozen water ice), lemonade, tea, and cakes. In carnival time these weekly receptions turned into more or less formal dances. And besides these there were the different Embassy balls, and occasionally an extra entertainment given by some resident foreigner.

Balls were very exciting. One went with a certain delicious trepidation. Would there be partners for every dance? Would the right one engage us for supper? For the cotillon? There was a certain hazard about each one; so many things might go wrong — things that at the time seemed all-important. The flutter of anxiety only added to the rosy joy of having everything go well, as it sometimes did.

The cotillon was the great opportunity, the time and place for confidences, when our young men could talk to us without being overheard.   The music, the calling of the dances, the many-voiced throb of the ballroom, created complete isolation.   Seated in full sight of the world and his wife, your conversation was private and unsupervised. After other dances you were returned to your chaperon, but during the cotillon your chaperon lost her authority over you, and you stayed with your partner.   The chairs were lined up, two and two, in a hollow square around the four walls of the ballroom.   The man was supposed to engage your seats by tying two chairs together with his handkerchief; he attended to this during the supper, while the ballroom was being prepared for the cotillon.   There were two kinds of partners: the simple worldling, who chose his seats in an exposed place where favors would be likely to fall thickest (seventeen was the most I ever got in one figure — I dare say others got more), and those who preferred a more secluded corner where their partner would not be so constantly reft from them; where they could tell her all the pleasant foolish things that form, after all, much of the pattern of life.   The thrill and excitement of the cotillon sprang from the carefully sequestered life of the *jeune fille* of those days; it was a feast enhanced by a preceding fast.   It would be impossible for the boys and girls of to-day, who see each other where and when they please, to find it anything but tiresome.

The American girl, who is brought out with alarums and excursions, and plunges at once into a maelstrom of highest possible social activity, misses many advantages of the more gradual unfolding favored by the old foreign system.   A girl of eighteen should not have the heavy responsibility of testing her powers. Too much is made of the success or failure of her first season. There is little use in expressing opinions on these matters. They are ruled by forces as far beyond our control as Sirius and Aldebaran, and the fashion of the hour overrules all reason. But when the American girl of to-day pities the restricted social life of the foreign girl of the '80s, she fails to realize that it had its compensations.

There were, to be sure, dull stretches, when we felt cut off from all that makes life interesting or exciting, but during these the cistern of the spirit had time to fill, and when good times came they were the more exhilarating, the more brilliant, for the periods of moping *Weltschmerz* that may have preceded them. Imagination was quickened by the variety, the contrasts, of experience.

The Roman season was governed by the liturgical year: It did not begin till after Christmas (no dancing was countenanced in Advent), and it ended with Shrove Tuesday, Mardi gras, when the masks of the Corso carried lighted tapers (*moccoletti*) which were constantly blown out by other masks, and as constantly relighted, only to be again extinguished, a symbol of our ephemeral earthly pleasures.

Then came Ash Wednesday with its *Memento, homo, quia pulvis es,* the reminder of the dust to which we must return; the Lenten sermons, the "Stations" in the various churches. These Stations are appointed to take place in a different church on every day of Lent. On the day of its Station the church is hung with damask and decorated with crystal chandeliers, holding innumerable wax candles, hanging all about the Altar where the

Blessed Sacrament is exposed.   There is a sermon followed by music, and Benediction.

We continued to see our friends, in a lower key, at afternoon teas, small dinners, and the usual weekly *ricevimenti*. As the soft Roman days lengthened to spring, *campagna* picnics were in order, expeditions to Ostia, to Castel Fusano, to mountain towns in the Abruzzi or in the Alban Hills, to Santa Maria in Galera, that strange deserted city in the plains; to Veii, the Etruscan stronghold; to all the legendary places of the Roman *campagna:* the *Bosco Sacro*, where Numa Pompilius visited the nymph Egeria; a grove of immemorial ilex trees on a knoll from which the view stretched over miles of solitary pastures away to the blue hills.   Egeria's spring still pours its tinkling waters into an antique marble basin under the hill.

Another of our favorite picnic grounds was the ruins of *Roma Vecchia*.   Browning's "Love among the Ruins" must surely have been inspired by these, with the remains of its ancient circus, and

> . . . the turret whence the charioteers caught soul
> For the goal. . . .
>
> And such plenty and perfection, see, of grass
> Never was. . . .

It would be hard to measure the ardor with which Rome's lovers enjoyed her.   The successor of St. Peter carries the keys of heaven and hell — the single key to our hearts was held by the City on the Seven Hills.

For the summer of 1886 we went to Vallombrosa.   The lordly Benedictine Abbey had long since been turned into a Bureau of Forestry, the *forestieria* or guest house into a pleasant, rather rustic summer hotel. Milton may have been entertained there by the hospitable monks; if he was, he must already have been blind, or he would never have written his lovely line about the spirits, "Thick as leaves in Vallombrosa," for there is not a deciduous tree in the place. Hardly more than twenty miles from Florence, Vallombrosa lies in a high valley of the Apennines surrounded by miles and miles of magnificent forests of tall firs. It is always cool and there are endless lovely walks and rambles in every direction. The company at the hotel was friendly and pleasant; some Romans whom we knew and some Florentines with whom we soon made friends, all there to spend the summer, formed a congenial circle. There were no tourists; these had not yet begun to devastate mountain solitudes.

The Spanish Ambassador's wife and two daughters were there, the two *Señoritas* adding much to our pleasure with their guitar playing and singing of Spanish songs, and amusing us with their high-pitched sisterly quarrels that sounded like the chattering of angry parakeets and were always followed by pious reconciliations. Both were small and lean, dark and full of inward fire. They suggested grasshoppers crossed with glowworms. I delighted in their songs, which seemed to liberate their ardent spirits from the discipline of ambassadorial constraint. The Wagnières, a Swiss family who lived in Florence, were also there; young Georges Wagnière was something of a poet and had a delightful repertoire of French, Swiss, and Italian songs that he too accompanied on the guitar, with considerable skill, but, of course, nothing like the

warmth and vigorous rhythm of the Spanish girls' playing. He read and recited French poetry very well and
introduced me to the works of Sully-Prudhomme, Leconte
de Lisle, and other "moderns" of those days. He was a
charming youth, gay and witty, besides being very cultivated and just a little romantic. He was a great addition
to the paper-and-pencil games that were much in vogue
with us. He could always turn out amusing unexpected
lines that fitted and enhanced the occasion. He later
went into the Diplomatic Service and I saw him again after
many years. He was by that time Swiss Minister
Plenipotentiary to the Italian Court, and I a grandmother. We had a pleasant meeting.

Then there was the Marchesa Origo, a Russian married
to an Italian who was Master of the Horse to King
Umberto, and their two daughters, for whom the
Marchesa was anxious to find husbands. She was a very
outspoken old lady and asked Mamma how she had managed to get two daughters married, adding that Olimpia,
the younger of hers, was a *bocconcino da principe*, a little
morsel for a prince. Olimpia was nearly six feet tall,
handsome and rather phlegmatic. She did not find her
prince, but married an American named Pearson (with
whom she was very happy), and they had a handsome
villa at Vallombrosa, the only one in those days; I hear
it has since been turned into a hotel.

Wintie Chanler joined us in July and was at once voted
a welcome addition to the little group that represented
so many different types and nations. Everyone liked
him; that seemed to be his natural prerogative, he was
so gay, *tanto simpatico;* the old Marchesa adored him.

I found him as delightful as ever and it did not take us long to discover what the stars had known from the first. We became engaged early in September.

We had a few happy weeks together; then he went back to America to break the news to his brothers and sisters, and we to Rome to make wedding preparations against his return.

XVI

VITA NUOVA ON HUDSON

Wintie arrived in Rome at the end of November. His family had taken the news kindly, all but the fact that I was a Catholic. To warn and protect him from the dangers of conversion he had been provided with a quantity of anti-Catholic books and pamphlets — *Plain Reasons against Joining the Church of Rome* was the title of one; the others I forget. Wintie showed them to me to see what I thought of them; he had not read them. It was crude stuff, full of absurdities written by the misguided for the unintelligent; the usual misrepresentation of fact to which fanaticism was ever prone. It seemed incredible that anybody should believe such things, but obvious that if they did believe them there could be no blame attached to their not becoming Catholics. The Church wisely holds that men may be saved by their blameless lives and their invincible ignorance. Wintie was very light-hearted about the matter. I am afraid he would have been just as light-hearted had I been a Buddhist or a Mahometan.

We wanted to be married before Christmas. To do this we had to obtain three dispensations: the first because marriages are prohibited in Advent; the second because we

were cousins; the third, and most difficult of all, because
Wintie was not a Catholic, and stoutly refused to make
the required promises. Monseigneur Puyol managed
to obtain all three of them for us, though at times the
obstacles seemed almost insurmountable and I grew profoundly discouraged. He would put heart into me saying, "Remember, my child, we are in Rome, *où beaucoup
de choses s'arrangent*" (where many things arrange themselves).

He took us to see the Cardinal Vicar, who gave us his
blessing, and consented, no one could imagine why, to
letting me alone sign the papers, promising that any children we might have should be brought up as Catholics.
He was evidently much taken by Wintie's good looks
and air of spirited candor, for he kept reiterating in a
barbarous Italo-French jargon, "*Je sais que vous êtes ung
bonn Yak et que vous ferez votre devoir.*" By "Yak" we
discovered he meant "Yankee"; it is impossible to transcribe the heavy Roman pronunciation of the French words,
rendering them all but unintelligible. Yet he was kind
and gave us what we wanted. Monseigneur Puyol was
radiant as we came down the broad marble stairs. He
had hardly hoped for such complete success. He opened
his two hands, raising them shoulder high, "*C'est que votre
fiancé a séduit le Cardinal Vicaire!*"

Then he took us with my father and mother to the
office of the Apostolic Notary; a strange place and a
strange figure of a man. The walls were lined with
thousands of vellum-bound volumes in which were reg-
istered all the marriages that had ever taken place in
Rome — centuries and centuries of records. The old

priest looked like an ascetic Don Basilio, with a very pale face and a very long nose. When we told him of our errand and showed him the signed approval of the Cardinal Vicar he shook his head and adjusted his big spectacles. He asked no end of questions. My father's name was Luther — that made him wince; and he counted off on his long bony fingers all the good reasons why we should not get married: a mixed marriage; between cousins; in the forbidden season of Advent. But the Cardinal Vicar's orders were explicit and not to be gainsaid.

There may be sound reasons for prohibiting or discouraging the marriage of cousins, but they often turn out happily. There is a similarity of fibre, a coincidence of wave lengths, which make for good understanding.

We were married on the sixteenth of December, very quietly, in Monseigneur Puyol's private chapel at San Luigi dei Francesi, and went to Algiers for our honeymoon. We hired a little villa at Mustapha Supérieur and I kept house for the first time, with a very bad cook and Cecilia, my faithful maid, who was always ready to meet any emergency.

Algiers was disappointing; the tawdry Moorish veneer on the modern French town was unattractive. The interesting excursions into the interior, which are now so easy to make, were not thought of in those days.

I have but one memory of the place that seems worth recording. We went to a great ball at the Governor's house and there saw, lean and tall, with haughty aquiline features and an air of silent superiority, a magnificent Arab Sheik, dressed in plain white woolen robes with a rope turban over the veil which hung from his head. He was, we were told, a direct descendant of Mahomet, the head of all the Mahometans of Africa. Silent and wholly aloof, none of the rather second-rate civil and military crowd there present held the smallest interest for him, the descendant of the Prophet. I never saw such high pride expressed in any man's face and bearing.

We spent two or three months in our little villa; I had for several winters been subject to bronchitis and the mild climate of Algiers proved very beneficial. But we were both glad when spring came and the time to start for America, which was to be my new home.

It was June when we reached Rokeby, the old family place on the Hudson. A winding avenue leads through a park laid out by an English landscape architect of the 1830's to the roomy old-fashioned house surrounded by broad lawns with fine trees; the land sloping away on the west to the splendid view of the Catskill Mountains across the river.

The house was built in the beginning of the nineteenth century by General Armstrong, at the time of his marriage to Margaret Livingston; the land was part of the original Livingston grant. When their daughter Margaret married William B. Astor, the house was redecorated and a large octagonal tower added to it. The Gothic library was on the ground floor of this. The Astors painted the woodwork throughout the house in imitation golden oak according to the fashion of their times, with perhaps a touch of thrifty German taste for *Ersatz*.

The library was filled with excellent books. Baron de Bunsen had been William B. Astor's tutor and had taken him on the Grand Tour before his marriage. Bunsen had been a friend of Alexander von Humboldt and had doubtless sat on the knees, if not at the feet, of the great encyclopædists.   The shelves were well stocked with their works in fine Princeps editions, as well as with a good collection of French and English classics in dusky brown-gold calf bindings.

There was a large unused drawing-room with chairs ranged along the walls as for a funeral; it had for many years been used for nothing else, though it had three French windows opening on to the lawn and was in itself a charming room.   There was a dreadful little "home parlor" where the family would gather around a very bad square piano.   The large dining room was hung with family pictures by mediocre artists.

When William B. Astor died he left Rokeby and a daughter's portion to his granddaughter, Margaret Ward Chanler.   She had grown up there and loved the place, but was not long to enjoy the possession of it, for she died shortly after inheriting it, having contracted pneumonia at her grandfather's funeral.   She left ten children, of whom the oldest was barely twelve.   The marriage had been a very happy one, and the life of her husband, poor Winthrop Chanler, seems to have been shattered by her death.   He established the family at Rokeby under the care of his cousin, Miss Mary Marshall, from Charleston, South Carolina, and himself died two years later.   This cousin, Mary, devoted her life to bringing the children up in the fear of the Lord.   She was morally well qualified for this task, being deeply religious and heroically conscientious, but quite devoid of social grace or mental elasticity. There was a tutor, also appointed by their father; he, too, had been chosen for his moral rather than his intellectual qualities. He knew his Latin grammar and elementary mathematics, but little else. There was also a dim English governess in a black wig, who knew little more than Cousin Mary and less than Mr. Bostwick; she conducted the girls' studies, but no one paid much attention to her.

Before his death their father also appointed a group of guardians. These had been selected rather for their impeccable respectability and their social and financial prominence than for their knowledge of children; most of them had no families of their own. Uncle John Astor had one son, later Lord Astor; Rutherfurd Stuyvesant was then a childless widower; "Aunt Teeny" Griffin, a widow equally childless. There were three or four others, whose names escape me. They sat like gods together at their monthly meetings, deciding and decreeing what should happen to the Chanler children and how their fortune should be administered. Their father was haunted by the fear that at his death the children's grandfather, the brilliant but not wholly reliable Uncle Sam, should, as their natural guardian, take a nefarious hand in the conduct of their affairs. He had run through three fortunes in the varied course of his career, and one cannot blame Winthrop Chanler too much for building a Chinese Wall of unimpeachable probity about his children's inheritance.

They were brought up in this curious seclusion, amply provided with all the necessities, but with nothing to stimulate taste or intellect. Cousin Mary did her duty with all her might and inculcated her own very high, though somewhat narrow and rigid, principles to the best of her ability.

The older boys went to school and when at home had their ponies to ride, and so escaped the oppressive gloom of this orphaned family life. The younger boys were kept at home. Marion, the third oldest, had died of pneumonia contracted at St. Paul's School, and the guardians had decided that none of the younger ones should run a like risk. But the girls were satisfied with their lot. They clustered contentedly around Cousin Mary, dressed in the dreariest of homemade clothes. There was a great deal of praying and hymn singing in the home parlor.

Sundays were observed with Puritanical rigor; lawn tennis and croquet were barred. The boys used to take their dogs on to the servants' porch at the back of the house and fight them all Sunday afternoon. Discordant howls and yappings marred the peace of the Sabbath, but dog fighting was not forbidden.

At the time of our arrival they had all been living at Rokeby for a dozen years. Alida, the youngest, was now about thirteen. They were good-looking, high-spirited girls and boys, some of them gifted with artistic talent, all of them courageous and generous to a fault. There have been quarrels and dissension in the family, but never about the usual subjects of family quarrels — property and its distribution; always about theology, morals, questions of passionate opinion. It took me some time to get used to the sudden vehemence of the family temper; the brothers quarreled like angry dogs and were the next

moment the best of friends.   On one occasion the dispute
at the dinner table grew so hot and so personal, so many
disagreeable things had been said, barked, shouted, by one
brother to the other, that I felt sure the breach would be
permanent and that we had better leave the house by the
first morning train.   I went upstairs as soon as the ladies
left the dining room and told my good Cecilia to start
packing at once.   One could hear the raging brothers all
over the big house.   When Wintie came upstairs for
the night he was surprised and amused at my preparations
for an immediate departure.   Dear me no, what an idea!
Their angry talk meant nothing, it was a form of sport,
they loved one another dearly.   And the next day relations were perfectly friendly.

Elizabeth, the oldest sister, alone remained always
apart from, and above, these differences.   Bad health
and the pious resignation inculcated by Cousin Mary,
combined with a great sense of responsibility towards the
younger brothers and sisters, had developed in her a
character as perfect as her face.   She was very beautiful.
When John Sargent painted her portrait some years later,
he told a friend that she had the face of the Sistine Ma-
donna and the eyes of the Child.   She was, and continues
to be, the centre of all family affection.   She combines
to an extraordinary degree intelligence and great goodness, wit and sensibility; all these suffused with the
radiance and fire of a great spirit.

That their older brother, the first to marry, should
have brought home a Catholic wife was felt by the Chanler
children to be a calamity of the first order.   Cousin Mary
did not try to minimize it, but feeling sure that they could

only speak ill of me, she had, before I arrived, issued orders that I should never be mentioned. I found this out from the boys, who were less scrupulous in their loyalty. It was disconcerting to come into a roomful of people to whom I was a sort of voodoo, to know they were watching and criticizing me in enforced silence.

They led what seemed to me a desperately meagre life with a great sense of their own importance. This had been accentuated by the forecasts of a phrenologist by whom Miss Marshall set great store. All these children were taken to him in turn, and future eminence was promised each one from the shape and conformation of his head. One was to be a Bishop; another a leading statesman, and so on. Robert, the youngest son, was perhaps the one who suffered most from this very empirical régime. His gift was for painting, and Art was not among the phrenologist's categories. One day he had been left alone in the schoolroom to write lines to make up for some ill-accomplished task. When the tutor came to release him he found a well-drawn horse on the blackboard. Robert, on being asked who had done it, acknowledged the authorship, which in Mr. Bostwick's eyes proved him a liar. Miss Marshall and the family were called to see it. How could Robert have done it? A counsel of war was held and Robert was condemned to a three days' ostracism. No one was to speak to him till he confessed his sin. Winthrop, the older brother, then a student at Harvard, happened to arrive, and suggested, what seemed simple enough, that Robert should be asked to draw another horse; which he did; and the judges in Israel were for once confounded.

But it never occurred to anyone that this child should be encouraged in his gift. He was poor at his lessons; Latin and mathematics were not for him.

A few weeks after our arrival at Rokeby the family moved to Lake George for the midsummer months, leaving Wintie and me in possession of the roomy house. But the boys preferred being at Rokeby and, as I remember it, were with us most of the time. I had a good piano which I put into the big drawing-room, pulling the furniture about and making it look habitable with flowers and books. I was fresh from Sgambati's hands and my Santa Cecilia examinations, and played a great deal of Bach. The *Well-Tempered Clavichord* had always been a sort of daily bread. Robert used to listen to it by the hour. He often told me that Bach's fugues had been the first revelation of beauty in his life; that their changeful repetitions, their interweaving motives, ordered to intricate unity, had fixed a pattern in his mind that served him well in the composition of the screens and panels which made him famous — one of them hangs in the Metropolitan Museum in New York and another in the Luxembourg in Paris. And I like to think that I was the humble transmitter of the great Master's lesson, a scrap of the multiplied loaves and fishes that served to fill at least one of the many who are hungry for miraculous food.

When the family returned from Lake George, they were shocked beyond measure by the liberties I had taken with the drawing-room. One of the sisters refused to set foot in it; if we sat there after dinner she retired to the religious gloom of the home parlor to mark her

disapproval.   One or other of the children would join
her and sit with her for a while, as with one bereft.

My first baby, Laura, was born at Rokeby on September
30, and baptized by the village priest.   This same sister-
in-law suffered even more acutely from this than from
the desecration of the funereal drawing-room.   I heard
she told one of her brothers that the kindest thing one
could do to the infant would be to kill it in its innocence.
If the rosy child, bright-eyed and, to me at least, adorable,
was brought into the room, her pious aunt would solemnly
leave the family circle, so as not to lend the approval of
her presence to the disgrace.   One afternoon we were
having tea by the tennis court, watching a game.   Cecilia
wheeled up the baby carriage in which Laura sat, all fair
and fluffy.   M. rose and fled, as at the approach of a
leper.   She once sent me word, through one of her sisters, that she loved the child better than anything on
earth, had even gone into the nursery one night to kiss
it in its sleep, but that she could not acknowledge it in the
presence of others.

XVII

LODGE AND ROOSEVELT

WE were advised by friends that, with my foreign bringing up and my tendency to catch bad colds in winter, I
should find Washington easier and pleasanter to live in
than New York. Accordingly we hired and furnished
a little house on Dupont Circle and settled ourselves
there in the late autumn of that year.

Washington was at that time far from being the handsome, prosperous-looking city it has since become. The
great avenues were more than half empty and disfigured
by the fact that the good houses were neighbored by
unsightly hovels standing in waste spaces, inhabited by
the dregs of the negro population. I was told that this
was land to which there was no clear title, so that the
squatters who lived there in such slovenly fashion could
not be evicted.

Major L'Enfant must have had great confidence in
the future of the new republic when he laid out his fine
plans for its capital, with the vast system of diagonal avenues intersecting the rectangular streets, forming, where
several of them meet, centres and circles of radiation, to
be embellished by monuments and parks. He has been
proved a wise prophet, but in 1887 the city looked as

though he had seen too big.   The next forty years did much to make his intelligent French dream come true, and the gaping spaces have been built up into architectural vistas.

Our house was sunny and comfortable and we soon found ourselves surrounded by friendly acquaintances, many of them old friends of Wintie's parents who had lived in Washington when J. Winthrop Chanler was Member of Congress from New York.   One of Wintie's earliest recollections was of being taken as a very small boy with his brother Archie to a children's party at the White House.   The rooms were crowded with grown-ups and the ladies all wore immense crinolines; the two children got completely lost, hidden as they were among the great ballooning skirts.   They could not identify their mother's gown nor were they tall enough to catch sight of any familiar face.   Some friend of their parents finally sighted them, hand in hand, with scared faces, wandering in the vast forest of furbelows, and took them back to their anxious parents.

That winter in Washington laid the foundation of many lasting friendships.   Henry Cabot Lodge was there for the first time as Congressman from Massachusetts.   It did not take many meetings with him and the beautiful Nannie, his wife, to ripen acquaintance into a friendship sealed for life.

Forget any praises I may have bestowed on others. She was the most charming woman I have ever known; an exquisite presence in this workaday world.   She had unusual beauty, a pale face with regular features, and dark eyes the color of the sky when stars begin to twinkle.

MRS. HENRY CABOT LODGE

She had great wit; it was the only weapon she ever used in self-defense, and Cabot was a little afraid of its winged shafts. Daughter and sister to Admirals, she had perhaps caught from them a certain sense of discipline, some secret code of high behavior that guided her action but was never imposed on others. Gay and hospitable, she took delight in all that was delightful, yet never lost her bearings in fogs of enthusiasm. She combined the usually contrasting qualities of keen intelligence and warmheartedness. I never found another human instrument so delicately tuned to understand and sympathize. She was one of the shining ones.

Cabot Lodge was made of ruder stuff. He was a militant politician and his nature bore some of the battle scars of his encounters with the enemy. Many of his Boston friends had turned against him when, in the campaign of 1884, he had taken the stump for Blaine after having done his best to defeat him at the Republican convention; a question of loyalty to his party. The harsh criticism and disavowal of Boston's Back Bay element may have done something to accentuate a certain ready-to-fight element in Cabot's character. In discussion he was one of those who care more for downing his adversary than for discovering common ground for possible agreement.

His was the complete irreligiosity of his generation. As it was said of someone else, "born in Boston and educated at Harvard, what should he know of religion?" He never missed an opportunity to snarl and gibe at it. The Catholic Church was his favorite "straw man" and he demolished it to his own satisfaction several times a

week, leaving *Mater Ecclesia* quite unscathed.   I am not
painting an agreeable picture of Cabot Lodge, yet under
the captious crustiness there was a very real man whom one
could not but like, respect, and grow to love.   He was a
true scholar and a true friend; I do not know two
qualities that please me more, and he was, besides, an
accomplished horseman.

His fine library was an essential part of him and he
was at his best when, at the end of an evening, — there
might have been a dinner party at his house and all but
two or three of the guests departed, — he would take
down one volume and then another, reading some rare
lines of prose or verse with an intimate sense of their
meaning and beauty.   He then thawed into a most
sympathetic and "belovable" person, representing no
longer the harshness of Plymouth Rock, but the pleasant
laureled dingles of Parnassus.   He knew and loved books
with most intelligent affection.

Theodore Roosevelt had, in his domestic misfortune,
been politically more fortunate.   His young wife, Alice
Lee, died shortly before the Blaine-Cleveland campaign,
and the sincerely stricken widower escaped the dilemma
by going West and playing cowboy on his ranch for those
difficult "mugwump" years.   He sought and found consolation in the primitive life, had splendid adventures
with cowboys and sheriffs, shootings, hangings, raidings;
enjoyed it all hugely, wrote the *Winning of the West,*
and brought back a collection of wonderful stories with
which he regaled his friends.   After his return to civilization he married Miss Edith Carow, who, it was said, had

waited for him since schooldays, having never swerved from her first girlish attachment.

Theodore Roosevelt was Civil Service Commissioner when we first lived in Washington. He and Mrs. Roosevelt lived in a tiny house on Jefferson Place. Theodore, Junior, was just the age of my Laura; Alice, later Mrs. Longworth, daughter by the first marriage, a little girl in pigtails. The Roosevelts used to give Sunday-evening suppers where the food was of the plainest and the company of the best. Theodore would keep us all spellbound with tales of his adventures in the West. There was a vital radiance about the man — a glowing, unfeigned cordiality towards those he liked that was irresistible. When he eventually became a world-famous figure and a popular idol, he kept intact this great gift of friendship; but he lost, which was natural enough, some of the light-heartedness of the old days when we were all young.

One of his charms lay in a certain boyish zest with which he welcomed everything that happened to him. I never knew anyone more pleased with things as they were — life was the unpacking of an endless Christmas stocking; honors and high office were elaborate toys one must learn to understand; a cantankerous opposing Senate was a jack-in-the-box that popped out and made faces at him. He sometimes had trouble in shutting down the box on the ugly face; then he took pleasure in calling it names. He loved the caricatures of himself. When he was Police Commissioner in New York (we were living in New York at the time) he came to dine one

evening in great glee.   He had gone to his office that
morning and found the personnel at Police Headquarters
gathered around a letter delivered by the postman; clerks
and stenographers were tittering nervously, and hesi-
tated to show it.   "And here it is," he said, pulling it out
of his pocket.   It bore no other address than a pair of
glasses over a double row of clenched teeth.   He was
enchanted.   "Few men," he said, "live to see their own
hieroglyph."   The Spanish War, the Battle of San
Juan Hill, were glorious boyish experiences.   He assured
us that, considering the number of men engaged, the
battle had been one of the bloodiest on record.   As for
being President, it was the greatest fun in the world, and
we, his friends, all shared in the fun.

I leave to others the task of describing and doing justice to his more serious sides: his great political acumen,
his qualities as a leader of men, his unusual knowledge
of and keen interest in a great variety of subjects.   This
latter made his house a centre where the most distinguished and interesting men of his time were glad to
gather.   Explorers (he had an undeniable weakness for
these), scientists, historians, men of letters, all came to
give of their best.   It had indeed always been so; when
he lived in Jefferson Place, or in New York with his sister, Miss Anna Roosevelt, later Mrs. Cowles, during the
Police Commissioner years.   The White House had
merely given him more facilities for entertaining them.
The Muses attracted him less; his sense of the Arts was
primitive.   My husband gave him a picture, a geyser by
Twachtman.   It had real merit, and Twachtman was an
excellent landscape painter.   I have the letter in which

With best wishes
from
Theodore Roosevelt
May 25th 1902

THEODORE ROOSEVELT

Roosevelt thanked him for it with great warmth, saying he was delighted to have a Western picture painted by an American!

I was once staying with the Lodges, during Roosevelt's Presidency. Cabot came home for dinner tired and irritated; he was Senator then and had been wrangling with his fellow legislators all day. After trying various subjects of conversation I mentioned a book I had lately come across, *The Lives of the Dukes of Urbino.* Cabot flew out at me: "A pack of unmitigated ruffians and blackguards!" (Which of course they were.) "I would rather read the lives of the Selectmen of Nahant." After dinner we went to the White House to hear some music, which was followed by a little supper. The President had put me next to him during the music and I had amused him with Cabot's sally about the Dukes of Urbino. When the music had stopped and supper was announced, the President called out in ringing tones, "Now the Selectman of Nahant will lead the Duchess of Urbino in to supper." Cabot gave me his arm rather sheepishly and growled through a reproachful smile, "You went and complained to him!"

The White House entertainments, especially the informal luncheons, were always delightful. Some members of the "lawn tennis cabinet," Mr. Stimson, Mr. Elihu Root, General Wood, or others, were generally present. At one time the President was interested in jiujitsu. He would allow himself to be tossed about by the skilled Japanese instructor, and would insist that his friends also have a taste of the sport. At another time, it was quarterstaff practice that interested him. I re-

member one luncheon party at the White House when
he and Mr. Root had whacked at each other so hard
that both had painfully bruised and swollen wrists.
Skis had just been introduced from Norway, and after
an adequate snowfall, the President, Cabot Lodge, and
my husband went to experiment with them in Rock
Creek Park. Cabot Lodge felt that his life was too
valuable to his country and decided, after the first two
or three falls, to leave skiing to others; but Theodore
and Wintie plunged and tumbled bravely and ignorantly
and came home rather battered, but pleased with themselves for having broken no bones.

It is easy to talk about Theodore Roosevelt, delightful
for us who knew and loved him to recall his life-en-
hancing presence, but much will yet be said and written
about him before he takes his definite place in history.
Clio is biting her pencil while she looks for the final word.

There were years when his figure on the world stage
seemed legendary, larger than life. The enthusiasm
for him was unbounded; he seemed to embody an ideal
of manly vigor, good faith, and good sportsmanship. He
was genial and communicative; his life was an open book;
its pages were printed in every newspaper, and every
detail eagerly read by a delighted public. Everyone
wanted to know all about his children, his sporting trips,
his rides and games and entertainments.

We were in Rome for the winter of 1908–1909. As
soon as Taft had been made President, Roosevelt left on
his great tour. He landed in Naples and telegraphed us
to join him for the two days he was to spend there before
sailing for Africa. We were delighted to go and greatly

enjoyed the occasion. There was a hubbub of delegations and all-important visitors, the whole place seemed full of the bustle and excitement of Roosevelt's presence. At the two big lunch parties in the hotel he made me sit beside him, which seemed rather careless of precedent, as there were wives of Italian generals and high officials present, but it gave me a delightful chance to talk to him and I suppose he trusted to their ignorance of the fact that I had no official rank whatever. During one of these meals I remember saying to him, à *propos* of his successor, that it was dull for us to have an uninteresting functionary take his place in the White House. "Oh," said Roosevelt, "he is ever so much better than that. Taft is a very good man, an excellent man, but of course it amuses people more to watch a crusader than a jurist."

When he came back to America the following late summer, after shooting lions, visiting crowned heads, and attending King Edward's funeral, we happened to be visiting the Cabot Lodges at Nahant. A telegram signed "T. R." announced that he would come out to spend the day at East Point, their country place. He was attending some political convention in Boston that night. He came unaccompanied, and no other guests were invited. He was bursting with the things he wanted to tell us. He always liked to talk from a rocking chair; so one was brought out on the piazza, and the Lodge family, including the three children, who were by this time grown up and married, and Wintie and I, sat around him while he rocked vigorously and told one story after another, holding us enchanted, making us laugh till we cried and ached. He had arrived long before luncheon and he

stayed till late in the afternoon.   Some of his best stories
were about King Edward's funeral, or "wake" as he
irreverently called it, the latest of his experiences.   How
he was put in a royal carriage with a foreign minister
who resented not having been given a gala coach with
hammercloth and footmen standing behind, and pointed
out that they had not even been treated to the handsomest
liveries.   Roosevelt had answered him in rather broken
French that he was so glad to be there at all that he would
not have minded had the liveries been bright green with
yellow spots.   One should beware of trying to make
jokes in a foreign language.   The unknown diplomat had
reported that Mr. Roosevelt had concurred with him in
his complaint about the liveries, but on the ground that
they should have been bright green with yellow spots,
presumably the ex-President's own colors!

He had much to tell of Emperor William's friend-
liness, which did not seem to have beguiled him over-
much, though he had enjoyed his visit to Kiel and all
the hospitality shown him in the imperial palace.   He
saw him again at the funeral party, where Roosevelt had
met for the first time and taken a great fancy to the handsome Czar of the Bulgars, whom he found intelligent and
attractive.   They were holding an animated conversation when the German war lord shouldered his way
through the crowd of royalties there present, took hold
of his arm and said imperiously, "Come with me, Roosevelt, I will present you to somebody worth your knowing, my cousin, the King of Spain," scowling the while
at the Bulgarian monarch.

He also told us about the special train that took the

funeral party to Windsor, where King Edward was to be laid beside his royal ancestors; of how one king, whose private car happened to be next to the dining car, was cross with the other kings and would not let any of them go through when luncheon was announced, so they all had to wait and grumble until the train could be stopped at a station. When this was finally done, kings and potentates scrambled out on to the platform, hurried past the car that was closed to them, and reached their food only to find it getting cold, and with hardly time to eat it before the train was due at Windsor.

These and many more he told us with infinite zest and humor, in the long monologue. I do not think the rest of us spoke a hundred words, but no one had a moment's sense of boredom, all were amused and excited. It was a manifestation of that mysterious thing, nth-powered vitality, communicating itself to the listeners.

His popularity waned from the time he opposed the renomination of Taft for President in 1912. I believe he had good reason to feel that he had been jockeyed by the convention and that he was the rightful candidate. By heading a second Republican (Bull Moose) ticket with the cry "My hat is still in the ring," he split his party and gave the Democrats a plurality that elected Woodrow Wilson. I felt at the time and still feel it had been better for him had he considered the words of Teufelsdröckh in *Sartor Resartus:* "Hast thou any contention with thy brother, I advise thee, think well what the meaning thereof is. If thou gauge it to the bottom, it is simply this: 'Fellow see! thou art taking more than thy share of happiness in the world, something from my share; which, by the Heavens thou shalt not; nay I will fight thee rather.' . . . Alas and the whole lot to be divided is such a beggarly matter, truly a feast of shells, for the substance has been spilled out: not enough to quench one Appetite; and the collective human species clutching at them! . . . Can we not, in all such cases say: 'Take it, thou too-ravenous individual; take that additional fraction of a share, which I reckoned mine, but which thou so wantest; take it with a blessing; would to Heaven I had enough for thee.' "

There were many who fancied that, if he had let the nomination go and not split his party, Roosevelt might have been elected by acclamation, so great was the majority that wanted him for President. These are the inscrutable might-have-beens of history. His last years were darkened by this defeat; embittered by inaction and hatred of the new face at the door.

I saw him in the hospital shortly before the end came; he did not think it was near. As I was about to say good-bye he held my hand and said very seriously, but with none of his old gay fire, "I seem pretty low now, but I shall get better. I cannot go without having done something to that old gray skunk in the White House."

With the passing of years the perspective has shifted: Woodrow Wilson was trying to many of us; his defects were antipodal to Roosevelt's virtues; we were impatient of his hesitations, his academic serenity while the civilized world was crashing about our ears, his unwillingness to hear the truth about what was happening abroad. We had no use for his well-rounded sentences, his Messianic visit to Europe; but perhaps there was in him an element of noble survival. If the League of Nations ever becomes a practical reality, and countries learn to adjust their differences without bloodshed, Woodrow Wilson's name will be connected with the opening of the millennium. Could one but look into the seeds of time!

While Theodore Roosevelt's personality invites description and indiscretion, Mrs. Roosevelt's eludes the one and defies the other. She is more difficult of access; praise does not reach or define her. Just as the camera is focused, she steps aside to avoid the click of the shutter.

She always seemed deeply detached from the external accidents of life. No "first lady of the land" ever lived in the White House with less trepidation, with more simple dignity and inner indifference. She cared as little for its grandeur as she minded the exiguity of the house in Jefferson Place. Her family life was the all-important *continuum*. Apart from that she looked on the changing aspects of existence with a detached, intelligent curiosity; her warmth and passion lay far beneath the surface. One felt in her a great strength of character, and ineluctable will power. We used to think that Theodore, whom she adored, was a little afraid of his "Edie." A very long way after her husband and children came a small group of chosen friends to whom she was staunchly loyal. She has always been a great reader and has a fine critical sense of letters. Her taste in books and judgment of their merit *qua* literature were always far more reliable than were Theodore's. He read books for information and amusement, but would occasionally take fire at odd little sentimental booklets and press them into one's hands as containing some spirit-stirring new thoughts. The stirring had come from his own abounding enthusiasm. Edith's compass was safer to steer by.

XVIII

WASHINGTON FRIENDS

ONE afternoon I was having tea in my little house on Dupont Circle when a stranger walked in — a young man with interesting gray eyes and rather untidy clothes. He came up to me and said in a low, Eton-pitched voice, "I am Spwing-Wice of the Bwitish Legation" (he never could pronounce his *r*'s, but I shall not further disfigure his speech by phonetic spelling). "Beauclerc [the First Secretary] has received a cable telling him his wife is dying and, as he sails for England to-morrow, he sent me to ask you to return the Nell Gwyn miniature he lent you."

Mr. Beauclerc was descended from the famous beauty, and later became Duke of St. Albans, the title granted to Nell Gwyn's oldest son by Charles II. He had lent us the miniature to compare with a Lely portrait of the same lady that my husband had inherited with a number of other old English pictures. They did not look in the least alike, although the miniature had been in the family since it was painted, supposedly from life, while our Nell Gwyn is very like the portrait of her that hangs in Hampton Court. This was our first meeting with the beloved

"Springy," Cecil Spring-Rice, another friend forever, and I have always had a kindly feeling for the "orange-girl" duchess, since she brought it about.

Had Nell Gwyn not introduced him we would surely have come to know him in some other way, for he became a great favorite with all the people we liked best; and with them, as with us, the acquaintance soon ripened to charming intimacy. With some of us he grew to be the *enfant de la maison,* free to drop in for a meal, to come and stay with us in the country, to ride our horses and amuse our children. For this he had an especial gift. My oldest daughter was one of his pets and she still remembers the wonderful Japanese fairy tales that were carried on from one telling to the next and listened to with rapt interest.

Spring-Rice was a scholar and most pleasantly bookish. He made himself write a sonnet on every book that had interested him, summing up its contents in the narrow limit of fourteen lines. He never showed us these sonnets; they were merely an exercise of synthesis to assist his memory.

I asked him once what I should read, having a quiet summer in the country before me. "Read books of which you know the names," was his answer; an excellent piece of advice that I have followed for many years. His letters were always delightful; I remember one in which he told of visiting some place in Scotland where Wordsworth wrote a poem about dancing with nymphs or dryads. Spring-Rice's comment was, "I saw a few goats."

He was in Washington for many years, with interruptions of other posts, in Athens, in Teheran, in Egypt, and finally in Berlin, where he married the Ambassador's daughter, Miss Florence Lascelles.

It was said that he asked her to marry him in characteristic "Springy" fashion. He had called on her to say good-bye (he was about to leave Berlin), and after talking for an hour of this and that he shook hands and was about to go, when, with his hand on the door knob, he turned round and said, "By the way, Miss Lascelles, will you marry me?" And she answered, "Why, yes." The wedding took place soon afterwards and the marriage was of the happiest.

When Theodore Roosevelt became President he invited Cecil Spring-Rice to visit him, and later asked that he might be sent as Ambassador. There were delays in granting this request and postponements of its execution. Mr. Bryce was settling some Panama complication and stayed on for months after his successor had been appointed. When Spring-Rice finally arrived, in March 1913, Woodrow Wilson was President, a Pharaoh who knew not Joseph. All his friends were overjoyed to welcome him back and to meet his wife, of whom we all grew very fond. She fitted admirably into the circle of his old intimacies. "Do you know my wife?" he would say. "She is very plain." She was plain only in the sense of being unembellished, inconspicuous-looking. I never knew a woman less interested in herself or her personal appearance. The ladies of Washington had organized some kind of benevolent society for helping impoverished gentlewomen, stranded governesses and the like. They once held a meeting at the British Embassy at which one of the ladies, seeing a young woman dressed in very plain

Cecil Spring-Rice

clothes sitting by herself unnoticed, went up to her with kindly patronage and asked what the society could do for her, only to find she was speaking to the British Ambassadress. When one came to know her she was anything but dim and insignificant. Indeed she had discernment of spirit and great knowledge of the world, for all her indifference to it; was a good musician, a wise and devoted woman. She never made us feel that we had in any way lost Spring-Rice as a friend (and this must have required rare tact on her part), rather that we had gained a new one in her.

She was the ideal helpmate to him through all the hard times that were to follow. The heavy years of the Great War, which he fought in the Chancery of his Washington Embassy as manfully as did any of the Cabinet Ministers or indeed the soldiers in the trenches. At the end of it he was a broken man; he died soon after, leaving his post in 1919; the strain had been too great. The zeal of his devotion had literally devoured him. I never knew anyone with such passionate love of his country; a frail body dominated by untiring energy, stormracked by bursts of fiery indignation that would find vent in lightning flashes of bitterly sarcastic wit, not always suitable for a diplomatist, but always atoned for by his essential honesty of purpose and his keen intelligence.

His poem, "I Vow to Thee My Country," was written with his life's blood. It was sung or recited at the great peace celebration held in Westminster Abbey in honor of those who had died in the war. It was meet and right that it should be. But how little we dreamed of all the coming tragedies when we were seeing each other every day that long-ago winter. There was no end of pastime in good company, high talk, and merry fooling. He had many strings to his lyre, none better tuned than his delicately ironic humor.

Miss Mary Leiter, who afterwards married Lord Curzon, came out that year in Washington; her father was immensely rich and they had a handsome house on Dupont Circle. Spring-Rice was vaguely sentimental over the beautiful Mary, who looked like the Duchess of Towers in *Peter Ibbetson;* he used to write poems to her and about her. These generally showed a certain note of bitterness, for he knew from the first that she was not for him. The rest of us thought her uninteresting; she could be tiresome when she "unpacked her library" and tried to talk books and ideas; but she had a divine swan-like way of walking into a ballroom and great taste in dress. She was always *Zielbewusst* (aim-conscious), as the Germans say, and never swerved from her intention of making a great marriage. The somewhat scornful term "highbrow" had not been invented in those days. The London "Souls" all aimed at being intellectual, and a woman with social ambitions liked to be thought clever. A pretty woman would inevitably try her hand at being soulful and bookish, just as she is now apt to disclaim all intellectual attainments and to conceal the fact that she has been to college and can read Latin.

A couple of years later Spring-Rice went round the world with George Curzon, who told him he had never loved Mary Leiter more than the moment he first saw her walk into a great party. He took some time to make

up his mind. Perhaps his talks with Spring-Rice helped
him to do it, for he cabled his proposal to her from Japan
and was accepted by cable. The marriage turned out
well and she made an ideal figure of a "vicereine."

There were many stories about her mother, Mrs. L. Z.
Leiter, who was something of a Mrs. Malaprop and,
though a kind and well-born woman, a little too conscious
of her vast wealth. "Let my third footman take your
coat, Mrs. Lodge." "Now help yourself well, Mr.
Roosevelt, you don't get anything like this at home."
"Mr. Leiter is going to the fancy ball in the garbage of
a monk." "What a pity dear Sally Loring is so obscene"
(meaning obese — Miss Loring was very stout, but entirely respectable).

Recounting the glories of their first London season:
"Yes, we were invited to the ball at Devonshire House
and Mary danced in the Duchess's own caviar." On
referring to her absence from some official entertainment,
held on a very hot day, she said she was sorry to have
missed it, but that she was not going to "fester" for
anybody.

These were some of the pearls that fell from her lips,
over which we made merry. Of course, many other
solecisms were attributed to her, and of many she was
probably innocent.

Amélie Rives published a much-talked-of story, *The
Quick or the Dead*. It had a certain *succès de scandale*
in those innocent Victorian days; that a young girl should
have written it added severity to the censure which it
received. I cannot remember anything very shocking

about it; there was a good deal of long kissing and, in a final scene, the heroine sat on the floor with her head on the young man's knees, her tear-wet cheeks on the rough tweed of his trousers; this was considered most indelicate. Armstrong Chanler, my husband's older brother, was supposed to be attentive to the fair novelist, and so were many others. She lived at Castle Hill, the old Rives place in Virginia, with her mother and two younger sisters.

That spring my husband, William C. Endicott (whose father was then Secretary of War), Spring-Rice, and Arthur Herbert, another English secretary, made a riding tour through Virginia. I could not be separated from my baby, but joined them by train at Charlottesville. Miss Louise Thoron accompanied me; she soon afterwards married William C. Endicott. We visited the fine old University of Virginia, Monticello, and other places of interest; but what we all really wanted to see was Amélie Rives. We had a letter of introduction to Mrs. Rives and drove over to Castle Hill in a body late one morning. We were received with kindest cordiality and invited to stay for luncheon.

This fine old Virginian house was the first of its kind I had ever seen and I was charmed with its appearance. It was built early in the eighteenth century with bricks brought by sailing ship from Holland. The well-proportioned rooms had the original woodwork, wainscots, overdoors, and mantels; there was an air of civilized taste and ancient leisure. The beautiful Amélie did not appear for some time; when she finally did the effect was dazzling, especially to the young men. She had the largest dark blue-gray eyes; the longest black lashes; the most wonderful halo of loosely curled ash-blonde hair; very regular features, and a shapely, well-curved mouth. A romantic white tea gown draped and flowed from her shoulders in most becoming fashion, all but concealing her want of stature. She was full of life and had a slight Southern drawl that was attractive. A siren, a goddess, perhaps a genius — at all events we were well repaid for our expedition.

Amélie's two sisters were like her, only less superlative. They had the same brilliant coloring, the same beauty of face, but in her presence they became part of the background. Our young men were heaving with excitement as we drove off. They wanted to spend another night at Charlottesville in order to see her again the next day. William C. Endicott's black eyes were rounder than ever; he kept exploding with enthusiasm, almost throwing himself out of the carriage in his ardors.

The men had some amusing experiences on their ride. There were practically no inns in those days and they would spend the night either in some village elder's home or in a farmhouse. As bathrooms were at that time unknown in such places, they had brought with them a rubber tub. One member of the party had just finished his ablutions when, without waiting for an emptying and refilling of the tub, Spring-Rice jumped in, saying: —

> "For by the grace of God 't is seen
> That dirty water maketh clean!"

In one place they stopped with a judge, and were much embarrassed by the family prayers and Bible reading.

The father of the family read a particularly plain-spoken chapter of Holy Writ after supper to a large company of boys and girls gathered round the family board. It was explained to our young men that he made it a practice to read the Bible through to his family, a chapter at a time. He took the chapters "as they came at him."

Not very long after our expedition to Castle Hill Amélie Rives married my brother-in-law, Armstrong, who later changed his name from Chanler to Chaloner, the old English spelling of the name. It was not a happy or a permanent marriage, and ended in separation and divorce. Amélie afterwards married Prince Pierre Troubetzkoy.

We were all very much under her spell when Archie brought her to Rokeby the following autumn. I think they were married towards the end of the summer. She was an unusually gifted creature; she drew, she modeled, she wrote poetry and composed little songs, and there was much beauty and imagination in all she did. But she lacked discipline and her work suffered from a certain absence of technique. She was warmly friendly to me and wrote me a number of letters which, when I received them, seemed inspired. I put them away, but when in after years I found and read them again they were, alas, little more than shriveled flowers.

We met but did not come to know Mr. Henry Adams that winter in Washington, although our friends the Lodges, Roosevelts, and others were constantly telling us what he said and thought about this and that; he was looked upon as wise and witty above others. His wife had died a year or two before and he had lately returned from his voyage round the world. I knew much about this voyage from Mr. John La Farge, who made it with him and had a great deal to say about their wonderful adventures in the South Sea Islands, where La Farge painted some of his best water colors and where Henry Adams was adopted into the royal family and made *ipso facto* to descend from the original royal shark, founder of the dynasty.

Mr. Adams went out very little, never for meals; he saw his friends in his own house, chiefly at his twelve-o'clock breakfasts, to which they were privileged to invite themselves. Wintie and I were taken to one of these, but the occasion was not a success. We were received with ceremonious aloofness and there was no intimation that we were expected to come again.

St. Gaudens, who made the beautiful monument for Mrs. Adams, also made for his own amusement a charming medal of Henry as *Porcupinus Angelicus* — his head in profile (an excellent likeness), with cherubic wings composed of porcupine quills. Only three copies were struck of this soul-portrait: one for the original, one for Mrs. Lodge, the third St. Gaudens kept. We happened to strike the quills first. It was not until much later that we saw them moult into angelic feathers. I will come to that in another chapter.

XIX

ROME REVISITED

WASHINGTON was pleasant enough, but we did not take root there; it was no place for a young man — Wintie was only twenty-four — with no occupation and no desire to hold office. His Etonian education had in a sense unfitted him for American life, which has no place for charming idlers; yet he was essentially American and never wished to expatriate himself, only to move about the world in search of fun and adventure, and they generally came his way. I was unfeignedly homesick for Rome.

The Chanler sisters had gone abroad, leaving the younger boys with their tutor, the good uninspiring Mr. Bostwick, at Rokeby. We decided to go there for the summer and liked it so well that we stayed on through the autumn and into the winter. In February we took passage to Naples on a German steamer.

Oh, but it was good to be in Rome again, to feel the caress of Roman sunshine, to breathe the delicate Roman air, to hear the splash of fountains and the dear sound of bells. What joy to walk the Roman streets again! I could go out alone now that I was married, and linger in my favorite churches smelling of incense and old marble, or take Wintie for a morning stroll on the Pincio, stop on the broad terrace that overlooks the city, and wait to see the black ball come down over the tower of the observatory at noon to give the signal for the Castel Sant' Angelo to fire the cannon by which Rome sets its watches. The sound of the cannon promptly sets off the midday Angelus, and the air is filled for several minutes with its many-voiced clangor, ranging from the solemn boom of St. Peter's and St. Mary Major's, through every diapason of rich sonorities, to the humble tinkle of little convent bells that add their quavering treble to the great harmony of prayer.

We had taken our old friend Mr. Hooker's apartment in the Palazzo Bonaparte, overlooking the Corso and the Piazza di Venezia. It had belonged to Madama Letizia, Napoleon's mother, and had a beautiful great drawing-room hung with painted silk, the gift of a Chinese Emperor.

Wintie enjoyed the Roman scene nearly as much as I did. Everyone liked him; Giovanni Borghese mounted him on his best horses to hunt with the Roman foxhounds; he had good shooting with his friend Waldo Story at the *Capanna,* Story's shooting box near the sea, some twenty miles south of Rome. It was all unbelievably pleasant.

I found my old friends as congenial as ever and we made many new ones. The Roman world, with its very permanent social structure, has at the same time a larger element of change than other capitals. It has in the first place a duplicate diplomatic corps; two ambassadors from most of the major countries, two ministers from the lesser ones, each with a separate staff of chancellors, secretaries, and attachés. One set is for the Vatican, one for the Quirinal; the one will belong to the Black, or clerical, society and be received by the Pope; the other will be White and go to the Italian Court. But there has always been plenty of neutral ground where the two could meet, and there was never much hostility between the two camps. In later years few if any of the *Neri* (Blacks) held out whole-heartedly against United Italy, and the ground was well prepared for the Mussolini compromise that made the Pope the independent sovereign of Vatican City.

Then there are always those who come to Rome to enjoy it for a season and decide to stay on, perhaps for the rest of their lives, and the many who come because they want to and leave because they have to, always hoping they may come again. All these make a motley crowd that is in a perpetual state of change and flux, forever forming new groups and coteries as this or that personage emerges, attracts attention, and becomes a centre of interest and influence. So the changeful human stream flows through the same old palaces, mounts the broad easy staircases, and passes through the long suites of halls, antechambers, and reception rooms that have seen so many generations go the same way.

Lord Dufferin was British Ambassador in Rome; his previous appointment had been as Viceroy of India, and in recognition of his services there he had recently been created Marquis of Dufferin and Ava. He and Lady Dufferin were charming hosts and we came to know them and their pleasant family well. Lord Dufferin was at

once a very great gentleman and a delightful human
being.   He could look very imposing, as became his high
position, but his official dignity was seasoned with a rare
sense of humor, derived, one liked to think, from the
Sheridan blood that ran in his veins.   He knew the way
of the world and how much amusement could be derived
from watching it go by.   His talk was brilliant and his
fine intelligence had a distinguished amenity all its own.
He would sit down beside one and say: "Would you
like me to tell you a story?" and then unfold some Indian fairy tale or Persian romance with a kind of envel-
oping charm.

At the big embassy dinners the table was decorated
with golden horseshoes and golden roses, a great many
of them; the roses stood up on little stands and the horseshoes lay flat; the effect was very pleasing.   Lord Dufferin explained to me that one of his ancestors had
quarreled with a neighboring Lord of the Marches
over some land to which both laid claim, and had finally
ceded his right on condition that the other should send
him every alternate year a golden rose and a golden
horseshoe.   This pact must have been faithfully kept
for a great many years to judge by the abundance of the
table decorations.

One of the best of our new friends that winter in Rome,
and forever after, was Count Hans Coudenhove; he was
then attached to the Austrian Embassy to the Quirinal.
He was a delightful and interesting companion with a
passion for animals.   When he eventually tired of the
Diplomatic Service and gave up the *majorat*, or entailed
estate, to his brother, he went to live in what used to

be German East Africa, surrounded by his pets — mongooses, zebras, monkeys, and I do not know how many others. He and I corresponded faithfully for many years and his long letters are full of amusing tales of wild life. His book, *My African Neighbors,* was published by the Atlantic Monthly Press. When the Great War broke out the English took over the German possessions and Coudenhove was interned in a concentration camp.

While being taken to this he had his first ride in a motor and was outraged with its excessive speed. He was allowed to take with him his two favorite mongooses and one of them died of excitement. This was enough to damn all motor cars forever in Hans's eyes. Living in solitude, he had time to write very long letters, a part of which was always filled with reproaches that mine were too short, that I told him too little. He counted the words on my page and found them too few. How little he dreamed, in the long leisure of the wilderness, of the ever-accelerating tempo of Western life. He made friends with the natives and gained their confidence; practised medicine (which he had never studied) — helped to bring their babies into the world, and for other ailments distributed simple drugs, calomel, quinine, restoratives; and gained such reputation for his good offices in this line that when the war was over, and the concentration camp was dispersed, the English protectorate gave him a small salary as physician to the natives. His Austrian securities had lost all value, so this was his only means of support during the last years of his life.

He was found dead in his camp; he had sent one of

his "boys" to his nearest neighbors, some English people living many miles away, to say that he felt ill. When they reached him the end had come. He died alone with his friends, the mongooses and monkeys, about him.

Buffalo Bill brought his Wild West Show to Rome that winter and the city gave him the waste land of the Prati di Castello, west of the Tiber and north of the Castel Sant' Angelo, in which to camp and set up his circus. This has since been covered with streets and squares — the Palace of Justice, Piazza Cavour, and many modern palaces and tenements.

Miss Rachel Sherman, daughter of the Civil War General, happened to be in Rome, and when Colonel Cody learned of this he put a whole section of the improvised stadium at her disposal. She invited a large party of us to help fill it. Buffalo Bill had been her father's chief scout. We saw "little Annie Oakley" as a middle-aged woman in cowboy suit shooting glass balls, the Indians tearing about in their war paint, whooping and yelling, and Buffalo Bill riding his old charger, shooting glass balls from an easy canter, but missing more of them than he hit. The most interesting part of the show was the horse breaking and bronco busting. The Wild West Show had challenged the *butteri* of the Campagna to a contest in horse breaking and the different methods were exemplified. The cowboys rode their bucking broncos to a standstill; the *butteri* threw them, tied them up, and did not mount them till their resistance was broken. It was difficult to judge from one perform-

ance, but on the whole the Roman horse breakers seemed
to show more science — they certainly made it easier and
less dangerous to themselves and more convincing to the
horse.

After the performance Rachel felt that she must take
us all to the Colonel's tent to thank him for his kindness
in inviting the party.   Poor Buffalo Bill was in no condition to receive us.   He came towards us majestically,
with his flowing moustache and military air, but he could
hardly stand, and after shaking hands very pompously
"with the daughter of his Great Chief" and mumbling a
few incoherent words, it was evident that he could do
no more, and he reeled back into the seclusion of his
tent.

His whole company was received at the Vatican by
Pope Leo XIII.   The Indians gave a blood-curdling
yell as the frail and venerable figure was carried into the
Sistine Chapel.   They looked and sounded terrifying,
but we were told they were all devout Catholics and
that their uncouth noises were an expression of loyalty.

Dr. Axel Munthe was in Rome at this time and we
saw him often and always with pleasure.   He was a
somewhat enigmatic figure, at once a doctor, a hypnotist,
an unrivaled story-teller, and a Nordic hero.   His stories
transported one into a magic world of mind-over-matter
experiences and were always exciting and momentarily
convincing to his hearers; to question their veracity was
beside the mark.   He had studied under Charcot at the
Salpêtriére and had there developed his natural gift for
hypnotism.   He knew how to take a sort of psycho-

romantic possession of his patients. The late Queen of Sweden could hardly live without him, and there were others, not quite so august, in the same case, and completely under his spell. We heard of this or that one being madly in love with Dr. Munthe, never that he had lost his heart or his head. It was part of his psychopathic practice to gain such an ascendant over his patients that he would become indispensable to them; he was all the more successful in that he himself seemed to be invulnerable; they felt that he controlled them at a distance.

I remember his telling us the case of a Roman princess who had lost her mind and whom he had restored to sanity. When her mental disorder had subsided, and he was able to leave Rome, he continued to carry her in his thoughts. It happened that in Capri he went out for a sail and was overtaken by a sudden storm. He and his sailors had a hard time to get safely back to port, and the strain and exposure to which he was subjected brought on a hemorrhage followed by a prolonged fainting fit. When he recovered consciousness he was in his bed at San Michele and there received a telegram from the distracted family of the princess, who during his swoon had become uncontrollable and needed his immediate attention. The time when her trouble overtook her was found to coincide precisely with the moment when he had lost consciousness.

Then there was a strange story of an Italian tenement in Paris, where Munthe had known some workmen's families and attended their sick children; he was very charitable and compassionate and had great understand-

ing of the Italian peasant soul.   One afternoon he found
that the family in which he was particularly interested
had been told they must leave that day, having failed
for some time to pay their rent.   Two small children
lay dangerously ill.   They had nowhere to go.   The
padrone knew no pity.   They were gathering up their
few poor belongings to take along with the sick children
out into the gathering darkness, facing despair.   Dr.
Munthe reassured them.   Who was this hard-hearted
man?   Where did he live?   He told them to stay where
they were, he would go and plead for them.

He found the owner of the tenement and gave a grim
description of him, sitting like an ogre in his den, before
his ledger.   The little room was bare of all ornament.
A crucifix hung on the wall.   The man looked inhuman
and unapproachable.   Munthe laid the case of the poor
family with the sick children before him; he would not
hear of relenting.   Then the doctor felt a great heat
rise in him and, standing up, he pointed to the crucifix
and spoke eloquently of mercy and compassion and
finally of judgment.   As the man continued to shake
his head with set lips he brought his speech to a climax
by shaking his finger at the hard face and saying: "Perhaps this very night you will be called to answer for
what you are doing!" and left the room.

The next morning he went back to the tenement to
see the sick children and to find out what had happened.
The whole place was in an uproar of excitement.   "*Il
padrone s'e impiccato!*"   The man had hanged himself
that night in the very room where Munthe had talked
to him.

I was never one of his patients nor one of his particular ladies, but enjoyed nothing more than having him to dinner and listening to his stories.   If in his treatment of psychological cases he seemed to show, and indeed almost to claim, occult powers, this did not prevent him from being well able to cope with what might be called normal diseases.   He pulled Mr. Robert Crawshay through a dangerous typhoid.   But as a physician I preferred our dear Dr. Montechiari, who was no mystic, but a plain wise doctor and devoted friend.

I have mentioned Mr. Robert Crawshay.   His wife, whom I first met about this time, soon became one of my favorite friends.   A woman of rare wit and exquisite gentleness, whose kindness never wavers.   Her nephew, Mr. Shane Leslie, draws a charming picture of her in his *End of a Chapter*.   She too was a great friend of Dr. Munthe, but not one of his psychic possessions.

There are people whom it is hard to describe apart from their surroundings.   Prince and Princess Doria-Pamfili lived in one of the most beautiful of the Roman palaces.   The sight-seer is familiar with the state drawing-rooms and the handsome gallery that contains so many world-famous masterpieces; these are open to the public twice a week.   Adjoining them are the private apartments where the family lived surrounded by rare and precious objects — the unrivaled private collection of pictures, furniture, tapestries, and treasures of all kinds, accumulated through the centuries.   Were not the splendid gold-enwoven tapestries that hung in the dining room a gift from the Spanish King to Andrea

Doria after the naval victory of Lepanto? I once took our cousin, Alphonse de Stuers, to see them; he was himself a passionate lover and collector of beautiful things, and he was lost in admiration. He said they were among the best in the world.

The Dorias were proud of their high tradition and felt they owed it to themselves and to the world to take a prominent part in its doings. It was said of the Prince's sisters, the Duchess Massimo and the Countess della Somaglia, that when they came into a ballroom they had the air of saying: "Look at us well — we are Dorias." Prince Alfonso was a connoisseur and a man of fastidious taste. His mother was a Lady Mary Talbot and the house was run in the English grand manner, which is more elaborate, more formal, and yet far more comfortable than were most of the Roman establishments of those days. He took pleasure and pride in his many wonderful belongings and had the art of giving the sumptuous rooms an air of pleasant livableness. He was not otherwise an interesting man.

His wife, the Princess Emily, on the contrary, lived among the grandeurs with an elusive detachment. She was English, a daughter of the Duke of Newcastle. She had a small lovely face with radiant blue eyes, dark hair, and a silent, sphinx-like mouth. She had a vivid quietness, the attraction of a highly charged magnet; under the still surface there were passion and courage, and even a sort of waywardness. Like the famous Duchess de Longueville, sister of the "Grand Condé," who was also wayward in her day and a great *frondeuse*, "she spoke little, she listened attentively, she never inter-

rupted, she never said aught to her own advantage." I
quote from memory.

That winter in Rome when I first came to know her
well she was very gay; she rode to hounds and led a
worldly life, surrounded by many admirers; these had to
be witty and amusing, for though she said so little she
appreciated the fun made by others. Giovanni Borghese
was one of her most devoted friends.

After we left Rome her life was darkened by the loss
of a child, a little second son on whom she had set her
heart. When I saw her again some eight years later
she was another woman: she had renounced the world
and devoted herself to good works; she had built a children's hospital and spent most of her time there. Every
afternoon she drove to the villa and put fresh flowers
on little Giannettino's tomb in the family mausoleum.
It was then several years since his death, but she wore
perpetual mourning and saw only her friends and intimates. I found her as charming as ever. Why did she
so resolutely turn her back on the pomps and vanities
that went with her station in life? Her husband was
distressed by her withdrawal; a good confessor would
probably have told her it was her duty to go out with
detachment of heart and play the part assigned her by
Providence. There was something harsh and irrevocable in her break with the world. Many years later,
long after she and Don Alfonso had been laid beside
their little boy in the Doria-Pamfili mausoleum, a
friend in East Africa sent me a faded letter he had found
among his papers. It was a farewell from a dying man,
his best friend, who found it doubly hard to die when she

whom he had so long adored had perhaps relented. I barely knew the writer of the letter, but I well knew whom he had so long adored — it happened while I was in America. This threw light on the renunciation: Emily had taken her child's death as a judgment and devoted her life to expiation, but she always wore the ruby ring given her by the dying man.

How many delicate shadows have passed over the earth's rough surface! Pia de' Tolomei asks Dante to remember her when he returns to the other world and has rested from the long journey. The few wistful words she added to what the second spirit had said are all he tells us of her, but the grace and pathos of her slender outline can never be forgotten. *"Ricorditi di me che son la Pia!"*

That spring Giovanni Borghese organized a delightful expedition for us. It was at the time of the *Merca,* the rounding up and branding of the cattle on the big Campagna farms, and he took some eight or ten of us to a number of the great Borghese *tenute* (holdings) to see the Spring Festival. The Dorias and the Theodolis were of the party.

The marking of the cattle was very interesting. The young steers were led into the corral one by one between two old oxen called *mandarini.* The *butteri* (equivalent of our cowboys) would then rope them, throw them, and brand them. They did it with much skill. The long-horned Campagna cattle are rather savage, and there are many scuffles and a certain danger when a young bull is

"LILY," MARCHESA THEODOLI

The famous Roman beauty

restive. After the cattle had been rounded up and all
the yearlings branded, a great feast was spread *al fresco*
for everyone who had taken part. There was the high
table for the lord of the manor and his guests; the
ragioniere or steward had his; and so on down to the
farm hands.

The next stop was made at Fossanuova, the property
of another Borghese brother and his wife, the Prince and
Princess di Rossano. Fossanuova was anciently a Cister-
cian Abbey. The convent church, built about 1225, is one
of the earliest examples of Italian Gothic. St. Thomas
Aquinas died there in 1274 on his way to Lyons. His
body was taken not to Lyons but to Toulouse, where
it rests to this day. I think the pious intention was to
carry it to Lyons, the goal of his last journey, and that the
Dominicans of Toulouse would not let it go by them.
But in those days mediæval studies did not interest me
as they did in later years, and my memory of Fossanuova
is of the very pleasant evening we spent with the Ros-
sanos in their charming house which nestled comfortably in a wing of the old monastery.

Their *curato*, who came to dinner, was a picturesque
type of Italian village priest. The family all seemed
very fond of him and much friendly fun was made with
and about him. My husband was the first Protestant he
had ever seen and he found him very puzzling. Wintie
was one of those people who are never without the Rose
or the Ring. Everybody was attracted by him, and the
good *curato* could not bear the thought that this charming young man was in peril of damnation. It seemed

to him such a simple matter to convert him to the true
Faith.   He tried to make Wintie promise that he would
say a Hail Mary every time he embraced his wife.

He had unbounded respect, admiration, and affection
for the Borghese family.   Under cover of general conversation Giovanni whispered to me how lenient he was
with their shortcomings.   He had himself been to confession to him and the good man could not find it in his
heart to condemn anything he had to tell him.   His only
comment on grievous sins was, *"Troppo naturale, Eccel-
lenza."*   How he would have shocked my Chanler sisters-
in-law!   Yet he was a good, faithful soul and Wintie
understood him perfectly.

We left Rome soon after making this expedition, and
did not go back for many years.   It was always hard
to leave it; there my spirit was deeply rooted and drew
life from the soil; in other places I was a plant in a
tub or a flowerpot, "a guest and a stranger."   We are
told to keep ourselves from idols; perhaps Rome was
mine, and I must learn to do without it.

We went to Venice for a few weeks before leaving
Italy.   Hans Coudenhove joined us there from Sicily,
where he had left his yacht, and Giovanni Borghese came
all the way from Hungary where he was visiting friends.
They had both been away from Rome when we left it
and they wanted to say good-bye to us.   Nothing could
have pleased us more and we spent delightful days together; the old sorceress of the Adriatic knows how to
entertain her guests; she has done little else for centuries.   Ever since she lost her supremacy of the sea and

her great financial and political importance she has amused
herself weaving spells out of moonlight and deep shadow,
broken reflections of palaces and churches on the waters
of her canals, the drip from the oar of the gondola, which
makes no other sound as it passes.

Venice made the best possible *coda* to our Roman
winter: it charmed away the pain of departure and made
a transition from one reality to another.   Venice is made
of dream-stuff, and dreams take us softly from one day
to the next.   Reality came upon me with a pang when
we got into the train for Paris, the first stage of our
journey home.   It was good-bye, Italy — *Addio, mia
bella, addio!*

XX

NEW YORK SOCIETY

WE planned to spend the summer in England, where
Wintie had enjoyed happy years at Eton and had a few
relatives and many friends. But soon after we reached
London he ran into Dr. Nevin of Rome and Dr. Rainsford
of New York, another sporting parson and muscular Christian, who were starting together for Colorado on a big-
game-shooting expedition. They were sailing in a few
days and begged Wintie to join them. He was all on
fire to go and I had not the heart to deny him the adventure. I was left in London with two babies (a son had
been born to us in Sorrento the summer before) and felt
rather stranded. My old Roman friends, the Theodolis,
had come to London. The Marchesa, the beautiful Lily
of my earliest memories, was suffering from the results
of a serious operation and had come to put herself under
the care of a famous English specialist. Her husband
and five children came with her. After she had spent
some weeks at a private hospital it was decided to move
her to Yarmouth for an after-cure of sea air, and I, not
knowing of any better place and clinging to the com-
panionship of people I had always known and liked, decided to follow them there. It was a dreary experience,
for Yarmouth has little to offer in the way of beauty or

interest. The fine beach was overrun by holiday crowds. " 'Arrys" and " 'Arriets" lay all over the place fondly locked in each other's arms, to the great distress of the Theodolis, who did not like the children to see such things; in Italy they are not done in public. Mine were too young to be corrupted, but the good Cecilia's sense of decorum was deeply outraged, and she formed the poorest opinion of English morality. I fully realized that I was seeing England through the wrong end of the glass, which made it seem very remote. I took the babies back to New York in the early autumn. There Wintie met me, having had a glorious time in Colorado with the sporting parsons, who had proved excellent company. He told me of a talk he had with Dr. Rainsford. Wintie had spoken to him of my religion and asked him if it would not be possible for him to bring me back into the Protestant fold — not that he himself cared, but that the family would feel so much better if I could be weaned from Catholicism. He asked Dr. Rainsford if he would not try his hand at reasoning with me. "My dear fellow," exclaimed Dr. Rainsford, "I would not dream of doing anything of the sort! All the good arguments are on their side."

We returned to Washington the following winter and were happy to find ourselves back in the charmed circle of our dear friends there. These were delightful as ever, but for some reason the place was not sympathetic to me. The soil seemed shallow; there were no interests outside of politics and society, little or no music, no theatres to speak of, no opera, no university, hardly a native society. People from different parts of the world lived there for

a given time as ambassadors, secretaries, members of the
Cabinet or of Congress. Those one liked stood out
against a blank background, detached from their surroundings. It was a very idle place for an idle man.
Wintie and I both felt restless and ready to try some
other experiment in home-making. But the next was to
be on the whole even less successful.

Wintie's great friend, Amos Tuck French, lived in
Tuxedo Park. We spent a week-end with him and his
wife; it was bitterly cold and stiflingly dull. Wintie went
back there soon after for another visit to his dear Amos,
who was indeed a witty and delightful man; but what
was my dismay on being told that "we" had bought a
house in Tuxedo, that it was to be our home for the rest
of our lives!

Before taking possession of the new abode we spent
the winter of 1891–1892 in New York. The three Chanler sisters had lately returned from England, where they
had spent several years completing their education at
Miss Sewell's School, and were now ready to make their
curtsey to society. The council of guardians decided that
my husband and I were to bring them out. So we hired
a large furnished house in West Thirty-fourth Street,
one of a row of white marble "high-stoop" houses be-
longing to the Astor estate. It seems hard to believe
that Thirty-fourth Street was then pleasant and habitable,
without shops or street cars. It was soon to be invaded
by both. Dwellings were abandoned as such, to be replaced by business; it became a fashionable shopping
centre, and now even this has moved a mile or two
further north into the fifties and sixties.

The Chanlers had not lived in New York since their parents died. The old Chanler house was on the corner of Thirty-fourth Street and Madison Avenue, on the block now occupied by Altman's department store. The three girls had been brought up in the austere seclusion of Rokeby, and had from there been sent to Miss Sewell's most conservative and highly recommended school. This was well enough in its way, but had rather incompletely prepared them for the arduous experience of a New York season. They were handsome girls with rare qualities of mind and temperament; but they were not tuned to ballroom pitch, and lacked a certain social light-heartedness. They danced and dressed badly. They were related to everybody in New York, but had no circle of familiar friends. They were in truth not worse prepared than I, who had never lived in New York at all, had even fewer friends than they, and hardly a single acquaintance. Wintie was better off; he had his college classmates and clubmates, some intimate cousins, and his gay wit, and was at home, as he often said, wherever he found his hat. With him to give us heart we entered the lists.

A cousin gave us her visiting book, and we sent out hundreds of invitations to people we did not know: —

Mrs. Winthrop Chanler

The Misses Chanler

at home

from 4 to 7

A crowd duly came on the appointed day. We shook
no end of unknown hands and smiled politely at no end
of faces we had never seen before.   One old gentleman,
who had evidently prepared his little speech as he came
into the house, took me for my mother-in-law, and told
me he well remembered my coming-out ball in Lafayette
Place.   This ball must have been given a good many
years before I was born.   He suddenly realized his mistake, put his two hands over his face, and rushed out of
the room in confusion.

Then invitations began to pour in; we went to many
parties, hardly knowing the hosts, and feeling rather lost
among the guests.   It took us some time to get our
bearings.

New York society was still a closed circle to which one
either did or did not belong.   Ward McAllister announced to the world in a series of widely read articles
appearing in a Sunday paper that it consisted of four
hundred members, including the smaller group of the
ultrafashionable.   He mentioned them all by name and
made a sort of diagram of the hierarchy, not unlike Dante's
description of Paradise, with the greater and lesser saints
circling in their appointed places about the Mystic Rose.
He was laughed at, called a snob and nicknamed "Make-
a-lister," but the expression "the Four Hundred" passed
into current usage and has not been forgotten, although
the latest issue of the *New York Social Register* contains
over a thousand pages closely filled with names, passed
on by a watchful committee.

Mrs. William B. Astor was the acknowledged leader.
She always sat on the right of the host when she went

to dinner parties; she wore a black wig and a great many
jewels; she had pleasant cordial manners and unaffectedly
enjoyed her undisputed position.   She gave very grand
dinners and the great Astor ball was the social event of
the season.   Mrs. Ogden Mills was the other leader;
she was much younger and her house was the centre of
the inner, smarter circle, without in the least detracting
from Mrs. Astor's supremacy.   Mrs. Mills was a Livingston and had some years before this, our first in New
York, married Ogden Mills, the son of D. O. Mills, a
"forty-niner" millionaire.   They had built themselves
a really handsome house on upper Fifth Avenue and
furnished it in the new imported style, Louis XV and
Louis XVI.   It was much talked of as a bold innovation.
Most of the great houses were naïvely and sumptuously
ugly.   Ours was even uglier than the average.   The
new era of period furniture had hardly dawned, and the
high noon of the Interior Decorator was undreamed of.
Drawing-rooms were full of massive upholstery, and
there were heavy knotted fringes on the damask curtains.
Tables wore fringed tablecloths, and were covered with
indiscriminate *bibelots* and innumerable framed photographs.   These prevailed everywhere, in the Roman
palace, the English country house, or the French château.
They had succeeded the antimacassar, the keepsake, and
the photograph album of earlier Victorian days; they
were not peculiar to New York.   But the houses of the
Old World had the grace and dignity of old houses;
New York's mansions were built for the most part in
Pullman-car style, whole streets of them absolutely uniform, as their owners had followed the northward trend

of the rapidly expanding Megalopolis.   My grandfather, a well-to-do bank president, had, in his day, moved uptown from the Battery and built himself a fine big house in Bond Street near Broadway, with a picture gallery and well-stocked library and cellar; the Astors had begun their grandeurs in Lafayette Square.   Washington Square must for years have marked the uptown limit of where it was possible to live.   Uncle Sam Ward, as a boy, used to shoot woodcock on the land that was to be Union Square, only six blocks away.   Rutherfurd Stuyvesant, to be sure, still lived in Stuyvesant Square, which had once been part of Governor Stuyvesant's farm; but there was no trace of the first Dutch Governor's habitation; his descendant had built himself a new one in the taste of his day, and held out there for many years, in fact as long as he lived; it was pleasant in the city of perpetual changes to be Mr. Stuyvesant of Stuyvesant Square.   His widow, however, eventually lost heart and moved up to the Ritz-Tower, where she can see her friends without going through miles of slums.[1]   But enough of topography.

I found the great New York dinners for the most part extremely unrewarding.   Nothing was done for the guests' entertainment beyond providing them with a vast amount of elaborate food, often served on silver or silver-gilt plates, and with many varieties of wine.   Roman punch was served in the middle of the meal — after soup, fish, entrée, and a first course of meat had satisfied all natural appetite — to stimulate our courage to eat what was yet to come.   One was rarely amused by

[1] She has lately married Prince Caraman-Chimay.

one's neighbor. I invented a secret insurance company against bores. Everyone could hand in his private list; it would of course be strictly confidential. If one happened to find oneself again seated beside the flower of them all, there would be the cheering consolation that one could, with the well-earned premium, buy oneself a new hat, a nice engraving, or what not. After dinner the men retired to the smoking room in true Anglo-Saxon style, and stayed there until it was time to go home.

When Milton's Archangel visits Adam and Eve in the Earthly Paradise, and stays to dinner, Eve leaves the table after the fruit has been served, to let the men have their talk. Had Dante described such an occasion, we may be sure that Beatrice, I mean Eve, would have taken part in the serious conversation. The Latin likes to know what women think of what he thinks; the English-speaking man is curiously indifferent to this, the average American even more so than the average Englishman. He, the American, generally a hard-working man, is content to let his wife or daughter spend all the money he can make, and asks few questions as to where it goes, so long as she makes him comfortable; her business is in the shops, as his is in the down-town office, and there is a great gulf fixed between their thoughts and preoccupations. There is a deplorable habit of *tête-à-tête* prattling that spoils the usual dinner party; people seem to feel that saying anything to their neighbor is politer than listening to anything that is being said by someone else. There may be an interesting question under discussion at the other end of the table; you would like to hear, perhaps to put in a word, if you happen to know something about it; but your inexorable neighbor has to ask you if you like the new play, or if you are going to Newport for the summer. It is mere civility on his part; it is the convention that is universally followed here; there must be no pauses.

The New York world of those early nineties was based on a sort of untitled but long-established social hierarchy, from which all random elements were rigorously excluded. It held many attractive people, good-looking, agreeable, well-dressed women and men; but as a society it seemed flat and arid, a Sahara without lions or lion hunters. The Four Hundred would have fled in a body from a poet, a painter, a musician, or a clever Frenchman.

There were some eight or ten young men, known as "the Dudes," who set the fashion in dress and manners. The two Rutherfurds (who were Rutherfurd Stuyvesant's brothers and my husband's first cousins), the two Howards, the two Cuttings, the two Cottonets, — all these pairs were brothers, — and Dick Peters and Woodbury Kane, gay bachelors all. They were flawlessly well turned out, and comfortably conscious of being the best of their kind, handsomely representative of American aristocracy, and as English as possible in dress. My friend Edith Wharton tells a story corroborating this. She was once walking down Piccadilly with an English friend, discussing the comparative appearance of the fashionable British and American young man. The Englishman maintained that his compatriots had better taste, wore their clothes better, looked smarter. "Look at those two coming toward us," he said; "I do not happen

to know who they are, but you will never see two Americans looking like that." And behold! tall, lean, proud,
and magnificent, they were none other than Winthrop
and Lewis Rutherfurd — Edith Wharton's next-door
neighbors in New York, and intimate friends from childhood.

The beautiful Marion Langdon had come out in New
York before I was married. The fame of her brilliant
success and many conquests reached us in Rome. I met
her first in Washington after she had married Royall
Phelps Carroll, a great friend of Wintie's, a classmate
and fellow Porcellian. She and her husband lived in
New York and had come on to attend a ball given by his
father, Governor John Carroll, for the coming out of his
daughter Helen, later married to Herbert D. Robbins.
I did not come to know the Royall Carrolls well until,
some time after this, they took Wintie and me on a few
days' cruise in their fine sailing yacht the *Navahoe*, built
for them to compete at Cowes for the famous *America's*
Cup, then still in England. She won several races in
English waters, but it was another American yacht that
captured the much-coveted trophy that same year and
brought it back to America, where it has stayed ever
since.

On the cruise — it was off the New England coast
in lovely sailing weather — Marion and I became fast
friends and have remained so ever since. She had a
crisp and spirited beauty and high charm; she was and
is a very great lady. To my regret I see little of her
in these our later years, chiefly because we live in different places, but she was a bright spot for me in the New

York of the early nineties, although she was satisfied to move gayly and exclusively among the purely fashionable and could not understand my joy, as of a cat with catnip, when I found myself in the society of an artist or of the wise and learned.

New York society obtained at about that time a nation-wide publicity. Ward McAllister's articles were reprinted far and wide, and many more were written about the Four Hundred. No other city in the United States could boast of such a round number of prosperous social units, presenting so solid a line of exclusiveness. Their doings were recorded all over the country: so it happened that "the Dudes" were talked about in Western towns; Woodbury Kane, a favorite leader of cotillons, was better known than the Secretary of State or the Speaker of the House. Kane had been in the West shortly after he graduated from Harvard, and had greatly enjoyed himself there — as he managed to do wherever he went, for he was a truly charming fellow and an excellent horseman. He made friends with congenial cowboys. Some years later, a friend by chance met one of these, while on a Western trip, and was asked if he knew Woodbury Kane. He happened to know him very well indeed; he was his college classmate, fellow Porcellian, and intimate friend. The cowboy pointed to the New York society news in a local Wyoming paper, and shook his head: "Too bad, too bad; he was a good guy and could handle a horse, too, and now it seems he has turned into a 'society man,' and leads cotillons, whatever they are."

Town Topics had a very wide circulation, and gave

lurid accounts of fashionable scandals. People living in little frame houses in bleak Western places loved to read of the shocking corruption prevailing on Fifth Avenue. Theodore Roosevelt used to tell us of one of his cowboy friends, who wrote him that he was coming to New York, and would like to stay with him. They had been as brothers in the West. Theodore was at that time living with his sister Anna; he was still a widower, and she had not yet married Admiral Cowles. Miss Roosevelt's house was furnished with substantial old family pieces, and heavy dark upholstery. One could hardly imagine anything more soberly respectable in the way of household decoration. But there hung over the mantelpieces, in the dining and living rooms, large gilt-framed looking-glasses, and these the future President did not dare let his cowboy friend see. To him they would have denoted a house of ill fame, and stamped Miss Roosevelt as a lost woman. So he engaged a room for him at the Fifth Avenue Hotel, full of gaudy mirrors and exuberant decorations, which the good man could admire with an easy mind, without feeling that they implied wickedness in the home of his best friend. Roosevelt called on him the next morning to see if he had been made comfortable. "Well," said the hardy son of the West, "I found it rather cold, sleeping on the floor, but I finally rolled myself up in the rug and managed to get to sleep." The man had been too proud to ask questions, and the large ambiguous piece of furniture, which was neither sideboard nor cupboard, had not revealed its hidden nature; it was a folding bed.

But seen from the inside, the New York world of
those days seemed guilelessly proper and well-behaved,
censorious and dull. There were one or two flagrant
divorces; the "guilty parties" were scratched from their
friends' visiting lists that they might expiate their fault.
It was still what Edith Wharton aptly names the Age of
Innocence. Scandals must needs arise, but these things
"were not done" by the well-bred. How would my three
sisters-in-law have felt could they have looked into the
seeds of time and foreseen that in the course of the next
two or three decades two of their brothers would marry
actresses, three of them would be divorced, one of them
twice? Happily such foreknowledge was withheld from
their fond sisterly eyes.

My four brothers-in-law were, I think, universally
liked and well thought of. They were all good-looking,
quick-witted, and high-spirited; differing widely from
one another, they all shared a genial warmth of temperament that made their presence as exhilarating as a draught
of oxygen.

William was perhaps the most promising of the four
brothers. He was a brilliant creature, dark-eyed, ro-
mantic-looking, with great personal charm and flawless
courage. At twenty-one, as soon as he had come into
his fortune, he organized a successful expedition into the
wilds of Africa, and showed much ability, courage, and
perseverance in putting it through. He explored undis-
covered rivers, killed all sorts of big game, elephants,
rhinos, lions, and whatever seemed worth shooting at.
He made important contributions to geographical maga-
zines, and after his return to civilization wrote a good

book, *Through Jungle and Desert*, recounting his adventures. Harvard College, where he had been a student for about a year, and had done little beside becoming a member of the Porcellian Club, gave him an honorary degree, and a few years later, after his second African expedition, he was decorated by the Royal Geographical Society.

His mind was quick and resourceful and his conversation brilliant — more startling, perhaps, than convincing; but his most fantastic assertions were often based on fact, and his most improbable predictions had a way of coming true.

John Jay Chapman allows me to insert his verses on the snake charmer, which express better than I possibly can the bewildering fascination of his talk: —

THE SNAKE CHARMER

The tide of victuals was running slack
   (My interest failed at the canvas back),
But still the waiters circulate
   With wine on wine and plate on plate;
And the glasses yellow and red and green
   On the distracted board are seen,
Like an autumn garden stalk on stalk,
   When Willy Chanler began to talk.

What he said I 'll not repeat . . .
   For could a mortal understand
How he reached his sacred heat,
   Or what the meaning of his hand
As he raised it, and the eyes of all
   Followed its movements magical.

He talked of Egypt — how he slew
  In an afternoon ten thousand men,
And half a thousand women too!
  The last to frozen rivers grew, —
For they looked too long on his eyes of flame,
  And returned to their consorts never again!

And next a lion he did tame,
  And with the skin on Kruger smote
Till the mane grew fast to Kruger's throat
  And Cecil Rhodes gave up the game.
Now touching lightly on the Czar —
  And the Duchess of the Alcazar —
And what he won from the Shah in a fight
  And lost at faro in a night.

And even my visitors craned their necks
  And the waiters listened behind the door
To catch but a word if they could no more,
  Of that marvelous stream that might perplex
The brain of a Plato to unravel,
  Of history, legend, intrigue, travel.

Now a whisper about would go,
  "Does he believe it? — is it so?
We don't know and he don't know!"
  And still the continuous stream doth flow:
"Is it opium? Is it wine
  That makes his glassy eye to shine
And tinctures yours and dazzles mine,
  Till the decanters seem to dance
In tune with the flashing of his glance?"

He is telling the laws of the Boogla-Goo
  The secret clique that rules Bombay.
He himself was the chief they say,
  The very Pyjam of the How-do-you-do
That poisoned the Princess of Cathay
  And won the bride and rode the ride
And ran the race that turned the tide
  Of the Mongols in Baffin's Bay.

One at a time they came up the pass,
  One on an elephant, one on an ass,
While he with sorceries manifold —
  A handful of silver, a pound of gold —
And the hair that the witch of Atlas gave
  When Genghis Khan came out of the grave
To frighten them all away!

He talked till the brains of the men that night
  Like absinthe mixed with dynamite
Gave off blue sparks, and the lamps burned low,
  And still the murmur about doth go:
"Did he do it and is it so?
  We don't know and he don't know
If it be false or if it be true":

Nobody living ever knew
  Or in eternity can find out,
We only obey his call.
  He is merely weaving his charms about,
While the snakes crawl in, and the lights go out,
  And the charmer has charmed them all.

                JOHN JAY CHAPMAN

ROKEBY, *Christmas Day* 1900

Willie made several subsequent African expeditions, was elected Member of Congress, and, later still, married the gifted actress, Minnie Ashley; he became interested in horse racing and horse raising. He has now for many years lived in Paris, where he keeps in touch with politics both at home and abroad. He knew about the Chinese Revolution many months before it occurred; he had something to do with quelling the Senussi revolt among the North African tribes; he is an ardent anti-Semite, and holds the Jews responsible for the World War; he believes the Pope to be somehow run by the Jews, and many other strange things that cannot all be true.[2]

Few of the people I have tried to describe in these idle pages seem more worthy of mention than John Jay Chapman. I knew him first when he came to Rome, bringing us a letter from Wintie that ensured him a warm welcome. He had just graduated from Harvard and was spending a year in Europe before entering the law school. He was delightfully intelligent, bubbling with his own ideas, with a strong bias against those of others. His first reaction to my Dante-cult was to say that Dante was altogether overrated, and that anyone could write that kind of thing. He scratched off an imitation of a canto that did not exactly prove his point. A few years later he produced some of the best translations of Dante that have ever been made in English. The first flash was always a prompt and often ingenious refutal of any generally accepted proposition. I was very glad to see him again when I came to live in America. About that time

[2] While these pages were in the publishers' hands William Astor Chanler died in Cannes, March 4, 1934.

he married Miss Minna Timmins of Boston, a woman as original and interesting as himself. They lived in New York and were shining lights in their circle of intimates; both were great friends of the Chanlers. She died when her third son was born, leaving him very desolate and broken-hearted. Not very long afterwards he married my sister-in-law, the beautiful Elizabeth Chanler, who devoted herself to bringing up the three small boys and to taking care of the rather erratic and wholly delightful Jack. He became an integral part of the family and has, through all these many years, been one of my best friends.

While not always agreeing with what he writes, I read his books and articles with the keenest interest; no one on this side of the Atlantic seems to have his distinction and purity of style, and he has besides a lovely wit.

He wrote a comical skit on the "Sandwich Family," in which it was easy for us all to recognize ourselves. It was never allowed to circulate, but once in a while, when the right few are gathered together, it is brought out by request from its safe hiding place and read aloud amidst peals of laughter. His many published works speak for themselves, his books of essays, his admirable translations of Dante and of several Greek tragedies, above all his life of William Lloyd Garrison, a little classic that cannot but live.

Underlying his literary accomplishment he has an element of romantic mysticism that has called him to undertake unusual adventures. He betook himself to a Southern city when a horrid lynching had taken place, hired a room (it was a little empty shop), and announced in the local papers that a service of atonement would be held

there.   I believe only one old woman presented herself
when the time came, and Jack read propitiatory prayers.

He has no liking for Catholicism, though he admitted
to me once, many years ago, when we were having one of
our rare discussions on the subject, that it was the only
logical form of Christianity, but he has deep, unformulated
Christian faith.

He went into New York politics on a reform movement
that had nominated Theodore Roosevelt for Governor —
the Hercules that was to cleanse the Augean stables.
Roosevelt accepted the nomination and promised to run
on the forlorn-hope ticket, without any chance of being
elected, as the reform party represented a small minority.
When the Republican machine also chose him for its
candidate Roosevelt accepted the second nomination, argu-
ing, one must suppose, that the greater included the less.
But Chapman felt betrayed and outraged; he took the
next train to Oyster Bay and had a stormy interview with
Theodore, using such harsh language that the twice-
pledged candidate grew very wroth and told him that
he had no right to say such things to him, an able-bodied
man who could not hit back (Jack had only one arm),
and ordered him off the place.   Half an hour later Jack
returned, having missed his train, and rather sheepishly
asked to be allowed to spend the night — and might he
borrow a tooth brush?   Roosevelt was disarmed and
amused; it was he who told us the story.

Chapman did not pursue politics any further.   He was
too quixotic and too high-geared to submit to the discipline of party compromise.   He henceforth devoted himself to literature, where his real talent lies.   His books

should be better known than they are; perhaps they will be some day.

Jack and Elizabeth are a rare couple. They seem to have distilled from their long life together a certain quintessence of all their most endearing qualities. I often visit them in their seclusion; both are invalids and live away from the world; every time I see them I find them a little frailer, perhaps, and yet ever more interesting and delightful. Elizabeth's beauty has been silvered and etherealized by age and Jack has acquired from it dignity and a certain aloofness; but the shafts of his wit have lost none of their brightness. I always leave them feeling stimulated and enriched.

Alas, as I write these words, I receive a telegram saying that Jack Chapman died to-day.[3] Peace to his gallant soul!

[3] November 3, 1933.

XXI

NEW YORK'S COMPENSATIONS

WE soon learned to take the formal and formidable social activities in our stride and found that New York, apart from these, was full of interesting things to do and see, full indeed to bewilderment, as it has always been. There seemed no end to the concerts, theatres, exhibitions and shows of every sort. Then as now the pleasure-seeker had to be very alert not to let a day go by without missing an important event, very discriminating in his choice of what was offered. Above all there was the Metropolitan Opera. Most of us were opera-minded in those days. The box holders in the "Diamond Horseshoe" wore all their tiaras and jewels on Mondays and Fridays. Music lovers dined early so as not to miss the overture. *Carmen* was a recent novelty. There were excellent Wagner performances under the baton of Felix Mottl. The impresario Gericke was German, and German music still predominated. The next season, 1892–1893, Gericke was replaced by Maurice Grau, an Austrian. On the last night of Gericke's stewardship there was a gala farewell: a fine performance of *Die Meistersinger*, with Fischer as Hans Sachs, Mottl, of course, conducting. There were monumental laurel wreaths, speeches, and a great deal of emotion. *Deutsche Kunst* was about to be replaced by *Wälsche List*, German art succumbing to Latin guile. (There are words to this effect in the last Hans Sachs solo, which made it all very appropriate.) We were deeply stirred; many wept. Heine says the German soul is full of beer and *Gemüt* (feeling).

As a matter of fact, Grau did nothing to lower the standard of the Metropolitan performances; rather did he raise it. He imported great singers, the de Reszke brothers, Melba, Plançon, Emma Eames, Sembrich, and many more, for our delight. He gave more French and Italian opera than we had been used to, and, to some of us, *Rigoletto, La Forza del Destino, Norma,* and the *Hugenots* sounded rather thin; but he gave us quite as good Wagner as his predecessor. Jean de Reszke, as Walther in *Die Meistersinger,* was exceptionally convincing, in that his singing always greatly surpassed that of the rest of the cast, thus fulfilling the requirements of the plot. Most Walthers, including those to be heard in Bayreuth, give no assurance that they will not eventually turn into Pogners, Vogelgesangs, or any of the other old gentlemen in the long row of "Masters." As Tristan he was equally fine; he had great sense of form, and divided into intelligible episodes the long, the well-nigh interminable third act, when Tristan lies wounded under a tree in his castle of Tintagel, and comes out of his swoon to sing almost uninterruptedly for fifty-five minutes, waiting for Isolde and the *Liebestod;* marvelous music throughout, but requiring endurance both in performer and in listener. Someone has said that all great art has

stretches of august boredom.   We were all a little in love
with Jean de Reszke, so that he, at least, could never
bore us.

Jean de Reszke had a beautiful voice and sang with
distinguished art.   We had not yet heard Caruso and
asked for nothing better.   Caruso's was, I think, a more
astonishing, and perhaps a more natural organ, but Jean
had an incomparable stage presence, a charm and personal
distinction that Caruso lacked.   Melba's singing had the
purity and freshness of a most limpid spring, rising
among smooth pebbles in an Alpine valley.   It was not
her voice that first suggested this image, — while listening to her one did not think of images, — but once on a
mountain ramble I came upon such a spring, and its ef-
fortless flow brought Melba's singing into my mind.
There was never more exquisite voice production.   Jean
de Reszke said of it: "There is a wonderful bird in
Melba's throat."

The Kneisel Quartet was the joy of true music lovers;
it was recruited from the Boston Symphony Orchestra of
which Kneisel was the first violin.   They gave delightful concerts, very classical and impeccable in their style.
They were a good antidote to the rhapsodic, almost
visceral emotion of the Wagner operas, taking us back
to the sobriety of pure art.   A group of us arranged to
have them play us all the Brahms chamber music in a
series of afternoons in a private music room.   It is impossible to say how much better chamber music sounds
when heard in this intimate way, how much of its charm
is lost in a concert hall.   I look back on those Brahms

recitals in the dusky cosiness of winter afternoons with unfading pleasure. It was music for musicians. I do not mean to say that Wagner's is not, nor that he is not a greater composer, but Wagner's music is penetrated throughout by dramatic human passion, passion as irresistible as fate, that *is* fate, and in those days when the Wagner cult was at its highest many of his most ardent admirers were not in the least musical. The cult was for unrestrained emotion. I have seen individuals who knew nothing about music wallow through a Wagner opera, tasting forbidden joys and weeping over their sensations. This was great magic, but not pure music.

That winter in New York I was elected a member of a ladies' discussion club. Some thirty women met in each other's houses every fortnight. The card that told us where the next meeting was to be held announced the subject to be discussed; this was chosen by the governing committee, from a list sent in by the various members. We covered a wide field — literature, the drama, citizenship, divorce, woman's suffrage, the education of our children. As most of the members were young mothers, this last was naturally one of the favorite topics, and constantly returned to, under different captions. Parliamentary rules were more or less strictly observed; we had to address the chair, and at the end of the meeting something was always resolved, though no further action ensued. After this we went into the dining room, where tea was served, and we broke up into groups and talked to whom we pleased.

It was all very foreign to me, and I found it exciting and stimulating. I quite liked holding the floor and often felt I had something to say; we all did. There were some charming members. One I particularly like to recall was Miss Josephine Lazarus, sister of the poet Anna, who had died some years before. She, Josephine, was wholly inconspicuous-looking and dressed as if to avoid being seen, or as if to go out in the rain; but she had wise gray eyes that gleamed behind thick glasses, full of humor and deep understanding. She was a Hebrew of old Sephardim stock; she seemed to descend from prophets rather than from money lenders. We became close friends. She had chosen most of her best friends among Christians; yet Judaism was the thing that lay nearest her heart, and when she talked about it I used to feel that we younger races have nothing in our whole make-up, moral, spiritual, and intellectual, half so cogent, so real to us, so rooted in the essence of our very being, as Judaism is in the Hebrew soul.

Josephine Lazarus did not believe in Zionism. She wanted the Jews to give up their separateness, and would have had them mingle freely with, and eventually be absorbed by, the modern world around them. Were they all of her stripe they might indeed leaven the lump; but they are not, and the question is entirely beyond my competence.

Theodore Roosevelt's two sisters, Miss Anna Roosevelt and Mrs. Douglas Robinson, were also members of the club, and when both or either of them were present the meeting was sure to be interesting and amusing. They were unusually intelligent and had much of their brother's vital cordiality. Anna, the older, was wise and sympathetic; Corinne (Mrs. Douglas Robinson) had more poetic fancy and was brilliantly witty. No one ever told a better story. In later years some of us felt that the sisters took their brother's Presidency a trifle too seriously; I, for one, subscribed rather faint-heartedly to the foundation of Roosevelt House, the house where he was born, and where they had spent their childhood and early youth. It had been turned into a shop — East Twentieth Street had long since been abandoned as a "residential quarter" when their sisterly piety undertook to reconstruct the old family home and exhibit it for the edification of the public. The brownstone front had to be rebuilt with the "high stoop" flight of steps leading to the front door; all the 1860 furniture was collected and put in place, solid and comfortable, devoid of beauty. The sight of all this was supposed to incite the youth of America to leading manly, strenuous lives. The Roosevelt sisters were so universally beloved that one gladly forgave them their excess of zealous pride in their distinguished brother.

Mr. Chase, the painter, gave a party in his studio for Carmencita, the Spanish dancer whose jaunty grace still lives in Sargent's pictures of her. It was the first studio party ever given in New York as far as I know, at all events the first one I ever heard of or attended. The beautiful dancer had just arrived and was about to start on her tour of conquest. She had her first American triumph that evening in Mr. Chase's studio, and we were all carried away by her beautiful dancing and the almost savage intensity of the Iberian rhythms. Spanish dancing has a different vocabulary from that of other European countries; deeper roots in its native soil than the classic Italian and French schools from which the Russian Ballet was later developed. These were all produced by trained artists for the pleasure of royal patrons. The Court of Spain was too austere to countenance anything so frivolous as a ballet, and Spanish dancing remained a thing of the people. It never adopted the conventions of toe dancing and the sudden immobilizing of the dancer in an almost impossible position — things in themselves not beautiful, only unnaturally difficult.

Carmencita was infinitely alluring in the vigorous grace and lovely precision of her every movement. She also sang some popular ballads in amusing untrained chest notes, suiting action and dance to the words in a very captivating way. One can never forget her.

Stanford White, the well-known architect, was a brilliant and contrasting figure in the New York world of those days. He was a big red-headed man with a warm pleasant voice; he seemed to tingle with potential energy; there was something meteoric about his exits and his entrances. Restless as a whirlwind, he would flash into a roomful of people on his way from one show to another, shake hands here and there, tell us how lovely something was, or how much he hated something else, and rush out again into the white night of Broadway, leaving us all exhilarated and a little breathless, as if a foam-crested wave had swept through the room.

He and his handsome wife and their only son Lawrence, who was a child when we first knew the Whites, and who

later married our daughter Laura, lived in a large house
in Gramercy Park; it was full of beautiful and interesting
things collected in many lands: pictures, statues, tapestries,
old furniture, rich spoils of the past.   There was much
old Italian gilded carving on twisted columns, and elaborate picture frames.   Stanford White was the initiator
of the fashion for antique furniture that has since run
its course.   He started it with enthusiastic imagination:
in the music room, a half-circle of eighteenth-century
harps stood at the back of the stage; when there was music
they seemed to listen and vibrate.

He was a lively link between "Philistia *felix*" and high
Bohemia; he belonged to both countries.   Contrary to
American habits he always lunched at home.   Mrs. White
never lunched out, and her friends and his were asked to
drop in without ceremony.   We often saw them in this
delightful way; but he also gave gay parties in his studio
rooms, in the Madison Square Tower over which
MacMonnies's graceful young Diana stood with lifted
foot in virginal nakedness, aiming her arrow into the
wind.   Philistia had been shocked by her pagan simplicity;
the first casting of the charming weather vane was rather
too large; it aroused a storm of criticism and prudish
protest, and had to be taken down.   A comic paper had
a cartoon of the "*chased* Diana" running away from New
York with her crescent tucked under her arm.   A smaller
reproduction took her place, which looked better, and
nothing more was said.   We were all sorry to lose the
wind-blown goddess when the old Madison Square Garden
was torn down a few years ago to make room for more
lucrative erections; we were sorry to lose the building,

though I cannot say that I ever wholly liked it.   There
was to me something incongruous about the huge square
pile and its overelaborate decoration of minute terra-cotta
ornament, which had a look of dusty frosting on a titanic
cake.   It is difficult to make Spanish Renaissance architecture seem appropriate to modern popular gatherings.
The fine arcade that supported it was always defaced by
glaring advertisements of circuses, horse shows, shows of
every sort.   It was for many years the largest amphi-
theatre in town; during horse-show week it was the gathering place for the fashionable and sporting elements from
all over the country.   On its roof there was a hanging
garden, with a theatre, a restaurant, and coolness for hot
nights.   This was the first roof garden in New York,
another fashion initiated by the genial Stanford.   He had
been the architect and inventor of the whole combination;
it marked the end of the brownstone-front era; it showed
an artistic nostalgia for things of foreign beauty in the
rigidly monotonous streets of Manhattan, but since it
could not pay its dividends it had to go; more perfect
things have shared the same fate.

Writing of Stanford, I have perhaps said too much
about the vanished building; it seemed so much a part
of him, a realization of his dream, eventually the scene of
his death.   Long years before it was handed over to the
wreckers he was shot and instantly killed while sitting
alone at a table in the roof garden on a summer night,
listening to music.   His murderer was declared by the
courts to be criminally insane, and is now at large.

Stanford White was a kind gay pagan who enjoyed life
to the utmost and did much to make others enjoy it; he

hated convention, affectation, and pretense, and chose his friends in varied walks of life: artists, millionaires, and poor chorus girls shared his good will, and he was much beloved by all who knew him.   My husband was among his warmest friends and refused to believe the scandals that the press circulated after his death.   "Foul lies and willful exaggerations," he assured me; "Stanford never wronged a human being and was the kindest and most generous of men."

XXII

TUXEDO PARK

THE following autumn we moved into our cottage at Tuxedo Park. My husband had been persuaded by his friend Amos French that we should be happy there. I had not been consulted and was skeptical from the first; nevertheless I did what I could to make the best of it, though I never succeeded in disguising my dislike of the place. I found the life there fundamentally distasteful. A country-club community enclosed by a high fence; the entrance strictly guarded against intruders; only members and their guests were allowed to enter. I always resented the exclusion of random elements.

The landscape of wooded hills sloping steeply down to a long lake was pleasant enough, and the air was delicious; had we been Thibetan hermits we might never have found a better spot in which to withdraw from the world and meditate on the Non-Ego. But there was a big ugly clubhouse where parties were constantly given, and it was considered unfriendly not to attend them; there were a few large houses and a great many small ones, all inhabited by hospitable folk who hailed one another by their nicknames; to quote Mr. Charles Francis Adams's description of the Boston society of his youth, "it was a

Molly and Billy affair." It was not country life: there were no farms; cows and sheep, pigs and chickens, were rigorously excluded, with anything that might suggest rusticity. Few of the members had their own horses and these were only for driving, as there was but one hard iron road around the lake and the wooded hillsides were rocky and impracticable for riding, as for gardening. I did not play tennis or golf, nor had winter sports any attraction for me. I never learned to find pleasure in ice and snow.

There was a great deal of big poker playing at the club by the men and milder poker that the ladies played in their own houses. I cannot remember any other distractions. The men were all in business and took the early train to New York. Ladies' luncheons were of course in order.

In Tuxedo I was instrumental in getting a Catholic Church built just beyond the Park limits; even the Episcopal Church was outside the gate! When we first lived there Mass was said every other Sunday in a hall built for the entertainment of the club servants. The altar was dressed on a tawdry little stage; to receive Communion we had to climb over the footlights; it was incredibly sordid. The pious Irish congregation disliked it as much as I did, and the non-Catholic members of the club were generous in their subscriptions because it made their servants happier to have a decent place of worship.

Among the great changes that have taken place in America during the last forty years none is more noteworthy than the present status and prosperity of the Catholic Church, compared to its modest beginnings. Handsome churches have sprung up all over the country;

religious communities own great tracts of land in the most desirable situations. Much of the old patroon property on the shores of the Hudson has come into their hands. Gentlemen's seats and marble pleasure domes built by recent millionaires come under the hammer, and in five cases out of six are knocked down to an order of teaching nuns or friars. When I first went to church in America the congregation, in New York State at least, was made up almost entirely of Irish servants. The priests were not very cultivated; there were few opportunities for them to acquire scholarship. They ran their churches to suit themselves, and seemed less willing to put themselves out than the French and Italian priests I had known. On the other hand, they and their flocks understood each other perfectly, and the foundations of Catholicism in the United States were laid by single-hearted faith and generosity.

There were few rich and fewer cultivated Catholics; St. Patrick's Cathedral on Fifth Avenue was built for the most part with money earned dollar by dollar. So were the other churches in New York — St. Stephen's, St. Gabriel's, and many more. None of these are endowed; the priest must see to it that contributions be forthcoming for maintenance of the building and the salaries of the incumbents. This necessitates a great deal of housekeeping talk from the altar or pulpit; a great deal of urging and soliciting for special collections; card parties, fairs, dances, and church picnics.

To those who are not used to it there is something rather shocking in all this. I remember finding it almost unbearable, but have come to feel differently about it.

It gives the congregation a share in the worries and
responsibilities of the pastor; it makes them feel that the
Church's business is very much their business; they are
told how their money has been spent, how much more will
be needed to accomplish what they have set out to do, and
if it comes to looking into the lives and deaths of the
priests, it will be found that they live very simply and
for the most part die very poor. All that tiresome
begging is a stern necessity, and cannot be helped. Some
manage to do it with more grace and tact than others, but
it has to be done.

Fortunately Tuxedo was not out of reach of New York
and its many attractions. I think it took two hours in
the train to get there, which gave one good time for reading. One winter I read the whole of Schopenhauer's
World as Will and Idea on my numerous escapes to the
city. I had a convenient pocket edition of the admirable
book and found comfort in it.

One of the people I greatly enjoyed seeing in those
days when New York was my refuge from Tuxedo was
Mr. John La Farge, the painter and decorator. I met
him first at Mrs. Cadwalader Jones's, his great friend and
mine. He was different from others, not only in degree,
but very essentially in kind. He might have been of
another race. His head seemed carved in ivory, centuries
ago by a Chinese artist, with subtly significant lines and
planes. He wore very thick glasses, and saw everything; he told me he could use his eyes microscopically
without glasses by bringing the object very close. His
conversation was perhaps the most brilliant I ever listened

to. He had traveled much; he painted in every manner — great mural decorations, water-color sketches, easel
pictures in oils. He revived the making of stained glass.
He had read everything and written one or two delightful books. His *Artist's Letters from Japan* and his
Considerations on Painting are both classics in their way.
His talk had an indescribable richness; he knew all there
was to know and had besides "taken on himself the
mystery of things." He used to give me the feeling
that he was filling my lap with gold; after listening to
him one would be forever wiser. Alas, my treacherous
memory let most of the treasure escape, or was it fairy
gold, which cannot be carried home? I can remember
little of what he said, but just remembering him gives me
a quickening sense of interest in all things.

One story he told me I do remember: He was in Paris
when the Louvre opened the rooms devoted to the early
French school. He had gone to Paris to see them and
was seized by one of the heart attacks to which he eventually succumbed. The doctor in charge forbade his stirring from his bed; there could be no question of his
visiting the gallery: the exertion might easily prove fatal.
Mr. La Farge was willing to take the risk. He had himself carried down and put into a carriage; the doctor
must accompany him with his finger on his pulse, armed
with restoratives. At the Louvre a guide must be engaged to lead them to the right place, but pledged to
absolute silence. The patient was lifted into a wheeled
chair and the collection was visited, not a word being
spoken. When he had been put safely back in his bed
at the hotel, the doctor told him that it had been the most

interesting experience of his life to watch the rise and fall
of his pulse as they had paused before the different
pictures. "And may I tell you which of them you enjoyed most?   It was the '*Pieta*' of the school of Avignon.
Your heart positively leaped at the sight of it." The
happy imprudence probably aided his temporary recovery,
for La Farge survived many other attacks after that one.

It is difficult to gauge his place among the immortals.
He has done beautiful things. There is something tenta-
tive in his work, as if he were always looking for a more
perfect medium. It is intellectual rather than sensuous.
Yet he sometimes attains the high fusion of thought, feeling, and expression which creates such masterpieces as his
"Nicodemus," his great painting of the "Ascension" in
the Fifth Avenue Church of that name, his lovely Newport landscape with a lamb, and many others. In his
stained glass he obtained remarkable effects of color,
but made his figures too large and realistic for our present
taste. They impose themselves on the eye and intrude
on the light instead of breaking it into a space of many
colors. I prefer some of his small decorative pieces
which are just a pattern in jewels. Stained glass should
not tell its story too obviously.

While we lived in Tuxedo, Cecil Spring-Rice often
came to stay with us, as did Owen Wister and other old
friends. They brought a whiff of open air into the ex-
hausted receiver of our country-club atmosphere.

The Tuxedo experiment lasted four years; then came
an autumn when I felt that I could not go back. A fifth
baby was due in the spring; I should be imprisoned for

long icy months in the enclosure of the Park fence; my philosophy did not help me; my courage failed. Wintie thought me unreasonable but wanted me to be happy, and consented to look for winter quarters in New York. We had been spending the summer in Newport, and I was still there. His first choice fell on a suite in the old Brevoort House. I wrote back that it would be dark, stuffy, and noisy: could he not please find something better? He telegraphed back: "All right will look for a sunny silent palace." What he found was anything but this — a rather grubby little house in East Twenty-second Street, the best we could afford. We spent a pleasant winter there, seeing much of our friends.

One of these was Mr. Charles McKim, the architect, partner of Stanford White. He was a charming man of exquisitely fastidious taste and ardent classical convictions. He had just completed the Boston Public Library and was devoting all his energy to the founding of the American Academy in Rome, collecting funds and framing the plans on which the organization should be run. Mr. Pierpont Morgan had already given a generous endowment and other contributions were coming in. Mr. McKim was so enthusiastic about the scheme that he told me he would rather be known as the founder of the Academy than for his many architectural achievements. He asked me to give a little dinner at which he could talk things over with a group of experienced men, representing different arts — sculpture, painting, music; he would speak for architecture himself. He did not want any ladies invited. It was an interesting evening.

Mr. St. Gaudens was the sculptor and gave his whole-

WINTHROP CHANLER WITH LAURA

hearted approval to the undertaking. He told us how he owed everything to classic art; how Rome had opened his eyes to beauty and how hard it had been for him to leave it, after spending a few penurious months there as a poor student. He had come back to New York to make his way as a sculptor, had hired a studio in a grim office building, and was so homesick in the unlovely surroundings that his only consolation had been to let the water run in the faucet all night, and go to sleep making believe he was hearing the splash of Roman fountains. What would he not have given for a Roman scholarship!

McKim, himself a great music lover, was not sure whether music should be included with the other arts; not certain that Rome offered enough musical opportunities. Mr. MacDowell had been invited to represent music. He was not enthusiastic; he seemed to think that Germany was the only country where music could be studied with profit. Yet McKim felt very strongly that a few years' stay in Rome would benefit any artist, and his opinion eventually prevailed, for musicians are given scholarships at the Academy along with painters, sculptors, and architects, but are allowed to spend part of their time elsewhere.

Marion Crawford passed his winters in New York, leaving his wife and children in Sorrento. His publishers, the firm of Macmillan, put the top floor of their large business building on lower Fifth Avenue at his disposal as a studio-apartment, and there he lived and worked on his novels. It was a very different setting from the grotto of the *Calata*, with Vesuvius in view and the Bay of Naples, but it was spacious and quiet and he

liked it as a workshop, and had made it look homelike
with comfortable furniture and big tables strewn with
books. I remember a little dinner he gave there.
Monsieur de Montesquiou, the rather extravagant French
poet, was lecturing in New York and Marion invited
Wintie and me to meet him. Mr. John La Farge and
Mrs. Cadwalader Jones were the other guests. Montesquiou, a brilliant talker, was happy to find himself among
people who understood French and could follow the
rapid flow of his conversation; he knew little or no English
and there were few in New York to whom he could
communicate his cataract of ideas. We found him entertaining in his highly artificial way; he abounded in
paradoxes and hyperbole, yet his knowledge and taste in
all that concerned French art and literature seemed
thoroughly sound. He was tall and handsome, with
aquiline features and a haughty, almost insolent bearing;
but his face was painted and his figure was obviously
corseted. He was full of contradictions. Marcel Proust
filled many pages of his great novel with analyses and
comments on the character of this singular man *à la voix
jacassante* (with the ugly noisy voice), but the book did
not appear till many years later, and at the time we were
merely amused by his eccentricities and his conversational
fireworks. When I came to read *Du Côté de chez Swann*
and the many volumes that followed it to complete the
amazing work *A la Recherche du Temps Perdu,* it was interesting to compare my superficial impressions with the
careful masterly study of the ambiguous personage.

Those were hard years for my brother. The great
popularity of his novels chained him to his desk to produce

one best seller after another, leaving him little time to enjoy life. Mamma used to complain that her poor Marion was coining his brain into dollars and they did not seem to make him very happy. He had a few very good friends, chief among these the ever kind and devoted Mrs. Cadwalader Jones, who did much to alleviate his exile. Her house in Eleventh Street, full of books and old engravings, was an island of refuge for him, and there he met the interesting people she knew how to collect. Henry James was one of her intimates; he stayed with her all the time he was in New York. On the second story there were two pleasant rooms that she called her "Authors' Suite," where she made her friends very comfortable. I often stayed there on flying visits and could see why Marion enjoyed the atmosphere. It combined all creature comforts with a sense of civilized tradition and intellectual resource. All the books of the day on the table, all those of the past, well bound, standing shoulder to shoulder in ordered ranks along every available wall space.

Mrs. Jones represents the brave rear guard of old American tradition; she has stood and fought for good English, good manners, good citizenship; but her chief concern has ever been the doing of kind things. All who know her must agree that she excels all possible competitors in this endearing accomplishment; she is the typical Bee-Woman, praised by Pindar. Would there were more like her!

XXIII

AVE ROMA

IN September 1897 my mother died; we received the news in Bar Harbor, where we had taken a house for the summer. We had tried Tuxedo Park as a home and found it wanting. My husband generously suggested we should go to Rome and settle there for a few years to be near my father so long as he might live; he was then well past his four-score years. So we rented our Tuxedo house and went abroad for an indefinite stay, with our five small children, of whom Laura, the oldest, was ten. Rome was Paradise after the years spent in Washington, New York, and Tuxedo Park. I felt as though my body and soul had come together again after a long separation; for during my exile in the country that should have been my own some part of me was forever there, in the Eternal City, "alone and palely loitering" about the well-remembered places. In the midst of the hurry and high tension of American existence my living ghost had haunted the streets of Rome; at any moment, had anyone asked me the question, I could have told them just where I was — on the Piazza del Gesù, on the Spanish steps, in the Via della Scrofa or wherever. There was no particular spot to which my thoughts were anchored; my thoughts

were fully occupied with things and people about me and
had nothing to do with this uninterrupted shadowy consciousness of being in Rome. It was an idle trick of
memory and imagination and wholly involuntary on my
part. It was part of the great magic of Rome. To find
myself there again in the body, not living as a stranger,
but well established (for we leased and furnished a sunny
apartment in the Via Venti Settembre), seemed like a
lovely fulfillment of dreams. The children had good
Italian nurses who took them to play on the Pincio every
morning, just as we had done, and they soon talked Italian
among themselves and made friends with the children of
my old friends and fell in with the dear Roman pattern.
Happily Wintie also liked the pattern; he even brightened
and enriched it for me by bringing a new element into it.
He bought a couple of horses and for me riding became
a new delight. I had only known the country round
Rome from driving on the familiar highways and picnick-
ing in favorite places. No one knows Rome who does
not love the Campagna, but no one really knows the
Campagna who has not ridden or taken very long cross-
country walks over it, and this I had never done.

The Roman Campagna has a beauty all its own; it
spreads its miles of lovely solitude in every direction
about the great Urbs, the ancient mistress of the world,
and is part of her majesty. There are stretches where no
human habitation is in sight; you may come upon a
Virgilian shepherd tending his softly tinkling flock, dressed
as his father's fathers dressed, in his high cone-shaped
hat, his shaggy goatskin breeches and ample cloak. There
are blue hills in the distance to the east, south, and north;

to the west a shimmering line on the horizon, *"Il tremolar della marina,"* gives an occasional glimpse of the sea.

Sometimes the rise and fall of the rolling country reveals the dome of St. Peter emerging out of the hazy distance like a great blue bubble. The dear *cupolone*, beloved of all good Romans.

Wintie of course joined the Roman Fox Hunt, but I had never hunted and Wintie was afraid of the Roman post-and-rail fences for my inexperienced horsemanship, so he would take me out on off days to ride nearer Rome — the Villa Borghese, the Ponte Nomentano, the Acqua Acetosa. One day the meet was *fuori* Porta del Popolo, in the direction of the cork woods, not far from Rome. Wintie thought there would not be much sport, or perhaps he was just very kind, for he did not go to the meet but took me out for a ride in the general direction the hunt was likely to take,

It was in the valley Poussin loved and gave his name to west of the Via Flaminia, rolling pastures bordered by cork woods, no houses in sight save an ancient fortified farm that figures in many of Poussin's landscapes. We came out of the wood into the open on a little hill that commanded a wide view of the valley, when, faint and far, our ears were greeted by the music that Wintie loved best, the sound of a pack in full cry. He, of course, heard it first. It was coming our way, and presently we saw the hounds tearing along the valley at our feet, in diamond formation; you could have covered them with a blanket, as the fox hunters say. They were alone, neither Master nor huntsman, whips nor field, in sight. Naturally, we galloped after them as fast as we could, over the springy turf. After I know not how many minutes of sheer ecstasy we came upon a post-and-rail fence. Wintie pulled up and said ruefully, "I suppose this stops us." I was riding a Campagna-bred mare who had never been jumped, but she seemed full of spirit and over we popped after the streaming hounds. Presently the fox turned into a wood and there they killed. Another rider had joined us, the Count of Turin. He jumped off his horse and asked Wintie to hold it for him while he went into the thick cover where the pack was making a great joyful noise. He presented me with the brush and kept the mask for himself. Eventually the huntsman found us with his pack. The short winter afternoon was nearly over; we all went home, but I was not quite the same woman who had started for a ride that afternoon; an absurd new passion had suddenly sprung to flame — and fox hunting came into my life.

After this I hunted regularly with ever-increasing delight. My little bay mare turned out to be an un-defeated jumper, and negotiated stone walls and *staccionate*, the Roman post-and-rail fences, so light in appearance yet so strongly built of oak saplings firmly fitted together that if the horse hits the top rail he is very apt to turn a somersault in the air and come down with his rider under him. There are only two rails on the smaller fences, never more than three on those that measure over four feet.

Gabriele d'Annunzio used to hunt sometimes; he was not a brilliant rider, but he had showy horses that were led to the meet in handsome blankets, adorned with a large heraldic design, a shield bearing an Annunciation

lily argent on a field of gold.   He hunted for the sake
of extreme sensations, he said, and because he saw death
lurking for him under every obstacle.   Italians are not
ashamed of saying they are afraid, and are innocently
pleased with themselves when they have shown courage.
"Did you see me take that fence?"

I thoroughly enjoyed the fox hunting, and a good run,
of which we had many, was so exciting to me that I became
almost unconscious of what was happening.   Wintie
always knew just what the fox was doing and if, where,
and when a mistake had been made, while I, the blissful
one, galloped along after him in heedless rapture.   When
we had a blank day I would be far less disappointed than
he, for just to be out on the Campagna was pleasure
enough.

We did many things besides fox hunting during those
pleasant Roman years, saw many people, old friends and
new: Giovanni Borghese, the Dorias, the Caetani, my dear
Madame Helbig, and ever so many more. Count and
Countess Pasolini were among those that we especially
liked.   He was an interesting and charming eccentric,
a senator, a scholar and distinguished historian, a statesman and philosopher; he looked like a Perugino bishop.
He had the gift of devoted friendship and never forgot one
friend for another; they were all forever dear to him.
He had in his study a huge old glazed cabinet filled with
mementoes, a sort of shrine of memories, and loved to
show his guests the relics of old but unforgotten en-
thusiasms.   His writing of history was part and parcel
of his very human interest in attractive people; Caterina
Sforza possessed him with her beauty, her courage, her

vigor and reckless audacity; and he wrote a great book
about her.   He tried to write one about Louise de Savoie,
the mother of Francis I, and collected all the necessary
material for it, but found her on the whole too mild and
law-abiding, too much like other good women, to kindle
his flame, and he gave all the notes he had made to another historian working on the same period.   His admirable volume on the *Anni Secolari* gives vivid pictures of
Rome at the turn of each century since the beginning of
the Christian era, and his *Ravenna* is a classic and delightful history of his native town.

His wife, the Countess Maria, was no less interesting
than he.   She had grace, intelligence, distinction, and
warm enthusiasm.   Lenbach painted a head of her in
which he caught her Lombard smile, that sensitive half-
parting of the lips under the thoughtful brow.   She had
great taste and hers was one of the first houses to discard
the tawdry whim-wham of nineteenth-century decoration.   It was furnished for the most part with Italian
sei cento (seventeenth-century) pieces, sober and austerely
handsome.   She showed me how much beauty there is
in their simple lines and well-balanced mouldings.   For
years she collected photographs, most of which she had
taken herself, or caused to be taken, of the innumerable
lesser beauties of Rome — doorways, courtyards, gate-
ways, fountains that the guidebooks overlooked and the
casual sight-seer never sees.   Indeed, many of them have
been swept away by the opening of new streets and the
general march of modern life which has to sacrifice so
much old beauty to present convenience.   These photographs have lately been collected and published under the

name of *Architettura Minore* for the benefit of those whom
they concern.

The Pasolinis were very hospitable and gave many
pleasant dinners, where one was sure to meet interesting
people. Their house was a centre of friendships.

The Abbé Duchesne was at that time the director of
the French School of Archæology in Rome and had a vast
apartment in the Palazzo Farnese to which we were often
bidden. His great learned works on the *Ancient History
of the Church* and the *Liber Pontificalis* are authoritative
and in the hands of every student; they are admirable, but
not for the pleasure-seeker. He, our beloved Abbé, was
on the contrary wholly delectable; one could never see
too much of him. He had a priestly countenance and
wise brown eyes that looked on the world with keen understanding and saw that much of it was amusing. He
had the gift of captivating speech and was famous for his
wit; it sometimes ran away with him and he would say
funny, irreverent things about important people — things
better left unsaid, since they were bound to be repeated.
Among pious Philistines he was under some suspicion of
skepticism. He had in his learned works pulled down
certain altars, had traced the pagan origin of customs that
have, as it were, been built into the very structure of
Catholic practice, as fragments of classic sculpture are
built into the walls of the old churches, and he had above
all shown up historical discrepancies that had passed for
authentic relation of fact. He received the highest possible patronage and encouragement in his work; Pope Leo
XIII not only urged him to write the *Church History*
and accepted its dedication, but made it a textbook to be

used in all seminaries.   While the Italian translation was being prepared Pope Leo died and was succeeded by Pius X, whose interests lay rather in the line of encouraging the practice of frequent communion, promoting the study of Gregorian music, and doing away with the bad habit of singing opera airs during Mass, than in furthering historical research.   Some paragraphs of the translation were denounced to the Holy Office, examined, and found guilty.   It was a cruel blow to our dear Monseigneur,[1] who, at heart a devoted believer and faithful priest, had never dreamed of writing against the Faith.   He dutifully submitted to authority and retracted the offending sentences, but the *Histoire Ancienne de l'Église* was no longer the official textbook for students in seminaries, as Pope Leo had intended it to be.   Monseigneur Duchesne was deeply saddened.   All this happened some years later than the time I am speaking of. During those last four years of the nineteenth century he worked in the peace and sunshine of pontifical patronage, greatly beloved of his many friends.

He could bring his high learning down to the level of amusing conversation, and tell lovely old stories of saints and sinners that he brought out of his treasure-house of many centuries.   I remember one about a great Abbess of Fontevrault.   The beautiful Benedictine Abbey where the Angevin kings lie buried had been honored by a visit from the Pope (was it John XXIII?).   His Holiness had been grandly entertained, and as he was about to depart, the Abbess, kneeling before him to receive

---

[1] Leo XIII had given this title to the Abbé Duchesne since I first met him.

his blessing, said there was a great favor she would like to ask. The Pontiff was all smiles and benignity: "Speak, my daughter."

"Holy Father, some of my nuns are young, some of the priests sent here to hear their confessions are inexperienced and imprudent, scandals arise; human frailty, alas, creeps into relations that should be purely spiritual. Might it please Your Holiness to obviate all this by granting me the faculty to hear their confessions?"

"You ask a great thing, my daughter, and one that takes serious consideration; I shall be passing this way again in three weeks' time on my way back to Avignon, and will then give you my answer. In the meantime pray that Holy Wisdom may guide me, and do this other thing for me — I would leave with you this box, to which I give you the key, which you must on no account, however, fit to the lock. Promise you will not open it."

The Abbess promised and the Pope mounted his white mule and rode away with his court.

The Abbess kept the box but not her promise. She heard something moving inside, she lifted the lid, and a bird flew out and away. When the Pope returned at the end of three weeks she again kneeled before him.

"Has your Holiness considered my request?"

"Tell me first, daughter, what you did with the box I entrusted to your care."

The Abbess hung her head. "Alas, Holy Father, I opened it and the bird flew away and could not be recaptured."

"Oh, my daughter, and you who could not resist the temptation of unlocking the box you had solemnly promised not to open would have me trust you with inviolable secrets of the confessional?"

So the good Abbess did not get her wish and the nuns continued to have priests for confessors, and some of them were wise and some were foolish.

The first time I ever saw Monseigneur Duchesne was at Madame Helbig's. He was taking tea and talking to a group that gathered round him — Princess Bariatinski, Donna Laura Minghetti, and others. He charmed and intimidated me; should I ever be able to hold my own in such sparkling company? Experience shows that brilliant talking needs appreciative listening, as the positive needs a negative pole, as even the most precious wine cannot exist without a container. So I found my way into the friendship of the delightful Monseigneur, saw a great deal of him while I was in Rome and corresponded with him for some years after we came back to America. I have a most interesting letter in answer to one I had written in dejection, being very homesick for Rome. It was about Easter time and I mentioned one of the exclusively Roman functions I always loved to attend: the solemn blessing with the Major Relics given under the dome of St. Peter after the Office of Tenebræ on Holy Thursday. It was always deeply impressive: the crowd gathered from every part of the world all kneeling silently in the vast crepuscular basilica as, one by one, Veronica's Veil, the lance of Longinus, and finally the fragment of the True Cross appeared in their jeweled reliquaries, in the little balcony above our heads, and were raised three times, facing different directions, that all might receive the great benediction. Monseigneur

wrote me a sort of treatise on each of the three Major
Relics, their history and authenticity, too long to quote
here.   I treasure it as a precious document.

The next letter was all about his cats (his rooms were
always full of them) and told how an old favorite had
laid her litter of kittens on his bed while he was asleep,
and how it was not the first time that she had given him
this touching proof of her confidence.

The last time I saw him, many years later, was in
Paris not long before he died.   His health was failing,
but his spirit was all there; I like to remember the occasion.
My son-in-law, Edward Motley Pickman, great-nephew
of John Motley, the historian, and himself an ardent
student of history, had never met Monseigneur Duchesne.
I promised to bring them together if it were possible.   I
was spending the winter in a little rented house near the
Étoile.   Hearing through a friend that Monseigneur was
in Paris for a few days, I wrote and asked him to come at
any time that might suit his convenience.   He came at the
cosy hour of afternoon tea and we sat together by the
fire; the old historian, who had navigated the great seas
of backward time, telling the young one who was starting
off on the long voyage how to avoid certain perilous coasts
and treacherous currents, what places were yet uncharted,
what treasures might yet reward their discoverer.   He
was near the end of his voyage, but he was still full of
zest for the adventure and sympathy for the young man
about to undertake it.

Henry Brewster, the H. B. of Dame Ethel Smyth's
Impressions That Remained, was another of the new

friends. An American who had never lived in America, he was perhaps the wisest and most accomplished cosmopolitan I ever met. His childhood and youth had been passed in Paris, where his father had been dentist to the imperial court. It was said that his father had rescued the Empress Eugénie when the angry mob was storming and setting fire to the Tuileries in the red days of the Commune. That terrified woman walked out of the palace, disguised as a simple *bourgeoise*, leaning on the good dentist's arm, and found safety in his house, from whence she eventually escaped to England.

The young Henry had been given the best possible French education, had made brilliant studies at the Sorbonne, specializing in all known philosophies, had then lived for some time in Germany and Switzerland, and had finally settled in Rome. He had a handsome apartment in the beautiful old Palazzo Antici Mattei, where he gave excellent dinners and knew how to bring together the most interesting people. The Pasolinis and the Abbé Duchesne were among his favorites; Count Pasolini used to call him *il bel sauro* (the handsome sorrel), and complained that the ladies, his "Maria *cara*" among them, were all too partial to him. Brewster was indeed unusually attractive — tall, blond, distinguished-looking, he was at once friendly and remote. He had a romantic past that was never mentioned by those who knew about it, and naturally never by him. We only knew that after his German wife, the beautiful Julia von Herzogenberg, died he spent two years in complete seclusion. Of these he told me something in one of our long quiet talks, but he never alluded to the tragedy that had led up to them. He had chosen Paris as his retreat from the world and had buried himself there, avoiding all human contact by living among strangers and speaking to no one. He would not go to the same restaurant too often lest someone should recognize him from having seen him there before, and break in upon his silence. It was out of this dark night of the soul that he wrote *The Prison*, a remarkable book, written in the form of a journal or long soliloquy describing his solitary *psychomachia*, the struggle of the spirit with the powers of destruction; a *de profundis* without faith in God, but deeply felt and beautifully written.

At the end of two years a friend discovered him in his retirement and persuaded him to come with her to Rome. He came and saw that it was good and gradually started a new life. When I first knew him he seemed to have put away the past behind a curtain of despair, but his present was filled with highly electric worldly activities, and intercourse with many pleasant people.

Ethel Smyth used to come and stay with Brewster for a few weeks every winter, and during her visits there was much good music made at his house. She sang without much voice, but with such talent and understanding that it was a rare pleasure to hear. I never heard better interpretations of certain Schubert and Brahms songs. She sang and played her own accompaniments with dithyrambic fire; she seemed a very embodiment of music. She wrote a German opera, *Der Wald*, that was eventually performed in New York without great success, and later a French one, *Les Naufragés*, to a libretto by H. B. Her compositions lost much of their life when not played and sung by her. She played us parts of the *Wald* in Rome and they seemed very fine. When I heard the whole, some years later at the Metropolitan, I was disappointed. I never heard the *Naufragés* — it was given in Germany; but when her book, *Impressions That Remained,* came out it seemed to give fuller expression of her genius than did any of her musical compositions. English genius tends more naturally to letters than to music.

George Henschel, the first conductor of the Boston Symphony Orchestra, spent a winter in Rome; he was an old friend of Brewster's and often at his house. He was a most genial musician and a charming man. He and Brewster were both great chess players; they continually played a game that was carried on in their heads. In the middle of a dinner party one would signal to the other across the table and tell him his next move, then continue the conversation with his neighbor, who may hardly have noticed the interruption. They told me a game often lasted several days.

XXIV

THE SPANISH WAR

In the early spring of 1898 war clouds were gathering over the western horizon. On February 15 the United States battleship *Maine* was blown up in Havana Harbor; she had been sent to protect the lives and interests of American citizens in Cuba, where the insurgents were struggling to free themselves from Spanish rule. Rightly or wrongly, the people of the United States were convinced that Spain was responsible for the disaster; their blood was up and Red Gods were calling "the feet of the Young Men." Wintie could not but follow, and left me in Rome with the children. When he landed in New York sometime in March he found everyone in a fever of warlike excitement; placards with "Remember the Maine" were everywhere in view.

It will be remembered that on April 19 the Senate passed resolutions demanding "that Spain at once relinquish its authority and government in the island of Cuba and withdraw its land and naval forces from Cuban waters; that the President of the United States be, and hereby is empowered to use the entire land and naval forces of the United States . . . to carry these resolutions into effect." On April 20 the Spanish Minister in

Washington asked for his passports and we were at war.

All that was young and brave rushed to the colors; two hundred thousand volunteers were being hastily drilled into soldiers; ever so many more wanted to join the army. Did not President McKinley say: "I am sorry, gentlemen, but there are not Spaniards enough to go round"?

Wintie wrote me about this time in a letter dated April 29, 1898, from the Union Club, New York: "Theodore has resigned from his position as Assistant Secretary of the Navy and goes to Cuba before long with a regiment of cowboys from Arizona and New Mexico. I really think he is going mad. The President has asked him twice as a personal favor to stay in the Navy Department, but Theodore is wild to fight and hack and hew. It really is sad. Of course this ends his political career for good. Even Cabot says this."

Having left the Department, Roosevelt proceeded to organize, with the help of Leonard Wood, their regiment of "Rough Riders"; they recruited it among their friends from all over the country — cowboys, Indians, college classmates. Theodore invited Wintie and his brother, William Astor Chanler, to join them. The latter had already chartered a boat, collected a crew, and secured a quantity of ammunition which he intended to take to the insurgents. When offered a commission with the Rough Riders he asked Wintie to take charge of the filibustering expedition. This my husband was delighted to undertake; the hazard and adventure were entirely to his taste. He went to Tampa forthwith to collect the men and the cargo and assume command. He had some dif-

ficulty in doing this, met with endless delays and dis-
appointments, for in Tampa all was confusion, dust, heat,
and discomfort, but he finally succeeded and sailed for
Cuba in good order and high spirits. He went under
the unofficial protection of one of our cruisers whose
commander was his friend.

In choosing his landing on what seemed to be a deserted
marshy inlet he had overlooked a little masked Spanish
fort that opened fire on him and his men as they were
wading ashore. They spent a whole day in three feet of
water crouching under what shelter they could find.
Out of fifteen of them one was killed, a good many of
them were wounded; had the Spanish fire been more
accurate not one would have escaped. Wintie was shot
through the elbow. Night came and the fort ceased
firing; they managed to get back to the ship and sail away
under cover of darkness. The next day they found an
undefended spot where they landed their cargo and con-
signed it to General Gomez, who promptly made Wintie
a Colonel in the Cuban Army. He was in no condition to
take charge of a regiment, much as he would have enjoyed
doing it; his arm was giving trouble and he was forced to
abandon his men and go back to New York to have it
taken care of. By the time he was well enough to return
to Cuba peace was declared. How quickly it all went!
Looking back on those few anxious months across the
four long years of the Great War, it seems indeed a small
matter. As our friend Admiral Davis (Mrs. Lodge's
witty brother) said of it a year or two after our occupation of Cuba: "When I think of all the agony and bloody

sweat — it seemed like treading on a cockroach." But we did not know this when war was first declared.

European papers gave alarming accounts of the strength of the Spanish Navy. They printed in parallel columns the figures of the tonnage and armament of their ships and of ours; and on paper the Spanish sea power appeared to be far more formidable than the American. It should be easy for them to land an invading army on our unprotected shores.

The United States Ambassador in Rome came from Massachusetts, where he owned valuable cotton mills. I met him a couple of days after war had been declared, at a little tea party where, in the presence of other foreign envoys and "strangers of distinction," greatly distressed, he declared he was at a loss to understand his country's temerity.

"Our country must have lost its head to go and do such a crazy thing," he said. "Our coast is undefended, Boston and New York will be destroyed!" and gave vent to ever so much more of his defeatist foreboding from the sincerity of his dismay. Representatives of foreign powers listened with diplomatic composure, looking into their teacups; it was interesting wild talk for them and worth reporting to their respective Foreign Offices.

Fortunately for me I had a friend in the Italian Navy Department who, seeing me so anxious, copied out for me the Department's secret information on the relative strength and preparedness of the two navies; this showed that ours was by far the stronger of the two, that many of the Spanish ships were worthless, their artillery super-

annuated, their discipline poor.   This friendly act of indiscretion gave me great comfort.

Presently Admiral Dewey destroyed the Spanish Pacific squadron in Manila Bay and allayed our fears; but
before this happened no American I saw in Europe was
free from the terrors of bombardments and invasions and
"all the devildoms of Spain."   They were all terrified
lest the sources of their remittances should be seized or
destroyed, leaving them stranded in their exile, without
good American dollars to make it pleasant.   They accused
our government of having been meddlesome in the matter
of the Cuban insurrection; why not have left Spain to
attend to her own affairs?

I took the children to Geneva for the early summer
and there, sharing the same hotel balcony with us, was a
middle-aged couple of well-to-do Americans who actually
wore Spanish (red and yellow) cockades to proclaim
their disloyal sympathies and went so far as to fly a little
Spanish flag from the railing of their end of the balcony.
My children quickly countered with the Stars and Stripes;
they would gladly have climbed the bar that separated
our end of the balcony from that of these Spanish sympa-
thizers and raided their premises in a punitive expedition.

And the children were quite right in their instinct.   It
is an unseemly thing to disclaim your country, a true
misfortune not to love it; but the essence of American
patriotism is volatile: when exposed to too much foreign
contact it seems to evaporate, leaving a faintly unpleasant
flavor of flatness, easy to recognize, hard to define —
characteristic of what we used to call the "denatured
American."   *"Ame bien née ne renie jamais sa patrie."*

I should be the last to find fault with Americans who choose to live abroad, I understand them only too well. When they are by nature dim and dull the foreign veneer seems to intensify their insipidity, but how many have I known whose talent and personality have thriven in the richer intellectual soil of Europe. These make their own place in the country of their choice, lead interesting, often useful, and generally far pleasanter lives than might have fallen to their lot had they remained at home. The 100 per cent American looks on them with disapproval, as did the Western frontiersman on those who found pioneer life uncongenial and went back to the East.

Mr. James Truslow Adams in his admirable *Epic of America* explains how and why this has come to be the American point of view. For my own part I cannot see that any ethical question is involved in people's living where they like, so long as they have the good taste and decent pride not to deny their origin, not to wear Spanish cockades when their country happens to be at war with Spain.

When Dante and Virgil reach the second ledge of the *Purgatorio* they find dismal souls clad in stone-colored raiment, their eyelids cruelly sewn together with wire. They lean on one another, blind and woebegone. Dante asks if there be a Latin among them who would like to have speech with him, and he hears the voice of one of them who stands a little apart say: —

> *O fratel mio, ciascuna e cittadina*
> *D'una vera citta, ma tu vuoi dire*
> *Che vivesse in Italia peregrina.*

(O brother mine, each one is citizen
Of a true city, but thou wouldst say
One who has lived in Italy a pilgrim.)

Dante, the great expatriate, puts these words into the mouth of Sapia, a Sienese gentlewoman who had been banished from Siena and lived in Colle, a Tuscan village, eighteen kilometres away, where a battle was fought and the Sienese were defeated by the Florentines; and Sapia had rejoiced "like a thrush for a little fair weather" at seeing them beaten and had cried, "God, I fear Thee no longer!"

She was not punished for having lived a few miles out of Siena, but for siding with Siena's enemies and gloating over her defeat. On the ledges of Purgatory the warring factions are forgotten, and all the bitter hatred and malice; Italy has become for her the land of her pilgrimage, the stopping place on her way to the true city, the abiding habitation.

XXV

FRIENDSHIP OF HENRY ADAMS

In the winter of 1898–1899 the Cabot Lodges came to
Rome, the Senator, his wife, and their two sons — George
Cabot, the older of the two, better known to his friends
as "Bay," and John Ellerton, who has since made a name
for himself as a Chinese scholar and curator of museums.
Bay was something of a prodigy; he had suddenly
emerged from unkempt and rather uncouth boyhood into
an unusually attractive and accomplished youth. With
keen taste for intellectual things, he seemed to have absorbed a knowledge of them as a part of his growth; in
an incredibly short time he had acquired letters and was
at home in all that was best not only in English, but in
French and German as well. He had read a good deal
of philosophy, — Schopenhauer, Carlyle, Nietzsche, were
his favorites, as I remember, — and under the guidance
of Dr. Bigelow he had dipped into the occult psychology
of Buddhism. But poetry was his chief interest and
aim — he was himself to be a poet. Browning, Swin-
burne, Poe, Walt Whitman, Verlaine, and Leconte de
Lisle were his guiding lights; Carlyle was really his
prophet, and he loved to rant and growl with him against
"Gigmanity" — all the comfortable conventional world

of well-to-do people rolling about in gigs. He sympa-
thized with anarchists and revolutionaries, in the vague
hope that if the old forms were destroyed better ones
would take their place. He believed that the spirit of
man need only be set free to achieve great things; that
government, religion, family life, were so many forms of
bondage, shackles to the soul to be cast off as rags by the
Superman. There was nothing very original in all these
opinions, they were merely a symptom of intelligent ado-
lescence; but, tall, handsome, rather rugged-looking as
he was, with luminous laughing eyes and well-modulated
voice, he had so much life and radiant zest, so much
understanding beyond his years, it was natural to expect
great things of him.

He published a book of verses, *The Wave*, not long
after his visit to Rome, that was thought to show much
promise. Friends of the Lodge family declared nothing
so good had been written in English since Shakespeare.
And then appeared another, more ambitious, volume in
blank verse about Adam and Eve and their family
troubles, in which, without Bay's intention, it was easy
to recognize Senator Lodge in the rather crusty progenitor
of the human race, while the part of Eve could only fall
to the beautiful and infinitely tactful lady, his wife. Cain
was of course the spokesman for Bay's own feelings. The
work was dedicated to Jesus Christ, who, it appeared
from the words of the dedication, had been misunderstood
by all who had ever believed in Him. He later published
another volume of poems that showed more skill and
maturity, but his books were a disappointment to me; his
writing had none of the starry quality of his presence.

Bay himself was the poem, the shining youth, the arrow drawn to the head, the miraculous dawn that may turn into a day not unlike other days. He married a beautiful and devoted wife, he had three children, and died young, very suddenly, of heart failure. Adonais cannot live to be old; his youth is part of his tragic immortality; his beauty is that of the rainbow on the waterfall.

It is one of the hard predicaments of friendship when those we love and admire disappoint us in what they create. They detect the perfunctory note in our praise, they know us too well to be deceived by any amiable feint of enthusiasm, and they resent our failure to appreciate. Each had perhaps expected too much of the other. But that winter in Rome our friendship was free from these unhappy issues. Bay was the new planet swimming into our ken, perhaps a great star.

Princess Doria and I were studying philosophy with our learned Monsignor; the lessons took place in her boudoir, and Bay was invited to attend one of these. We were deep in the Thomistic-Aristotelian categories, of which he was, I imagine, quite ignorant, and as the lesson was given in Italian I do not believe he left it much the wiser, but it was amusing to see the contrast of personalities gathered in that quiet room: the silent inscrutable Princess, the overcertain expounder of ancient wisdom, who was so sure of the truth of what he taught that he who did not agree with St. Thomas must be talking nonsense, and the keen-eyed youth from the West who held the future as in a crucible of possibilities.

Mr. Henry Adams was traveling with the Lodges and,

as we saw them every day while they were in Rome, our company was somewhat thrust upon him. He began rather shyly by making friends with Laura, our lively eldest, then about eleven years old. He told her he was her little boy and that she must take care of him as he was growing smaller all the time; she must call him her "Deordy," as did one or two of his especially privileged "nieces." He paid her almost daily visits, going straight to the nursery while the Lodges called on me in the drawing-room. He took her for long rambles and gave her beautiful toys. She was not a little proud of his attention and puzzled by some of the strange things he told her about himself; could it be true that he was growing smaller? She knew of course that he was not really a little boy but a very small old gentleman — was he shrinking back into childhood? She asked me one day if she might bring her wonderful Deordy home to lunch with the family. He had shown so little desire to see us that, beyond the hospitable gesture of asking the Lodges if they would like to bring him to lunch or dinner (and they had not brought him), I had not tried to entertain him. On Laura's invitation he came, and from that midday meal sprang one of our warmest, most treasured friendships.

The prickly porcupine moulted his quills into angelic feathers; there was no intermediate hesitation. We discovered at once that we immensely enjoyed one another's company and that we must be together as much as possible. Whatever had been the cause of his first aloofness, it was forgotten and forgiven from the moment

HENRY ADAMS
After the crayon drawing by J. B. Potter

Laura brought us together. He liked and even loved us — Wintie for his sparkles and me, perhaps, for the religion I professed.

He had for the last few years passed his summers in France, and had amused himself with the French Middle Ages. He had discovered Our Lady of Chartres and her cathedral; Éleonore of Guienne, mother of Richard Cœur de Lion; St. Thomas Aquinas, St. Bernard of Clairvaux, the philosophers, the mystics, the troubadours, above all the master builders of cathedrals and makers of stained glass. At Chartres he lost his heart to the *Belle Verrière*, which taught him to understand the cult of the Virgin Mother and inspired that curious "Prayer to the Virgin and the Dynamo" found among his private papers after his death.[1]

He had approached the subject of mediæval Catholicism as a historian free from all bias might examine the Laws of Manu or the religion of ancient Babylon, believing it to be something long dead, of purely archæological interest. He found to his surprise that the thing was full of life, of beauty, of profound human significance; he discovered the Church as a living power shaping human destinies through the centuries, even to the present day, and not only among the unlettered and unreasoning masses, but among those with whom his high fastidious-

---

[1] It was found in a leather wallet with a few intimate papers and was written in pencil; Mr. Adams's niece, Mrs. Bancel La Farge, herself a Catholic, offered to send me a copy of the poem, and was surprised to find I had long possessed a fair copy in Mr. Adams's delicate scriptlike calligraphy, which I had treasured, without, however, knowing that he had never shown it to others.

ness had much in common.   The fact that I was a believing and practising Catholic linked me somehow with his
new interests.

His family never took his Catholic philosophy for more
than a literary pose — it was so remote from the things
they were used to, so contrary to the Adams tradition;
but to me it seemed a sincere intellectual adventure, a voyage of discovery into other-worldly regions, where Henry
Adams, the Harvard Professor Emeritus, author of a
standard work on American history, fell in love with the
twelfth century and used all his genius to get as near to
it as possible.   The mediæval pageant took him a long
way from the Jefferson-to-Madison Administrations, and
that, his first important work, he told me, had never been
a success, though it was highly approved by the professional world; its publication had cost him many thousands
of dollars, and it had never attained a second edition.   So
he resolved to write about Mont St. Michel and Chartres
for his pleasure and that of his friends.   The book was
privately and very handsomely printed and given away
to the favored few, not lightly bestowed for the asking;
a college president wanted a copy and, knowing me to be
a friend of Mr. Adams, wrote a beseeching letter after
sending several verbal requests, but Porcupinus Angelicus
put on his prickliest quills and blankly refused: "No, the
book was not written for college presidents."   When
Father Pardoe, a learned and eloquent Jesuit to whom I
had lent the volume, was so interested in it that he
wanted a copy for the college library, Mr. Adams was delighted to let him have one.   Father Pardoe told me
that some of the theological definitions were astonishingly

brilliant as well as perfectly sound; this cannot happen to theological definitions very often. It happened this time because Henry Adams brought not only a highly trained and gifted but a wholly fresh mind to the subject, kindled to brightest enthusiasm by his discovery of a new world.

Among his friends the *Mont St. Michel and Chartres* had the most immediate and unqualified success. We all loved it and sang its praises. I remember talking to Cabot Lodge about it and saying that I liked it too much to talk about it with outsiders, with people who had not read it, to whom my praise might sound fulsome and exaggerated. To my surprise Cabot Lodge said he felt just the same way about it, and that he did not know another book that gave him quite the same intimate pleasure.

It was taken for granted that the big public could never understand it, and must at all costs be kept away from the darling thing. How little any of us imagined that it was in time to become a popular favorite and share the honors of "best seller" with *The Education of Henry Adams,* the book that followed it, and that was by its author destined for an even more intimate circle. Only a hundred copies were printed in the original edition. Henry Adams did not live to see his volumes on every table, his writings discussed in every periodical. Not long before he died the American Institute of Architects obtained permission to publish *Mont St. Michel and Chartres.* They promised to have print and paper of the best, but produced a rather shoddy, commercial-looking volume, which disappointed its author by its undis-

tinguished appearance.   The public was not put off by
this — it was enchanted with the book and bought it by
the many thousands of copies, as it bought the *Education*
a year or so later; but Henry Adams died in his sleep and
did not hear the chorus of praise.   One wonders how it
would have pleased him: would he have revised his opinion on the average human intelligence, taking back his
favorite saying that it was impossible to underestimate it?
It could not but have embarrassed him to find so much
attention centred on him, who avoided crowds and was
only happy in the company of a chosen few.

After our meeting in Rome we never again lost touch
with Henry Adams.   He was a willing correspondent
and I have a bundle of his letters written in varying
moods.   Some are merely flowery exhortations to come
and visit him, or to answer his last, but some treat of
deeper subjects — of his interest in the Church, his pre-
occupation with the future of the human race, his search
for a mathematical formula that should express the curve
of the ever-accelerating tempo of modern life.   He made
dizzy calculations on the geometrical progression in man's
use of power, from the Merovingian ox cart to the motor car, the speed boat, and the flying machine.   He felt
that civilization could not stand the stress and strain
and prophesied that it must collapse under it in ten or
fifteen years from the time of writing.   Perhaps it did!
Only the Virgin could save us from the all-devouring
dynamo.   She represented all that was lovely and un-
mechanical; she was the embodiment of grace and mercy as
opposed to reason and justice.   He said a good deal of
all this in his chapter on the miracle plays.   His literary

executors had heard of these letters and asked to see them when his correspondence was being collected for publication; they saw them and decided that the public would not know what to make of them and that they had better not be included. Whether the public misses anything in not being shown this shy angle of an interesting mind is open to discussion, but the incident shows how the most well-meaning and intelligent of biographers or literary executors cannot help putting some of himself and his own preferences into the picture he is preparing for posterity.

There was never a moment's serious thought that Henry Adams might enter the Church; his interest was all intellectual and æsthetic, literary and historical; his sympathies were engaged, never his actual will to believe. But we, a small group of his friends who were Catholics, knew that he liked us to belong to the Faith, that he enjoyed the spiritual climate of our religion, that he approved our obedience to its laws, our practice of its customs and regulations.

I asked him once how it was that he did not become a Catholic, seeing he assented so warmly to what we believed.

"Do you think, my child, that Rhadamanthus would be less severe?" He said this half solemnly with a defiant twinkle in his eye.

Henry Adams lived the last years of his life in a rather ostentatious retirement: he did not go out into the world, but saw everyone who was worth seeing in his own house. He had a great influence with his friends and a very individual relation with every one.

When I meet any of them I think I recognize something of his point of view in theirs — a certain critical detachment foreign to the American mind, by nature more given to incredulity than to criticism or analysis.

He was delightful with children; he had an elaborate doll's house behind a sliding panel in his library, always ready for any little girl that might be brought to see him. I took my youngest son, Theodore, to lunch with him one day, and as I was presenting him I said, "This is your Uncle Henry [all my children called him that], and he knows everything." Teddy looked at him in round-eyed silence through part of the meal, watching his opportunity. During a pause in the conversation of the grown-ups the little boy leaned forward respectfully and said, "Uncle Henry, how do you feed a chameleon?" He had possessed one for three days and the creature had refused meat and drink; of course the all-knowing uncle told him just what to give it.

I often stayed with him in Washington, after we went back to America, in the handsome house he had built for himself and his wife, but that she had not lived to inhabit. It was designed by Richardson in the rather heavy New England-Romanesque style of Trinity Church in Boston and the Capitol in Albany, with a low carved archway over the entrance, and elaborately carved stone fireplaces of the same design. The rooms were large, sunny, and well proportioned; the walls were hung with good pictures, a fine collection of English nineteenth-century water colors, and a great many beautiful old Italian drawings *de haute époque*. He liked his house and was proud of it. The library, where he and his friends passed so many pleasant hours, was of course overflowing with books, but there were choice bibelots, Chinese bronzes, and flowers on his big table; the best of the water colors were hung there — the lovely Turner landscape, the curious Nebuchadnezzar crawling on all fours and eating grass, painted by William Blake — and all the rarest Italian drawings were disposed about the mantelpiece. The chairs and sofas had been built to his measure and were extremely low, covered with a dark maroon leather and, I need hardly add, superlatively comfortable, so that, once folded into their depths, one had no wish to move. The whole room had a mellow *patine* left by the much good talk it had harbored.

I was there once with Henry James and John La Farge, both very old friends and well beloved of our host. I sat next to Henry James at luncheon — he and John La Farge were staying with Mr. Adams. We were in a house we had taken for a couple of winter months to be near our Washington friends. Mr. James murmured under cover of the general conversation that the one thing he wanted to see in Washington was the St. Gaudens monument in Rock Creek Cemetery where Mrs. Adams was buried, but that he could not possibly make his wish known to Henry; so I offered to take him in my brougham, and after luncheon we slipped away together without saying where we were going. Mr. James was an old friend of my family and I had known him all my life, meeting him in Rome and elsewhere at long intervals, for we were rarely in the same place; but I had never had the privilege of his sole company for a whole afternoon. There was no one more delightful

to talk with, for all his mumbling hesitation in trying to
find the one matchless word that should precisely express
his meaning — hesitation that the irreverent compared
to a rhinoceros trying to pick up a pea.   The word when
found well justified the search: it was never a pea, nearly
always a pearl.   Besides having so much to give he had
the rarer conversational art of being, or seeming to be,
immensely interested in his interlocutor.   He would
have made a wonderful father confessor; he solicited
confidences, he wanted to know all you could tell him.

On the way to the cemetery we talked of this and that:
he asked me a great deal about my Crawford sisters,
whom he had known well in old Roman days when I was
still in the nursery; he had much to say about the talented
Annie, and wanted to hear about her married life and
how she fared in the *Junker* surroundings.   It was a
wintry day in early spring, and when we reached our destination and found our way to the tomb the trees that
surrounded the monument had a slight sprinkling of
snow on their boughs, and the sky was bleak.   Mr. James
stood for many minutes bareheaded before the solemn
bronze figure that seems to embody, more than any work
of modern art, that great calm that is beyond hope or
fear.   He seemed deeply moved.

On the way home he told me a great deal about Mrs.
Adams, whom he had warmly admired, and of whom all
mention was avoided in Henry Adams's presence, as he
had himself avoided it in his *Education,* passing without
a word over the years of his unusually happy married
life.   Mr. James abounded in her praises; it seems she
was a brilliant and charming woman, so brilliant that the

circle of intimates considered her the more interesting of the two: "We never knew how delightful Henry was till he lost her; he was so proud of her that he let her shine as he sat back and enjoyed listening to what she said and what she let others say."   In the volume of Henry Adams's letters we get an occasional glimpse of those little parties they liked to give — how good the talk had been, how pleased they had all been with themselves and each other (some wise Frenchman has said that he who leaves your company pleased with himself is surely pleased with you); but it was hard to imagine another focus than Henry Adams's own wit and wisdom in any group collected about him — not that he talked much, but that he was always the centre of interest and what he had to say was always what we most wanted to hear.

From Mr. James I gathered that Mrs. Adams had not been a pretty woman, but small and graceful and well dressed.   With all that the world could give to make her happy, she left it of her own choice, and the rest was silence.

One of the topics Mr. James had most at heart was that of Europeanized Americans; he felt so strongly about their dilemma that he developed it into a "case of conscience" in which right and wrong action were somehow involved.   He disapproved their divided allegiance and thought their duty lay in a deliberate and irrevocable choice.   He was a little shocked to hear that I had a son at Eton and daughters in the Sacred Heart Convent at Roehampton (that was on another occasion, at a meeting some years later in New York), and said I was shifting the burden of the decision on to the shoulders of the next generation. When, shortly before his death, he became an English subject, it was his very sincere declaration of faith, the result of long thought on the matter. My own case, that of an American brought up by expatriate Americans with a strong European bias, was to him an unusually lucid statement of the problem and he felt I should do something about it. I asked Mr. La Farge what he thought (he was much wiser and far more exotic than I), and told him all that Mr. James had said and with what earnest solicitude. "Dear Henry," was his reply; "he forgets how easy it has become to cross the ocean; the issue that so worries him does not exist." But then La Farge was not interested in ethical conundrums.

For my own part I have never found the whole answer to this one. Contact, sympathy, and close friendship with people of other nations may have sapped my patriotism a little, but it never occurred to me that my children had better belong to another country than their own, and this is the final test of a woman's convictions.

I must return to Henry Adams, who will pardon my having left him for a moment to speak of Henry James, whom he dearly loved. He at all events solved the Jamesian problem in favor of America, for in the last years of his life he passed his summers on this side of the Atlantic, and he told me how much happier they were than many that had gone before. He was curiously shy, self-conscious, and inaccessible with foreigners; during all those summers spent in Paris he never made friends or even bowing acquaintances with any of the lights of the Sorbonne or the Collège de France. He might have known Gaston Paris, Gebhart, Langlois — the list is too long to fill out, all great experts on the Middle Ages and the things he was studying at the time; he read all their books, but would not meet them, preferring the society of his own little group, consisting almost entirely of Americans. "There are no men in Paris," he would say to the well-dressed, good-looking women of his own race who would lunch with him at Larue's, and in whose dressmaking expeditions he took interest.

Fashions have their place in thought. To be surrounded by the young and gay, to avoid somewhat the fellowship of his learned colleagues, may have kept his spirit from gathering dust, his pen from scratching and rusting over unimportant controversies. His book was dedicated to his nieces; it was learned, although it was not addressed to the learned; it reached not only his nieces, but a vast public to whom it brought a new message.

One of the last visits I paid him was at Tyringham in the Berkshires, where I went to spend a few amber autumn days. He had hired Ashentully for the season, a white palace built on the scale of a great Italian villa across the end of a lovely valley, rather in the spirit of a "folly"; there were eight furnaces in the cellar to keep it moderately warm. Outside, the valley was all aflame with autumn, a mist of wild asters tempered the crimson and gold to a dreamy beauty; indoors, by the fire in the huge library, sat the little old gentleman who knew and understood so much, and was so wholly friendly and delightful.

His last years were the happiest since those of which he would not tell us, which had ended in such bitter sorrow; he took great comfort in the society of his devoted

secretary, companion, and adopted niece, Miss Aileen
Tone, an unusual young woman, who combined good
looks and breeding with much tact and faithful kindness;
she had a pleasant tuneful voice and sang old songs without pretension, but with nice musical feeling, to his great
satisfaction.   His mind kept all its healthy curiosity and
never rested from searching and pondering; a new theory,
a new discovery, was always given a measure of attention.
He had a wistful interest in higher mathematics and
always regretted his want of knowledge; he read Poincaré
and Bertrand Russell and all the expounders of the new
views on hyperspaces and the explorers of the dynamic
molecule, and linked them with things pertaining to the
spirit of man.   But what gave him the keenest pleasure
were the mediæval songs Miss Tone used to sing to him.
He had in the course of his studies for *Mont St. Michel
and Chartres* found many forgotten treasures in the old
French *chansonniers;* he had employed learned musical
archæologists to transcribe the melodies into modern
notation; MM. Expert and Gastouet [2] would send him
the results of their work among the manuscripts of the
Bibliothèque Nationale and the Bibliothèque de l'Arsenal,
and his friends were called in to rejoice with him when
some particularly lovely treasure had been unearthed
and rescued from the dustbin of oblivion.

There was great excitement when a package arrived
from Paris containing words and music of Richard Cœur
de Lion's authentic prison song discovered among the for-

[2] Both these gentlemen published much ancient music discovered
by them in the libraries here mentioned. Their work was greatly
helped by Mr. Adams's financial support.

gotten riches of the Bibliothèque de l'Arsenal. Aileen must learn to sing it; Dr. Richmond, President of Union College, who specialized delightfully in old ballads that he sang with much feeling to his own accompaniment on the harp (and was therefore forgiven for being a college president!), must find an accompaniment for it not too modern for Blondel to have strummed on his lute. Mr. Adams made an English translation of the verses and it appeared in the second private printing of *Mont St. Michel and Chartres,* in the chapter on Queen Éleonore.

He was essentially a teacher and had a great gift for communicating interest and imparting knowledge, or at least a desire for it, to those about him; but for all this he was keenly aware of the individual human predicament, the most understanding comforter, the most reliable counselor to his friends in trouble. Like most intelligent older people he took great pleasure in surrounding himself with the young; he knew how to charm them, to stimulate their half-awakened minds.

My youngest daughter went to stay with him in Washington and tells of a strange evening she spent alone with "Uncle Henry." Miss Tone, the "niece in residence," was dining out, and the sixteen-year-old Gabrielle, better known to the family and friends as "Bebo" (the first two syllables of her Roman nursery name of Bebolina), was rather afraid of him. She need not have been, since he was amused with her and soon made her feel at home. During the meal they chatted cheerily of places and people they had known, and then settled in the low armchairs of the library for the rest of the evening. There was a pause; Uncle Henry leaned back with his eyes half closed and his two hands joined at the upturned fingers. Then he began to talk, softly at first as if to himself; then, gathering momentum from his surging thoughts, he went on to speak of all that lay on his mind, the mysteries of time and eternity, man and destiny, his aspiration and helplessness. It was all way over her head, but she listened breathless, feeling that something great and wonderful was happening, though she could not understand it. At last he paused and came back to earth, looked at her, and said: "Do you know why I have told you all this?" Of course she had no answer. "It is because you would not understand a word of it and you will never quote me."

She could not remember what had been said, nevertheless something precious and unforgettable had been conveyed — a sense of the great problems that the human intellect is forever trying to solve; a contact with a high train of thought left her spirit deeply stirred, bubbling and luminous like the wake of an ocean liner in phosphorescent waters.

XXVI

TYROLESE SUMMERS

In summer we went to the Austrian Tyrol, where we liked to discover little rustic inns in remote valleys; there "Happiness lies stretched on all the hills" and we lived the simple life in great contentment. We took long walks, we climbed mountains, we ate *Kaiserschmarren*, a kind of glorified scrambled pancakes, and drank the thin wine of the country, *mit a' Spritzel* (the local name for a dash of soda water), and everything tasted delicious.

In most of these out-of-the-way places the inns were scrupulously clean, the board floors were scrubbed every morning by stout round-armed mountain maids, the beds were spread with rough homespun linen, the food was plain and plentiful, but what the guidebooks are agreed to call "modern comfort" (a euphuism for elaborate plumbing) was quite unknown. We made shift with our rubber tubs and felt none the dirtier. At Maistatt in the Pusterthal things were different; it was an ancient Tyrolese watering place and boasted a whole wing of bathrooms where one could enjoy the luxury of fragrant pine-needle baths. The water itself was soft and slightly peaty; it was supposed to have healing qualities. On the door of the bath house there hung a sheet of crabbed

German script, dating some hundred years back; it contained directions for taking baths.

"In the first place," it said, "let him who undertakes this cure commend his soul and body to God, prepared to thank His Divine Majesty if it proves successful and not to be downcast if it should profit him nothing; then let him use all prudence in taking the baths; he should not stay in the water for more than five minutes the first day, ten minutes the second, and so on, until he remains in it for an hour, after which he must reduce the bath by five minutes a day to the end of his cure, that by thus gradually increasing and decreasing the length of the bath his body may receive no violence."

There was also a crude old picture of Kaiser Maximilian, the head of the Holy Roman Empire, the grandfather of Charles V. He is said to have first discovered the virtue of these waters while on one of his hunting parties; he was a great sportsman and the Tyrolese still keep his memory green with tales of his bold adventures. The picture represented him lying in a huge tub covered with a red counterpane. It was set in an open meadow; one could not help wondering how it came there. All about it were the men of the imperial suite in gay hunting costume. The name of Maistatt was derived from Majesty— *Majestät*.

Wintie found that there was good shooting to be had in the neighboring valleys and became an impassioned chamois hunter, stalking the shy agile creatures along giddy precipices and rocky slopes inaccessible to all but the most sure-footed. Spice of danger was essential to his pleasure, and a certain gay courage was as natural to him as breathing. He made friends with Mr. Baillie-Grohman, a congenial Englishman who lived in a charming old castle in the valley of the Inn and had written good books — *Sport in the Alps*, and others on kindred subjects; he knew all there was to know about them. He very kindly asked Wintie and me to stay with him and his wife at Schloss Matzen, a delightful spot. The mediæval castle had been arranged with English taste and made thoroughly comfortable without losing its character of handsome austerity. There were open galleries or *loggie* around the inner court of the castle, two tiers of them, and these were all hung with trophies of the chase. Every head that had been killed on the property had a carved turnip in its mouth; some of them long antedated Mr. Baillie-Grohman's possession of the place, relics of the sport of former owners, long since gathered to their fathers.

The Tyrolese have always been great wood carvers, and our hosts had a fine collection of their work. Many of the rooms were beautifully paneled, the surfaces ingeniously carved in flat relief with conventional designs of plants, fruit, and flowers that grew in the neighborhood; a native form of art, practised by the peasants during the long snow-bound winters. Mr. Baillie-Grohman had found them in the old farmhouses for which they had originally been carved and was one of the first to appreciate their charm. Others were quick to follow his example, and antiquaries and interior decorators reaped a rich harvest.

For our last summer in the Tyrol we hired a cottage
at Igls, a heavenly spot on a high plateau overlooking
the broad Inn Valley and the peaked chain of the Kaiser-
gebirge, the Bavarian Alps beyond; the foreground a
rolling country of meadows and apple orchards dotted
with old farmhouses, here and there a tiny village clus-
tering piously about its church steeple. The peasants
wore their local costume and nodded and said *"Grüss
Gott"* when you passed them on the way; all the immediate surroundings were simple and smilingly rustic, and
away across the valley, separated from us by a great wash
of blue air, tall mountains towered in majesty, so beautiful that one could never forget them. A good landscape
for the soul of man, to teach him to live his little life
humbly and contentedly, drawing joy without envy from
the heights he cannot achieve, yet possessing them in a
certain measure through his sense of their beauty. "That
we may so pass through temporal things without losing
those that are eternal."

In September Wintie and I went to Munich, leaving the
children at Igls, where conditions were too primitive for
the arrival of a new baby. Everything went well with
the birth of the little man child, and while I was being
taken care of Wintie had a delightful adventure. He had
heard of two ladies, one English and one American, who
had in their youth been ardent chamois hunters and had
a little *Schloss* in the Ampezzo Valley, which runs between
the Pusterthal and the Dolomite country. It was called
Sanct Hubertus in honor of the patron saint of all venery,
being in truth little more than a fortified hunting lodge.
It had the best shooting in the Tyrol; the good ladies

who owned it and still lived there were no longer in their first youth and, although they occasionally had a shot at a chamois, the place was overstocked with game. Someone suggested that Wintie should call on them and ask them for the privilege of a day's shooting. So he went and presented himself and was received with the greatest kindness. He and the ladies soon found that besides the love of chamois hunting they had many friends in common; they made him stay to lunch, they put their two guides at his disposal, he must come and stay in the house. He gladly accepted their hospitality and they, as I later heard, felt well repaid by the gay presence of their impromptu guest. He spent long days in the mountains, walking the guides off their feet (the ladies had not worked them so hard in years), and got several handsome heads that still hang on the wall, tokens of his prowess. He came back to Munich just in time for the christening (I had arranged to have it in my sitting room at the hotel), and announced that the child's name should be Hubert; and Hubert it was and is.

News reached us from Rome that my father was ailing and we hurried back, taking the long journey rather sooner than was quite prudent, for I arrived in a high fever and could not go to see him. Wintie showed him his new grandson and 1813 kissed 1900 a few days before departing on the timeless voyage. When we arrived he seemed well enough to take a little drive, — the afternoon drive in an open carriage, the Roman *trottata*, down the Corso and around the Pincio had been one of his lifelong pleasures, — but there was a chill in the late October air and he caught cold and died without my see-

ing him again.   A grievous disappointment, all the more
cruel in that he could not understand why, being in Rome,
I was not at his bedside.

With my father gone there was no longer any good
reason for our living in Rome.   We stayed on through
the winter and spring, gathered up our belongings, and
came back to America the following summer.   We had
gone to Rome because my mother died, we left it after
my father's death, our going and coming were bordered
with mourning; but the four Roman years that lay
between were like a last kind gift from them to me, their
final parental blessing.

INDEX

INDEX